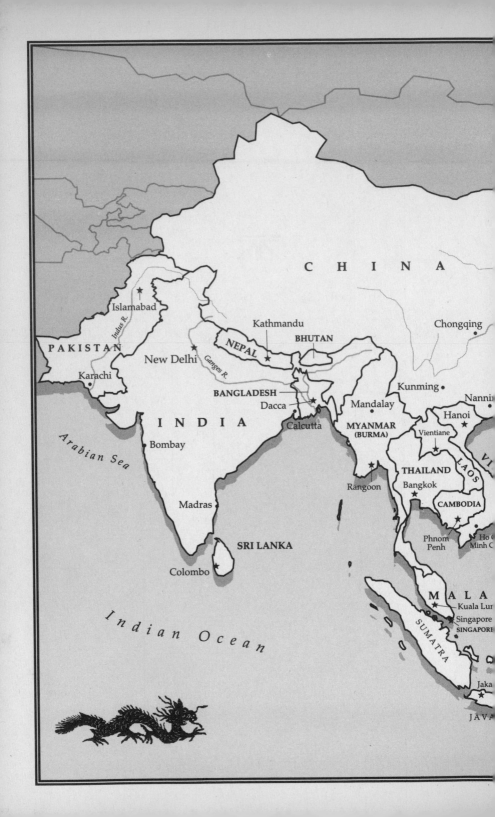

Harbin •

Beijing ★

Shenyang •

Pyongyang •

NORTH KOREA

SOUTH KOREA

Seoul ★

Huang (Yellow) R.

Qingdao •

Yellow Sea

Sea of Japan

Sapporo

JAPAN

Tokyo ★

Osaka

Nanjing •

Wuhan •

Yangtze R.

Shanghai •

Hangzhou •

East China Sea

Guangzhou •

Taipei ★

TAIWAN

HONG KONG ★★

MACAU

South China Sea

Philippine Sea

Manila ★

PHILIPPINES

Pacific Ocean

N

0   KILOMETERS   1000

0   MILES   1000

BRUNEI

SIA

BORNEO

Bandjarmasin •

I · N · D · O · N · E · S · I · A

Jayapura •

PAPUA NEW GUINEA

Port Moresby ★

Jeffrey L. Ward 1995

Also by John Naisbitt

Megatrends

Global Paradox

Reinventing the Corporation
(with Patricia Aburdene)

Megatrends 2000
(with Patricia Aburdene)

Megatrends for Women
(with Patricia Aburdene)

Japan's Identity Crisis
(with Shosaburo Kimura)

Megatrends Asia

Eight Asian Megatrends That Are Reshaping Our World

John Naisbitt

A Touchstone Book
Published by Simon & Schuster

TOUCHSTONE
Rockefeller Center
1230 Avenue of the Americas
New York, NY 10020

First Touchstone Edition 1997

TOUCHSTONE and colophon are registered trademarks
of Simon & Schuster Inc.

Manufactured in the United States of America

1   3   5   7   9   10   8   6   4   2

Library of Congress Cataloging-in-Publication Data
Naisbitt, John.
Megatrends Asia : eight Asian megatrends that are reshaping our
world / John Naisbitt.
    p.   cm.
Includes bibliographical references and index.
1. Economic forecasting—Asia.   2. Asia—Economic
conditions—1945–   I. Title.
NC412.N2433   1996
330.95—dc20   95-50102
CIP
ISBN 0-684-81542-7

for my grandchildren,

Rory, Lily, Jake, Abe, Sophie, Eli, Eric, Paul

and Hannah Rose, who will know a lot more

about Asia than we do.

CONTENTS

INTRODUCTION

Asian Renaissance

THE first time I went to Asia, I stayed a year. That was in 1967. On leave from IBM, I was an advisor to the Royal Government of Thailand on accelerating agricultural growth in the northeastern part of the country. I divided my time between Bangkok and Nong Khai. Nong Khai is directly across the mighty Mekong River from Vientiane, the capital of Laos, and I would occasionally engage some locals to row me in one of their long boats to the other side, to Vientiane, a distance of almost a mile. Today there is a gleaming new, $42-million bridge between Nong Khai and Vientiane, a symbol of the economic progress that has been made in Thailand. It is also a symbol of the progress that has been made in all of Asia. That progress and the momentum behind it constitutes a sea change in the economic life of the world.

In the almost thirty years since my year in Thailand, I have visited Asia at least annually, and in some years, as many as five or six times. For the past three years, I have been based in the beautiful, modern city of Kuala Lumpur, the capital of Malaysia, traveling widely in the region. Malaysia's ethnic, linguistic and cultural diversity creates a stimulating environment. English is widely spoken. Malaysians are comfortable with Chinese, Indian and Malay cultures, which make their country a convenient gateway to Asia's (and soon the world's) three largest markets: China to the north, India to the west and Indone-

Introduction

sia to the south. My academic bases are the Institute of Strategic and International Studies (ISIS), Malaysia, in Kuala Lumpur, where I am (the first non-Asian) Distinguished International Fellow, and Nanjing University in China.

From this vantage point I have written this book. With the help of my Asian friends, I engaged in a series of dialogues with key government, business, academic and community leaders in Singapore, Kuala Lumpur, Jakarta, Manila, Bangkok, Bombay, Hong Kong, Taipei, Tokyo, Seoul, Shanghai and Nanjing in order to gather Asian voices and insights (their names are all listed in the acknowledgments). In addition, my staff in Kuala Lumpur, conversant in many Asian languages, did a content analysis of the region's leading newspapers and periodicals. And from both spoken and written words a remarkable picture emerged.

What is happening in Asia is by far the most important development in the world today. Nothing else comes close—not only for Asians but for the entire planet. The modernization of Asia will forever reshape the world as we move toward the next millennium.

From 1945 to 1995, half a century, Asia went from rags to riches. It reduced the incidence of poverty from 400 million to 180 million, while its population grew by 400 million during the same period. The World Bank has pronounced that nowhere and at no time in human history has humanity achieved such economic progress, and concluded that the East Asia story is an economic miracle. My studies in Asia convince me of that miracle, yes; but it has not been purely economics. The story of the New Asia is a story of the miracle of the human spirit, driven by an awakening to one's own potential and propelled by the power of determination, and of the progress achieved by toil and sacrifice.

Asia is on its way. Asian economies have reached critical mass, from which there is no turning back.

In the 1990s, Asia came of age. And as we move toward the year 2000, Asia will become the dominant region of the world: economically, politically and culturally. We are on the threshold of the Asian Renaissance. If you have any doubts about the speed with which that megashift is occurring I believe they will be erased, one by one, as you read this book. It is not a change the rest of the world will accept readily.

Yet it is time for all of us to face reality, and to devise a strategy to adapt to it. This book will help you do so. It will provide the data and trend analysis, and it will describe the regional and cultural patterns that will empower you to seize the moment and profit from the cutting edge of change. If you are a small to midsize producer of consumer goods, for example, why should you consider Thailand, let's say, over South Korea as your next market?

Given the extraordinary changes in the works, it is high time for the West to try to see the world from Asia's perspective. In Asia, for example, it is widely believed that the West is losing moral standing internationally, as shown in its lack of leadership in the Serb-Bosnian conflict (the Bosnians are predominantly Muslims and there are more than 500 million Muslims in Asia). Given this perception, Asians are increasingly irritated by the West's lecturing and hectoring them about freedom and human rights.

America's moralizing may come back to haunt it. Down the road imagine a big, economically powerful China threatening to withhold Most Favored Nation status from the United States unless it does something about the slums in our big urban centers (or improves its SAT scores!).

A new commonwealth of nations based on economic symbiosis is emerging in the East: the Asian Commonwealth. The nations of the area are working together for mutual economic gain for the first time in their long history. And the catalyst is the free market.

The old Asia was divided by culture, language, political ideology, religious philosophies and geography. The new Asia, forged by economic integration, technology, especially telecommunications, travel and mobility of people, will increasingly look like one coherent region. My Telluride neighbor and friend John Lifton, an Englishman, remembers that in the 1960s young people in Europe began for the first time to call themselves Europeans, rather than English, French or German, just as many young people throughout Asia are beginning to call themselves Asians.

Reflecting this, *Megatrends Asia* is not a country-by-country inventory, but descriptions and predictions about subject areas that cut across Asia. It is a story about Asia as the continent it is and will become. All the more than thirty countries in the area are dealt with to one degree or another in this book, but the principal emphasis is on China, Hong Kong, India, Indonesia, Japan, South Korea, Malaysia, the Philippines, Singapore, Taiwan, Thailand and Vietnam. That is where the main dynamic of growth and change is located. I have visited and worked in all of these countries, some of them many times.

In thinking about and describing the world today, I want to let you know of my own bias. I have spent more than forty years in the business community. I am pro-business, pro-market, and I regard entrepreneurs as the true creators of new wealth, jobs and economic vitality. I believe in free markets and free trade. That's very much the direction in which the world is going. That is the context for this book.

Until the 1990s everything revolved around the West. The West set the rules. Japan abided by these rules during its economic emergence. But now Asians—the rest of Asia—are creating their own rules and will soon determine the game as well. Even Japan will be left behind as the countries of Southeast Asia, led by China and the Chinese Overseas, increasingly hold economic sway.

The West now needs the East a lot more than the East needs the West.

As far as Hong Kong is concerned, it sometimes seems as if Westerners think China is stealing a little European outpost. Hong Kong is China. Peking changed its name to Beijing; Saigon became Ho Chi Minh City; Burma became Myanmar. Just recently, Bombay was renamed Mumbai. How many people in the West took notice? These are changes symbolic of Asia's new independence from the West, and we will have more of them. When Macau returns to China at the end of this decade, a final chapter of Western dominance will have been written. For the first time in four hundred years, every inch of Asian soil will be controlled and managed by Asians.

The modernization of Asia must not be thought of as the *Westernization* of Asia, but the modernization of Asia in the "Asian way."

At the same time that Asia is modernizing, the Asian consciousness is rising. It is very much the *Asianization* of Asia. In the past a young Indonesian traveling in the West who was asked where she was from would have said, "Indonesia." Today, more likely than not, she would say, "Asia."

The Asian continent from India to Japan, from below the old Soviet Union down to Indonesia, now accounts for more than half of the world's population. Within five years or less, more than half of these Asian households will be able to buy an array of consumer goods— refrigerators, television sets, washing machines, computers, cosmetics, etc. And as many as a half billion people will be what the West understands as middle class. That market is roughly the size of the United States and Europe combined. As the widely placed Hong Kong Bank ad says, "There are 3 billion people in Asia. Half of them are under 25. Consider it a growing market." This is a consumer miracle holding vast economic consequences.

Many Asians have told me they believe that in the long run they will best the West competitively because they do not have, and will not have, a social security system, nor any of the other manifestations of the welfare state. Yet this is a competitive factor most Westerners have completely closed their eyes to. What does it mean? What does it mean in economic terms?

In Asia, families take care of themselves, above all else, and personal responsibility is emphasized. For Asians, the very idea of a central government being involved in family life is culturally unthinkable, horrifying. The idea of taking care of family first is why the savings rate in Asia is 30 percent or more in almost every country. Asia lives family values and self-sufficiency, and not only do Asians believe the cost of the welfare state is a heavy burden on competitiveness; they also contend that it undermines the importance of family and leads to out-of-wedlock children (in the United States, 30 percent of children are born out of wedlock, whereas in Malaysia it is 2 percent), high divorce rates, crime, loss of self-reliance and lower academic achievement.

This raises central questions for the West, especially for the United States and Europe. Are our welfare states now burdening our global

Introduction

competitiveness to a point where we must make some changes? Have our welfare states undermined the self-reliance of our citizens? Has our noble experiment failed? It is, I think, important to notice that today every country in the West, including now the United States, is trying to cut back on welfare state excesses.

What can Asia teach the West and its young people? Buried under a collapsed department store in Seoul for ten days, twenty-year-old Korean Choi Myong Sok became a hero in his country. Businesses were eager to cash in on his image of courage with lucrative media offers. But Choi would have none of it. "They don't understand my pain," he said. "They just want to make money. I don't believe in that." Compare that to America, where heroism—as well as crime, violence and human tragedy—is routinely commercialized. Can Asia's adherence to personal and family values help spark a global moral renaissance?

In the West, the least understood Asian phenomenon is the role of the Chinese Overseas, the ethnic Chinese who live outside the mainland of China, not only in Taiwan, Hong Kong and Singapore, but also in Indonesia, the Philippines, Malaysia, Thailand—and in Vancouver and Los Angeles and London. The most successful entrepreneurs in the world, they are the force that will catapult Asia to economic dominance.

Paradoxes abound in Asia's rapid ascent to global economic dominance. BMW is now assembling cars in Vietnam, paying its auto workers $1 a day, while the hotels of Asia's cities, including Saigon (Ho Chi Minh City) and Hanoi, are among the most expensive in the world. The picture is often cloudy, especially to Western eyes. But fifty years from now it will be clear that the most momentous global development of the 1990s and the early part of the next century was the modernization of Asia. It is the astonishing end result of the eight major shifts taking place in the region today, each described in the chapters of this book.

1. **From Nation-States to Networks**. Japan's economic dominance has reached its apex, and its relative economic position in Asia and the world is on a long downward slide. The power of Japan as a nation-state is giving way to the dynamic collaboration of the Chinese net-

work. Considerations about China and the Chinese Overseas now drive decision-making in Asia as China becomes central to the total Pacific region. But it is the Chinese Overseas network that will dominate the region—not China.

2. **From Traditions to Options**. Predestination is being replaced by diversity and a new individualism. In economic competition the West is handicapped by the heavy burden of the welfare state, which the East will not adopt, but new options in all aspects of life are now open to Asians.

3. **From Export-Led to Consumer-Driven**. Built on exports, Asian economies will increasingly be fueled by consumer spending and, with it, an emerging middle class. By the year 2000, Asia will have almost half a billion people who are what we generally understand as middle class.

4. **From Government-Controlled to Market-Driven**. Central government control and direction of the economies of the region have shifted to market economies, fueling an explosion of economic growth and opportunities. This shift has been accompanied by unprecedented economic cooperation and coordination among the countries of Asia.

5. **From Farms to Supercities**. Migration from rural areas of Asia to its cities is taking place at an astounding pace. This social shift is transforming Asia, moving it to the next era of development, away from agricultural societies to ones where cultural diversity and expanded opportunities will dominate.

6. **From Labor-Intensive to High Technology**. We are witnessing a dramatic shift from labor-intensive agriculture and manufacturing to state-of-the-art technology in manufacturing and services, most pronounced in the rush to computers and telecommunications.

7. **From Male Dominance to the Emergence of Women**. The shift from male dominance is most apparent in the increase of women entrepreneurs throughout Asia. In China, women make up 25 percent of all entrepreneurs. Women as voters, consumers and members of the workforce are now participating in all aspects of Asian life in unprecedented ways.

8. **From West to East**. The world used to mean the Western world. Today, global trends are forcing us to confront a reality: the rise of the

East. It is becoming apparent to the East and to some in the West that we are moving toward the Asianization of the world. The global axis of influence has shifted from West to East. **Asia was once the center of the world, and now the center is again returning to Asia**.

Those are the eight Asian megatrends that are reshaping the world. For the Chinese, the number 8 is a very lucky one. Some people in Hong Kong pay hundreds of dollars to get an 8 on their license plates or in their phone numbers. These eight trends will certainly bring luck to Asia. They will lead to an unprecedented prosperity. But how will they affect the West? Western nations long competed complacently among themselves until Japan suddenly took the field. The West is now confronted by not just another player but by a powerful new team of nations. And whether win, lose or draw, or whether everybody comes out a winner, will depend on how well we know our competition—and how well we play the game.

CHAPTER ONE

From Nation-States to Networks

For so many years it was the Japanese. The Japanese are coming. It appeared they were going to dominate the world economically. But now a remarkable transformation is taking place. The Chinese are coming. Asia and much of the world today is shifting from Japanese-dominated to Chinese-driven.

Japanese economic power has reached its peak and begun to recede as the Chinese prepare for the year 2000, the Year of the Dragon that will usher in the Dragon Century.

There are some people in Asia who are already aware of just how important this economic shift will be. But in the West, preoccupied with its own well-being, almost no one has the faintest idea that what is going on in Asia today will radically change the world. The economic resurgence of Asia, driven by an aggressive global network of Chinese entrepreneurs and offshore money, is moving in the direction of eclipsing the West. Unless the United States and Europe start to participate in the new Asia game, they will end up playing second fiddle to the new global leaders in Asia as early as the beginning of the next decade.

Yet the U.S. gaze (especially in the media-thick Northeast) continues to be toward Europe. And while what has happened in the old Soviet Union and Eastern Europe will in time have a great impact on the rest of the world, it will not compare with the impact that the changes taking place in Asia will have in reshaping the world.

The modernization of Asia—economically, politically and culturally—is by far the most important event taking place in the world today.

Meanwhile China, the Great Dragon, is flexing its economic and political muscle. Asia sees China as a major market now and in the future. In the context of Asia's rapid growth, I believe that companies must have at least a third of their revenues coming from Asia to remain substantial global players. China is now simply central to the total Pacific region:

• About 1,000 Hong Kong businesses are already controlled by Chinese state-owned companies, up from just 400 in 1992.

• In China, 3 million Chinese are employed in 25,000 Hong Kong company-owned factories—six times the number of employees the companies have in Hong Kong.

• By the end of 1995, annual two-way trade between Taiwan and China reached more than $25 billion.

• China's foreign trade in 1995 totaled $280 billion, an increase of 18.3 percent over 1994.

• China is also becoming an important investor in the region: 134 mainland China companies have invested more than $200 million in Malaysia.

• China's economy has doubled in just six years.

• Shenzhen, the Chinese city of 2.7 million on the border of the New Territories of Hong Kong, now boosts a GDP per capita of nearly $6,000.

But China's potential, as it usurps Japan's economic leadership, is not simply a matter of size. The true force that we must promptly come to reckon with is more dynamic, a secretive sophisticated network—invisible to most—that will make China and the Chinese the world's dominant economy. It is decentralized, Pan-Asian, increasingly global and family- and education-oriented. And most of all, fabulously rich. It is the phenomenon of the Chinese Overseas. There are 57 million of them, 53 million in Asia alone. They have been around for centuries, but only now is the world becoming aware of their awesome presence.

The Ethnic Chinese:
The New Great Economic Power

The dynamics of Asia's extraordinary growth cannot be understood without a thorough examination of the Chinese Overseas, the greatest entrepreneurs in the world. According to an assortment of estimates, **Chinese around the world hold between $2 trillion and $3 trillion in assets, and many believe the real figure is higher.**

In 1994, the Chinese-language *Forbes Zibenjia*, the franchised edition of *Forbes* magazine published in Hong Kong, analyzed the top thousand companies (those with the highest market capitalization) from ten Asian stock markets—Seoul, Taipei, Shanghai, Shenzhen, Hong Kong, Bangkok, Kuala Lumpur, Singapore, Jakarta and Manila. Their combined assets came to $1.14 trillion, or 89 percent of total market capitalization. Of the top thousand companies, 517 had an ethnic Chinese as the single largest stockholder. Thus, ethnic Chinese controlled $541 billion, some 42 percent of the total in these ten markets—quite a bit more than the $200 billion to $300 billion cited in other estimates.

Fujitsu Research in Tokyo looked at the listed companies in just six key Asian countries. As its findings below illustrate, the overwhelming majority were owned by Chinese Overseas.

Thailand	**81 percent**
Singapore	**81 percent**

Indonesia	73 percent
Malaysia	61 percent
The Philippines	50 percent

This astonishing revelation about the tremendous economic power of the Chinese is confined only to the publicly listed companies. What about the less glamorous small and medium-size enterprises that together make up 96 percent of all companies in the Asia-Pacific Economic Cooperation (APEC) realm? According to Bustanil Ariffin, the former Indonesian minister who co-chaired the Pacific Business Forum, it is believed that small and midsize companies employ half of the workforce in most Asian countries. Chinese own 90 percent of these companies.

The economy of the borderless Chinese Overseas is the third largest in the world.

If we counted the economic activity of all the Chinese Overseas as a country all by itself, it would be outranked only by the United States and Japan. Chinese Overseas dominate trade and investment in every East Asian country except Korea and Japan. Chinese in Hong Kong, Taiwan and Singapore supply more capital and foreign investment for the region than Japan. Ethnic Chinese—not the Japanese—are the largest cross-border investors in Thailand, Malaysia, Indonesia, the Philippines and Vietnam. The Chinese Overseas account for 80 percent of all foreign investment in China, the motherland. In 1995, estimates put the number of people in China employed by ethnic Chinese businesses at 20 million.

In the thriving new countries of Asia, Chinese Overseas control a huge chunk of the wealth—far more than their numbers might suggest. In Malaysia, they represent almost 30 percent of the population and control 61 percent of the economy. The numbers elsewhere are even more remarkable:

- Indonesia: 3.5 percent control 73 percent of the economy.
- Thailand: 10 percent control 81 percent.
- The Philippines: 2 percent control 50–60 percent.

Some historians go so far as to say that the economies of Southeast Asia were in a sense leased to the Chinese Overseas, while the natives concentrated on government.

The Chinese Overseas are not a nation-state, and the vocabulary and concepts used to think about nation-states will not help us understand the phenomenon. As science historian Thomas Kuhn has pointed out, we simply cannot understand a new paradigm by using the vocabulary of the old. For example, centuries ago, when scientists discovered the earth was round, flat-earth vocabulary and formulations were of no use in understanding a round globe, the new model. Contemporaneously, the Cold War is over, and market economies prevail, but we still think in the same vocabulary and concepts. Unless we adapt and create a new vocabulary and new concepts for new phenomena, we will never be able to comprehend them. Today's global economy is dominated by intercompany trade and person-to-person communications. Countries don't trade; people and businesses do. Networks are at the core of the new global economy.

The Chinese Overseas are a network of networks. That is a new paradigm, a new formulation within the framework of the world's economy. All the key players among the Chinese Overseas know one another. Their businesses stay singularly apart, but they work together when necessary. They are intensely competitive among themselves and exclude outsiders, especially those not of the same family, village or clan. When a crisis arises or a great opportunity presents itself, they will close ranks and cooperate. Chinese business boils down to people and contacts. As one Hong Kong banker puts it, "If you are being considered for a new partnership, a personal reference from a respected member of the Chinese business community is worth more than any amount of money you could throw on the table." All my personal experience in Asia certainly bears this out.

The family businesses of the Chinese Overseas are networks of companies and other enterprises. And they are, in turn, woven together to constitute a huge global Chinese network of networks. The Internet is the model for understanding. Just as the Internet is a network of thousands of networks, the Chinese Overseas networks number in the tens of thousands.

The number of networks and individuals on the Internet is not limited because the Internet is totally decentralized. There are now more than 89 million individuals on the Internet. And that number will be well over one billion by the year 2000. It is decentralized right down to the individual; only the individual can access the Internet. Because of this complete decentralization, the Internet can have as many members as want to join. Similarly, the Chinese Overseas network can get as big as it needs to be to transform Asia's economy.

The other general characteristic of both the Internet and the Chinese Overseas network is that no one is in charge; the marketplace is. With the Internet, it is the marketplace of ideas and information, though, more recently, the commercial marketplace as well. With the Chinese Overseas network, market mechanisms are the deciding factor. Motherland or not, economic decisions involving China are driven purely by dictates of the market and guided strictly by rates of return.

Individual Chinese Overseas networks of companies are completely decentralized from the whole and they are extraordinarily efficient parts. In *Global Paradox*, I posit that the bigger the system, the more efficient must be the parts in order to function as a successful system. And because autonomous parts are the most efficient, we could say that the bigger the system the more autonomous must be the parts. That clearly describes the Chinese Overseas network of networks. The Chinese function efficiently as individuals. By comparison, the Japanese excel and misbehave collectively. This mode of operation makes the Chinese, and their enterprises, immensely nimble in the competitive global economy. They react speedily to changing conditions, especially to political vagaries.

All powerful networks have one thing in common: each of the parts functions as if it were the center of the network. When I am on the Internet in my home in Telluride, Colorado, sending and receiving messages to and from others all over the world, I experience being in the center, just as does each of the other users of the Internet. That is very powerful. Chinese Overseas experience the same thing. As each individual deals with other people in his network in various parts of the world, that individual experiences being in the center of the network. Also, the individualistic Chinese want to have control of their own destiny. The Chinese proverb has it that "There is no prospect working for others." Everyone wants to be at the center and be his own boss. This inner entrepreneurial drive makes the Chinese very proactive, risk-taking and enterprising.

Joining the Global Network

The Chinese Overseas network is very self-aware. Yoji Hamawaki, who is famous in Tokyo for his spectacular success in the introduction of the BMW to Japan and is now with Digital, told me of his discussions with a group of ethnic Chinese who wanted to computerize their network. He said that the project would cost more than "one billion U.S. dollars." "That will not be a problem," he was told, and got an on-the-spot commitment. The Singapore Chinese Chamber of Commerce is committed to launch a computer network called the World Chinese Business Network, which will link Chinese chambers of commerce worldwide. This high-tech link in cyberspace will facilitate the flow of information for all Chinese entrepreneurs. A Chinese CNN based in Hong Kong, called Chinese Television Network, was launched in December 1994 to provide coverage of events in Chinese communities worldwide.

Now entrepreneurs on mainland China are joining the Chinese Overseas network. It is not that the Chinese Overseas are joining China. China is not the point. It is not who will become part of China. It is who will join the Chinese network—which parts of China, which entrepreneurs in China will become part of the Chinese network. Together they will drive the economic transformation of Asia—and the world. I am more and more convinced, as I wrote in my book *Global Paradox*, that the Chinese network is the organizational model for the twenty-first century.

The world is moving from a collection of nation-states to a collection of networks.

Who Are the New Billionaires?

Many of us already think of Taiwan and Hong Kong as part of China. Now we must extend the boundaries of "greater China" to include ethnic Chinese in countries like Singapore, Malaysia and Indonesia.

The world's 57 million Chinese Overseas, ethnic Chinese living outside the mainland, are dispersed among sixty countries all over the world, but about 85 percent reside in Southeast Asia. There are about 5.5 million Chinese in Malaysia, 6.1 million in Thailand and 6.5 million in Indonesia. More than a million Chinese live in Singapore, the Philippines and Vietnam. There are more than 1 million Chinese in California, the largest Chinese community outside Asia. More than 90 percent of the 57 million Chinese Overseas are now naturalized citizens of their adopted countries; only about 2 million people have kept their Chinese nationality.

The Chinese Overseas dominate in general trading and the service industries, and many big players are involved in banking and properties. In the last twenty years, expansion in banking and property development activities has become increasingly global. For example, the Chinese-owned Bangkok Bank, Thailand's largest bank, is expanding regionally. Asian-Chinese banks and property companies are taking up similar interests in North America and other parts of the world. Even the Bank of China, Beijing's main international bank, has a branch in the Cayman Islands.

All these enterprises operate through networks. And atop these networks—or perhaps I should say at the core—are a remarkable number of self-made billionaires. Among them are:

Liem Sioe Liong (net worth $4.5 billion). Liem left the south of China in the 1930s, moving to **Indonesia,** where he created a rural trading network. He began to supply the rebels fighting the ruling Dutch and met a young lieutenant colonel named Suharto. They were partners when Suharto overthrew Sukarno in 1965. This connection helped Liem build his Salim Group, which had sales of $9 billion in 1994, accounting for 5 percent of Indonesia's gross domestic product. Liem's personal holding company has evolved into a seamless network of enterprises with interests in banking and property.

Robert Kuok (net worth $5.7 billion). Kuok's father came to **Malaysia** from China in 1911 and opened a grocery store. Son Robert went into the commodities trading business in the 1950s, establishing the Malayan Sugar Manufacturing Company. By the 1970s he handled some 10 percent of the world's sugar trade. Known widely as "the Sugar King," Kuok now owns the Shangri-La chain of luxury hotels. In 1984 he built the China World Trade Center in Beijing. His joint venture with Coca-Cola includes ten factories in China.

Nina Wang (net worth $3.3 billion). In 1998 there will be a grand opening of the $1.3-billion, 1,594-feet-high Nina Tower in **Hong Kong,** which will then be, at 108 stories, the world's tallest building. She is Asia's richest woman, and is borrowing no money to finance the construction. "We have always relied on our own resources to finance our projects," says Wang, who took over Chinachem Group when her husband, Teddy Wang, was kidnapped and killed in 1990. She is the sole or part owner of about 200 buildings in Hong Kong.

Dhanin Chearavanont (net worth $4.2 billion). His family moved from Guangdong Province to **Thailand** in the 1920s, where Dhanin eventually took his Thai name. In the 1950s he set up a new company, Charoen Pokphand (CP), a chicken-feed mill. Today CP is highly diversified, with forty-nine of its more than two hundred companies in China. TelecomAsia, a joint venture between CP Group and the U.S.'s Nynex Inc., was recently listed on the Bangkok Stock Exchange.

Li Ka-shing (net worth $10.6 billion). Li's father, a teacher, moved his family to **Hong Kong** in 1940. He died two years later when Li was only thirteen. After some hard work in factories, Li struck out on his own at twenty-four, starting a plastic flowers business. In 1951 he began buying property and in 1972 took his main company, Cheung Kong, public. Today Li controls publicly traded companies that account for more than 10 percent of Hong Kong's total stock market value. He sold Star TV to Rupert Murdoch for more than $800 million. He is building China's Foreign Ministry offices in Hong Kong free of charge, according to some sources.

Kwek Leng Beng (net worth $5.7 billion). Kwek runs City Developments in **Singapore,** a property developer. The group made news in the United States when it was involved in the purchase from Donald

Trump of the Plaza Hotel in New York City. He is the eldest son of the late Singapore property tycoon Kwek Hong Png.

Chao Kwan Yuen. Chao, a professor of forestry at the University of Beijing, and his wife were on vacation in Bangkok when the communists took over China in 1949. They chose to stay in **Thailand**. Eventually Chao built the first sugar refinery in Thailand and the first oil refinery. By the end of the 1960s, he personally accounted for 10 percent of the taxes paid to the government. (In the late 1960s, I spent a year apprenticing with Chao in Bangkok. After each of an interminable series of business meetings, he would tell me, "Slowly, slowly; in the end we catch a big fish.")

These are just some of the visible bigwigs. Ethnic Chinese dominated *Forbes* magazine's 1996 list of East Asian billionaires outside of Japan and Korea. Many of the Chinese Overseas are rich and some are superrich. And it can now be said that they are running things economically in China—as well in Southeast Asia. What has recently become clear to most non-Chinese Asians is that what is good for the Chinese of Southeast Asia is even better for the indigenous people and cultures. In a world where capital and talent know no national allegiance, it will work in the host country's interest to have players in their midst who can access a network of capital, ideas, markets and talent.

The Cold War is over and the Chinese won.

Chinese Global Power

The great Yangtze River in China divided the Chinese people into two orientations. The northerners preferred the glory and glamour of the imperial court while the southerners sought wealth and money in commerce and trade. The seats of Chinese governments were almost always north of the great river; Beijing literally means "the northern capital." For centuries a feud existed between the merchant class of the south and those who governed in the north. The southern Chinese have always been wary of the government, hiding their wealth and keeping a low profile in order to be invisible to the governing class and protected from extortion by corrupt court officials. Southern merchants stayed away from the center and sought patronage with money and gifts so that they could be left alone to make their fortunes.

For centuries the merchant-class southerners were used to this mode of operation. They developed and ran commercial enterprises along the coastal areas, content to secure the economic well-being of their families. But when conditions at home grew worse owing to famines and natural calamities, many began to leave China and brought with them this distinct commercial ethic to their new homes.

The exodus from the south grew in size and momentum in the nineteenth century. Some brave young people who were determined not to let nature or system decide their fate set out from China to the South Seas to seek their fortunes. China was overcrowded and the backward farmlands could not support its huge population.

Because of the hardships the Chinese have endured for centuries, their minds are full of vivid images of instability and chaos. Yet the Chinese are also ethnocentric. They think of themselves as the children of the dragon, call their country the Middle Kingdom (suggesting the center of the universe) and take great pride in their civilization. But reality and hardship drove many of them to venture afar, hoping to bring back a fortune to enrich their motherland. Large-scale migration started at the time of the Opium War (1839–42) and continued until the Second World War.

The Han Chinese living along the coastal cities formed the dominant group of emigrants. Today, 85 percent of Chinese Overseas are from southern provinces—Guangdong, Fujian, Hainan and Guangxi— where among other dialects Cantonese is spoken. Cantonese, a broad term used to describe the people living in the Pearl River delta, formed the major group of Chinese Overseas. That's why most of the world's Chinese restaurants are Cantonese, although China has a wide variety of cuisines.

In the early days, apart from the wandering merchants, what is now the world's wealthiest network was little more than a slave trade. Families received a token sum from contractors, and their husbands and sons were shipped off to become laborers in foreign lands. Their only hope was that they would return someday with wealth.

Clan Networks

As emigration continued, familylike networks soon evolved. The migrants took care of one another and helped newcomers settle in their new homelands. They still worked backbreaking jobs but the clan associations they formed eased the burden with lodgings, contacts and communal support. Today, there are an estimated six thousand such clan networks in Southeast Asia, serving as contact points for employment, news and exchange and providing psychological support. Most now confine themselves to cultural and community activities, although some ambitious networks are transforming themselves into cooperatives and investment holding companies.

No mainframe. Just networked PCs. And as in all powerful networks, all of the Chinese Overseas experience being in the center of the network, which works well for the highly individualistic Chinese.

This vast network of clan associations is now serving as a ready platform that helps China attract the Chinese Overseas to invest in the mainland. For example, the International Hainanese Association recently convened a meeting of more than a thousand delegates from twenty countries in Haikou, a southern city in the province of Hainan. To date, the Hainanese Overseas have invested about $250 million in various projects in China.

Integrating Locally

In the past, one characteristic of ethnic Chinese enterprises was the avoidance of long-term investments or businesses with long gestation periods, which stemmed from the "sojourning" mentality, the desire to return to the homeland after making enough money. Interest in their temporary home was purely economic. That attitude is changing today. Chinese Overseas are tending to invest long-term in their adopted homelands. They have been involved in manufacturing, real estate and finance since the 1960s and in time Chinese Overseas assimilate into the local community and contribute to their adopted land.

Japanese businesses and people remain Japanese wherever they go. They live in closed Japanese communities and have less occasion to speak English. In contrast, Chinese, especially in Southeast Asia, have a working knowledge of many native languages and speak English well, even among themselves. They retain the ability to read and speak Mandarin and Cantonese. The Chinese take on local cultural habits, dress and food. The younger Chinese Overseas generation's command of the native language is indistinguishable from the native. Many no longer carry a Chinese name or speak Chinese, though they may still practice distinct Chinese ways and retain many cultural traditions (Chinese food, Chinese celebrations and festivals, Chinese customs and Confucian values).

Many government officials in Southeast Asia are of Chinese descent, including, for example, the just past prime minister of Thailand, Chuan Leekpai, and the current prime minister, Banharn Silpa-archa. Former President Corazon Aquino of the Philippines is another example. Chinese in Europe, North America and Japan are not as well-to-do as Asian-Chinese, so their influence in politics and government is not as strong. However, in recent years many have become mayors, senators and state governors. Some Chinese in South America are government ministers. Oddly, the president of Peru, Alberto Fujimori, who is Japanese, is called Chinese and affectionately known to the people as Chino (Chinese).

Hard Work and Thrift

One of Asia's most successful Chinese Overseas, Robert Kuok of Malaysia, says, "As children we learned about moral values—mainly Confucian. Terms such as 'business integrity,' 'honor,' 'your word is your bond' were often used by the elders and sank into our minds. We would hear from our womenfolk constant urging to remain humble and never practice ostentation. One other interesting thing I learned from my mother was a phrase which literally translates as 'morality of the mouth.' We were not to speak bad of others." Robert Kuok is known for adhering to these early lessons.

Hard work and thrift are the hallmarks of the Chinese. They work long hours and rarely rest, except for a break during the lunar new year festival. Making money is their preoccupation. Giving their children a good education is a universal Chinese obsession. Professor Wang Gungwu, vice chancellor of Hong Kong University and a noted authority on the Chinese Overseas, who himself is a Chinese born in Indonesia, says, "I believe that these Chinese attitudes towards wealth and culture are still with us."

Wang points out that the Chinese have been trading overseas for more than a thousand years without the support of their government in China. "They depended instead on their own daring, their skills and, most of all, their entrepreneurship." With no political power themselves, they would link up with those in power in order to achieve their commercial goals. "To achieve wealth while other people held the power was to accept that wealth could not be followed by power in the hands of the merchants themselves," Wang explains. They knew from Chinese history that wealth was safer when the wealthy showed no desire or ambition for political power.

Four Roads to Travel

These entrepreneurs entertained four possible strategies after they made their fortunes, contends Professor Wang. I have recast them somewhat as four archetypes:

1. *Returnees.* Accept that living abroad is untenable and therefore take their wealth and return to China.

2. *Assimilators/Connectors.* Recognize that total assimilation in the local culture is unavoidable and that to protect their wealth, they must be connected to those with local power.

3. *Sojourners.* Cultivate entrepreneurial activities in more than one country, ready to move wealth between various Chinese communities.

4. *Leaders.* Use wealth to achieve extensive influence as leaders in their adopted communities, remaining culturally Chinese while being loyal citizens of their adopted countries.

Successful Chinese entrepreneurs care deeply about maintaining cultural values in their local communities and strengthening cultural links with China. For example, the 5 million Chinese in Malaysia kept their Chinese education system alive entirely through private funding. Malaysia's Chinese community also supports a thriving media of more than thirty newspapers and magazines in the vernacular Chinese language.

The *first option*—returning to China—has almost universally been ruled out. Even with today's openness—and ethnic Chinese investments are welcomed with open arms—for most Chinese entrepreneurs it is still easier to make a fortune in Taiwan, Hong Kong, Malaysia and other parts of Southeast Asia than in China itself. Furthermore, the system of rule of law introduced by Western colonial powers in Southeast Asia has created an environment conducive for Chinese enterprise to thrive. Without both central authority looking over their shoulder and the unpredictability and vagaries of the "rule of man," the Chinese Overseas flourish in a much more secure environment than they had in the past.

Ethnic Chinese do extensive business with mainland entrepreneurs and send a considerable amount of wealth back to China to build schools and clan temples, and to support relatives. But most Chinese Overseas want to stay abroad to ensure their security and profitability.

The *second option*—assimilation in the adopted country—has been widely adopted. Most Chinese who settle abroad become citizens of their new countries. Some intermarry. But they guard against total assimilation. They continue to hold on to Chinese values regarding business practices, education in the Chinese language, and customs and social practices. For younger, well-educated Chinese, it is no longer an issue. After all, the world is becoming a global village. While one can still harbor pride for one's cultural heritage, there is a growing tendency for the young people to develop a global mindset.

The *third option*—remaining a sojourner—holds little attraction today. Wang Gungwu defines the sojourning mentality as "that cultural trait or habit of mind among the Chinese that treats every place outside China they may live in as but a temporary home." Ethnic Chinese entrepreneurs, however, sometimes act like sojourners, doing business from country to country, some commuting between Vancouver and Taipei, between Los Angeles and Singapore. With the gains in air transport and telecommunications, distance isn't what it used to be.

The very idea of sojourner suggests the Chinese Overseas have a very strong attachment to their homeland and its more than five thousand years of history. And they do. But today it is more of a cultural attachment than a physical one, although going back to visit your home village or the home village of your ancestors is still a journey that most want to make.

The *fourth option*—maintaining culture while affirming political loyalty to the country of residence—is the one most have adopted. While that loyalty is at times questioned, Chinese Overseas, the world over, affirm their identification with their country of adoption, but without turning their backs on their Chinese cultural roots. Their loyalty to Chinese culture is not political. They want to remain ethnically Chinese, but do not want to be citizens of the People's Republic of China. They tend to keep their heads down, observing the wisdom of the Chinese saying, "The big tree catches the wind."

Nationalist leaders in Southeast Asia have at times been suspicious of the ethnic Chinese. In Indonesia, in 1965, anti-Chinese riots killed tens of thousands of ethnic Chinese. At the Second World Chinese Entrepreneurs Conference held in Hong Kong at the end of 1993, Singapore's Senior Minister Lee Kuan Yew felt the need to voice a strong reassurance to the governments and people of the host countries of many Chinese Overseas:

Ethnic Chinese, who come from such "sensitive" countries, should take care that their investments in their own countries do not diminish as the result of their China investments. And they would do well to use their *guanxi* [personal connections] to increase China's trade with an investment in their home countries. We are ethnic Chinese. We share certain characteristics through a common ancestry and culture. We can build up trust and rapport easily between ourselves. But we must be honest and recognize the fact that at the end of the day, our fundamental loyalties are to our home, not ancestral, countries. After two or three generations away from China, we have become rooted in the country of our birth. Our stakes are in our home countries, not China where our ancestors came from. The Chinese-Thai is a Thai and in the end he wants Thailand to prosper so that his assets in Thailand can be secure. So, too, Chinese-Singaporeans, Chinese-Malaysians and Chinese-Filipinos. They may invest and visit China frequently, but few want to make China their home.

From Father to Son (and Daughter)

"The father makes the money," goes the Cantonese proverb, "while the son spends it." The late Malaysian tycoon Tai Chik Sen, whose family controls the big Soon Seng Group, maintained a humble lifestyle even after accumulating huge wealth. When local reporters asked about his modest lifestyle in comparison with his sons, who were breezing around Kuala Lumpur in flashy BMWs, he replied, "My sons have rich father; I don't."

The rise and fall of many family fortunes gives credence to the saying that wealth will not last three generations. The young man who has not known hardship and pain, or how to make money, will not know how to conserve it. But for many prominent Chinese Overseas families, a different adage seems to apply: the father builds the business, the son expands it. Many rising sons of Chinese Overseas families are not only expanding, corporatizing and consolidating family businesses, they are taking them to new heights, thanks to Western education, aggressiveness and global ambition.

A good example—and the talk and envy of corporate Asia—is Richard Li Tzar-Kai, twenty-nine, son of Hong Kong's number-one tycoon, Li Ka-shing. Listed as one of *Time* magazine's Global 100 leaders for the new millennium (December 5, 1994), Richard Li rose to stardom by founding the family's Star TV, the first satellite cable-television network, revolutionizing Asia's electronic media overnight. It was sold to Rupert Murdoch's News Corporation in 1993 for what eventually turned out to be more than $800 million. (Murdoch paid $525 million for most of it in 1993. He bought the balance in 1995 for around $300 million.) Richard Li studied economics and computer engineering at Stanford, and is now ready to take to the skies from his base in Singapore through his new vehicle, Pacific Century Group. He wants to provide satellite telecommunications services across the region. Businesses will buy a six-foot dish and receiver to get a twenty-four-hour dedicated circuit that bypasses local telephone systems by applying a Very Small Aperture Terminal (VSAT) license, a common service in the West. According to Li, "We want to provide Asians with the same basic access to services that the West now takes for granted." Target markets include China, India, Pakistan, Indonesia, Vietnam and the Philippines.

Y. C. Wang's Formosa Plastics Group is one of Taiwan's largest family conglomerates, with $9.1 billion in revenues. Wang's son, Winston, and his two daughters, Charleen and Sher, are pushing Formosa to greater heights in petrochemicals and electronics. Their global vision includes mainland China and they just plowed $1 billion into their Texas plant. Asia is watching to see how this second generation of Wangs carry on with their legendary father's enterprise.

Victor Fung, active in his family business and also chairman of the Hong Kong Trade Development Council, sees a changing mindset in the Chinese Overseas. At the Second World Chinese Entrepreneurs Conference, he said: "We are less inward-looking and more outward-looking. We may still value the family as the single most important unit of our success, but we are poised to move to the next threshold, whereby our small to medium-sized family companies acquire a multinational character and a global presence."

Asia's Own Name Brands

"My dream was to make computers available to everyone," says Stan Shih, chief of Acer, Taiwan's premier computer maker. He started with eleven people and just $25,000. Today, the Acer Group is the world's fourth largest maker of PCs and PC parts and had sales of $5.8 billion in 1995. "My vision for Acer in the year 2000," says Shih, "is to market Acer products as a global brand to countries all over the world." Acer is already the number one PC producer in several countries and expects to have twenty-one listed companies and revenues of $15 billion by 2000.

Shih is in the forefront of promoting Asia's own branded manufacturing. Chairman of Taiwan's Own Brand Federation, he is helping and educating local manufacturers to create strategies of developing their own brands. "We [Chinese] have never had our own brands. We are excellent at contract manufacturing for other brands. With the rise of Asian economies, manufacturers in Singapore, mainland China, Hong Kong and Taiwan must seriously contemplate creating world-class indigenous brands. This will be the aspiration of businesses in the region in the next century."

Expanding the Networking Model

The networking of the Chinese Overseas is a powerful phenomenon, and few have thought more about it than Singapore's Lee Kuan Yew, who says, ". . . it would be a mistake for Singaporean entrepreneurs not to participate in one of the greatest transformations of our age . . . And we would be foolish not to use the ethnic Chinese network to increase our reach and our grasps of opportunities."

In fact, Lee sees the Chinese Overseas networking model as a way to extend tiny Singapore's powerful reach into other ethnic communities. He wants Indian, Pakistani and Arab businessmen to "take up residence" in Singapore and serve, in effect, as Singapore's business ambassadors to their home regions. And, of course, Singapore has the best air links and telecommunications infrastructure in the region. Now Lee invites others to embrace the model. The Chinese Overseas can and do forge key relationships in international cooperation and between their host country and mainland China. That is appreciated—even by the region's most nationalist leaders.

There is yet another side to this networking model. The education-obsessed Chinese have been sending thousands of their children to the world's best universities and private schools in the West. The offspring keep company with the children of the world's business and political power elites at Eton, MIT, Harvard, Stanford, Oxford and Cambridge. Although not initiated by foresight, but more as a response to contingency planning, the ethnic Chinese have created another powerful worldwide network. And anticipating the future, I have heard talk in Taipei of Taiwanese parents who want to send their children to universities in mainland China, this time forming friendships with the children of the Great Dragon's power elites.

Japan's Long Downward Slide

The emergence of the Chinese Overseas onto the world stage is casting a shadow over the preeminence of the Japanese. Ever since Japan began to spread its economic wings, the rest of Asia has engaged in a need-hate relationship with the Japanese. Asians like Japanese money and know-how, but they still fear being dominated by Japan, partly because of residual hostility arising from the experience of colonization and war. Asians have looked to Tokyo, rather than Washington, to play a larger role in the region. But Japan has been reluctant to assume leadership except economically. Asia's response, in turn, has been fundamentally ambiguous. It looks to Asia as if Japan has reservations about genuinely embracing Asian culture. Today there are also complaints about Japan's reluctance to transfer technology and to localize management.

Japan is, of course, a powerful force in Asia and the world. Yet its influence in Asia has largely been confined to trade and investment. Japan is the biggest export market for most ASEAN (Association of Southeast Asian Nations: Brunei, Indonesia, Malaysia, the Philippines, Singapore, Thailand and Vietnam) countries. Beginning in 1990, Japan exported more goods to Asia than to the United States. Japan is also Asia's most important market and one of the region's biggest investors. But now even that strength is waning.

There are many signs that Japan's economic dominance has reached its apex. Between 1991 and 1995 the Japanese economy was in a kind of malaise.

• Japan's gross domestic product (GDP) suffered five consecutive years of stagnation.
• For the first quarter of 1995, Japan's industrial output was 7 percent below the 1991 peak.

- Excess industrial capacity now stands at more than 30 percent.
- At 3.4 percent, Japan's 1995 rate of unemployment is the highest since records began to be kept in 1953. Because of notorious overstaffing, this figure is unrealistically low. Among 1994 college graduates, unemployment stood at a stunning 17 percent.
- In 1995, Toyota announced it would lay off its first workers since 1951. As Japan's number-one auto maker, that paved the way for others to follow.
- Production costs in Japan are the highest in the world.
- In March 1995, Nissan's leading factory in Zama, outside Tokyo, became the first Japanese car factory to be closed since World War II.
- There probably will never be another new automobile plant built in Japan.
- Sony, the flagship of Japan's consumer companies, lost $2.5 billion in 1994.
- Japan's most expensive land in the Ginza shopping district of Tokyo has lost more than half its value in four years.

Only about 3 percent of Japan's personal computers are networked, compared with an estimated 50 percent in the United States. Less than 10 percent of Japanese homes have a computer. Japan has the lowest PC usage among developed countries.

The Bubble Economy

In Japan everyone talks about the economy "before the bubble," "during the bubble" and "after the bubble," as in "After the bubble, I lost everything."

The bubble occurred in the 1980s when industry overinvested and when banks and other financial institutions loaned too much both domestically and overseas, particularly to land and stock market speculators. Everyone was loaning and spending too much and prices went sky high, that is until the bubble burst in 1990. Real estate and stock prices took a nosedive and Japan entered a deadly deflation spiral with no end in sight. Today's stock market is 63 percent below its high and it is still overvalued. Property prices are down about 50 percent.

The big problem in Japan is massive deflation in stocks and real estate and no political will to fix it. Most troubling is the huge overhang of domestic bad debt. Japanese estimates of bubble bad loans were first made public in June 1995—$471 billion—or 8.6 percent of the nation's 1994 economic output. That is a bigger burden on Japan's economy than the savings-and-loan disaster was for the United States, and banking analysts in Tokyo immediately said the government's figure was much too low. Highly respected Yukiko Ohara of UBS Securities Ltd. said that estimates of the entire bad-debt load could be as high as $1.21 trillion, or about 25 percent of Japan's annual total economic output. If so, the Japanese banking system is in danger of collapse.

"Is Japan finished?" asks Edith Terry in *World Business.* "The Japan of the bubble economy was as unbalanced in its way as the former Soviet Union, forced to devote most of its human and material resources to creating national wealth. Faced with pressure for change, bureaucrats and politicians are falling back on hoary Japanese values, such as collectivism and obedience, rather than taking bold action. If that continues, a nation obsessed with becoming number one will have to settle for a position considerably lower on the list." The Japanese economy is emerging from five years of recession "as a misshapen monster—a dinosaur's body with the head of an ostrich," writes Terry.

Investors' Nightmare

In the 1990s a Japanese investor will soon have lost more than the American investor did in the 1930s. The Nikkei index of the 225 leading issues on the Tokyo Stock Exchange peaked at about $460 in December 1989 and plummeted to a six-year low of less than $200 in June 1992. There has been only a modest recovery since. In July 1995 it stood at $170. When the bubble was still expanding, many expected the Nikkei index would hit $1,000 by the mid-1990s. Now some predict it could fall to $120 before reaching bottom.

Since 1991 the number of foreign companies on the Tokyo Stock Exchange dropped from 127 to ninety-three. Daily transactions are one fortieth of the 1989 peak. Part of the blame goes to the abysmal performance of corporate Japan. Japanese companies quoted on the

Tokyo exchange in the year ending March 31, 1995, earned total net profits equivalent to only 1.9 percent of shareholder equity. In the same period the return on investment (ROI) of U.S. firms was 17 percent, British almost 14 percent and German 10 percent.

Japan was the star performer of the industrial world, but it is now the sick economy of Asia.

The Japanese lost more than half the domestic value of the money they invested overseas during the past ten years. (Remember the 1980s hysteria about "the Japanese are buying up America"?) Japan's GDP growth rate increased during the first quarter of 1996, but it is still questionable if Japan is finally pulling itself out of its worst recession since the 1930s.

Japan and East Asia

East Asia is replacing Japan as driver of the region's booming economy. Japan is losing market share to Asian neighbors and to countries of the Organization for Economic Cooperation and Development (OECD). Japan exports to OECD countries fell from 9 percent in 1986 to 7.7 percent in 1994. In the same period, the ten emerging Asian economies (China, India, Taiwan, South Korea, Hong Kong, Indonesia, Malaysia, the Philippines, Singapore and Thailand) increased their share to the OECD market from 9.8 to 14.5 percent.

In 1994, in these ten countries, Japan accounted for 24 percent of their imports, a little less than in 1986. During the same period, the group of ten countries increased their exports to this intraregional market from 22 to 35 percent.

The economies of most of Japan's Asian neighbors are growing at an annual rate of from 7 to 10 percent, thereby doubling every ten to seven years, respectively. And this phenomenal rate of growth is led by China, with an average of more than 10 percent for the last several years. Since 1990 the Asian Tigers (South Korea, Taiwan, Hong Kong and Singapore)—not Japan or the United States—have been the big investors in ASEAN countries. The first tier of Tigers is financing the next.

As much of its trade is intercorporate, unless Japan welcomes direct foreign investment, little hope exists for correcting its trade imbalance with the rest of the world. In contrast, the countries of non-Japan Asia are wide open to foreign participation in their economies. How much longer will the rest of Asia withstand one-way traffic in trade as their economies build? Japan has to rethink its Asian strategies, urgently.

Japan and the United States

But, one might argue, isn't Japan simply evolving into a more mature economy? You cannot expect sky-high growth rates forever. True enough. But look at these comparisons between the United States and Japan:

- Japan's industrial production at the end of 1994 was 5.5 percent below that of 1990. Industrial production in the United States was 15 percent higher.
- Japan's rate of growth in aggregate productivity over the past *eight years* has been close to zero. The United States has averaged 1 percent annual gain.
- Japan's labor productivity is 17 percent below that of the United States.

Japan's budget deficit relative to GDP is already as large as the U.S. budget deficit, and there are pulls and tugs to put money into the rebuilding of the earthquake devastation in the Kobe area and to otherwise spend more government money to stimulate the economy.

Japan trails the United States in the development and sales of electronics, computers and telecommunications. Its auto industry, confronting price hikes, trade wars and dwindling productivity, faces an uncertain future. Its once admired educational and managerial systems are now questioned in much of the world. And it has a huge identity crisis. In fact, I published a book in Japan in 1992 entitled *Japan's Identity Crisis*. That crisis has only gotten deeper.

In 1995, for the first time since 1985, Japan lost top ranking as the world's most competitive economy. The United States placed first. Singapore was second, Hong Kong third. Japan is now fourth.

There is also a growing sense that the Japanese model—an export economy with lifetime employment and tight regulatory control—is no longer working. The government is so paralyzed and chaotic that it is incapable of taking the measures necessary—that is, liberalizing regulation—to salvage the economy.

Perhaps the harshest judgment about the state of Japan's economy comes from Brian Reading, former economics editor of *The Economist*, who says, "This is no economic superpower bent on world domination. It is a hara-kiri economy set to self-destruct."

Japan's place in the global economy is further handicapped because:

• The postwar generation that sacrificed to build Japan's world-class economy is phasing out—and what appears to be a generation of "risk-averse" custodians has replaced it.

• Japan is extremely overregulated, which is a tremendous drag on growth. Japan pioneered cellular communications, but then regulated them so heavily that the United States and Europe soon surpassed Japan in production and use.

• Widespread sexism and ageism still exist.

• As a result of a very low birthrate, people living longer and virtually no immigration, Japan is aging faster than any other country in the world. By 2020 an extraordinary one quarter of Japan's population will be sixty-five or older.

• People at the top are overworked while the average workweek is being reduced. In 1993 the average number of hours worked weekly fell below forty hours for the first time. In Japan, the middle and the bottom are working less and less while at the top, people are working until they kill themselves.

• There is an overcentralization of money, people and information in Tokyo—at a time when decentralization and efficient parts make systems successful.

There is no sign in any sector of accelerating momentum in Japan's economy.

Social and Political Chaos

Japan has entered a period of political chaos from which I don't think it will soon recover. Ichiro Ozawa, the country's most powerful politician, calls Japan a "small-brained dinosaur." Economic woes are only part of it—or perhaps economic disillusionment is being expressed, or played out in the hearts and minds of Japan's citizens through some bizarre political decisions and a frightening public fascination with a violent, dangerous and apparently seductive cult.

The political establishment in Japan was humiliated in April 1995 when the huge body of unaffiliated voters elected comedic actors as governors (mayors) of both Tokyo and Osaka.

In Tokyo, Yukio Aoshima, a male comedian who played a "nasty grandma" on television, beat seven other candidates, including a deputy minister who had served seven prime ministers. Aoshima had no party backing, nor did he campaign, preferring to stay at home reading. He spent only $2,352. But his familiar stance against political parties and the central government was enough for voters.

The losing candidate, who was favored to win, Deputy Chief Cabinet Secretary Nobuo Ishihara, had the support of five ruling and opposition parties, and spent an embarrassing $360 million. Nevertheless, Aoshima, whose family ran a *bento* (boxed lunch) shop, is now the governor of Tokyo, one of the most powerful positions in Japanese politics.

In Osaka, Japan's second city, Nokku "Knock" Yokoyama, a storytelling comedian who in recent years has appeared on late-night television programs with scantily clad women, entered the election only three days before the campaign started. He beat former Science and

Technology Agency bureaucrat Takuya Hirano, who had the support of all major parties, and is now the governor of Osaka.

The outcomes of the elections in Tokyo and Osaka were stunning rejections of traditional politics and politicians. Never before has a governor been elected in either Tokyo or Osaka without party support. The number of voters who say they aren't affiliated with any party has doubled in two years, to 57 percent. Both new governors, however, had served for years in the quite meaningless upper house of the Japanese parliament.

"It's a revolution," said Takeshi Nagano, chairman of the Japan Federation of Employers Association. "For the first time since the Meiji restoration in the late 1880s," said political commentator Minoru Morita, "the Japanese people showed disappointment with the bureaucrats."

"People's anger against existing parties became my victory," said Aoshima, who had vowed that, if elected, he would cancel the 1996 World City Expo Tokyo, seven years in the making at an estimated cost of $2.4 billion, more than half of which was already spent. It was scheduled to open in the spring of 1996 for a ten-month run. Most opinion polls and editorial views agreed the billion-dollar city fair was far too expensive at a time when Japan is mired in its longest recession in fifty years.

True to his word, just months after the election, Aoshima called off the expo, causing widespread bewilderment and dismay among Japan's business and political communities. "The issue here is not money, but the validity of a public pledge," he said. "Any money lost, or gained, can be made up eventually. The bigger question is whether Aoshima is a man who keeps his promises."

Since the April 1995 elections Japan's political parties have been recruiting celebrities to run for office. The Liberal Democratic Party, the largest member of the ruling coalition, has gone for some sports stars, including an Olympic ice skating medal-winner, a former soccer star and a professional wrestler.

Castrated Country

Remember Shintaro Ishihara? He caused quite a stir in 1989 with his book *The Japan That Can Say No,* co-authored with Akio Morita, the former Sony chairman. A week after the Tokyo-Osaka political earthquake, he abruptly resigned the parliamentary seat he had held for twenty-seven years, saying he despaired of Japanese politics.

On the occasion of receiving an award for a quarter century of service in parliament, Ishihara surprised everyone by making a resignation speech. He said Japan now seemed like a "castrated country" unable "to express its will as a nation, like a man who is unable to function as a man." Strong stuff. Ishihara also said that Japanese politics is "despised by the people, and all politicians, myself included, are responsible. Although numerous problems threaten to disrupt a future that ought to be promising for Japan, hardly any politician today wants to touch any of these issues. All political parties and nearly all politicians act only for the most ignoble forms of egotistic self-preservation. I myself am ashamed, so I'm resigning as a Parliament member," he concluded.

Aum Supreme Truth

But few things in the postwar period have shaken the Japanese as much as the bursting into the public consciousness of the mystical cult Aum Shinrikyo, or Aum Supreme Truth. After the cult was suspected and subsequently charged with releasing a rare nerve gas in Tokyo's subway system that killed twelve and injured 5,500, it became an obsession with the Japanese. Ten days after the subway attack, Tokyo's chief of police was seriously wounded—shot in the back by masked gunmen —and Aum's senior scientist was stabbed to death outside one of the sect's buildings in downtown Tokyo.

When the cult's leader, Shoko Asahara, was arrested, all regular television shows were canceled and replaced with coverage of the cult, its history and activities. It was revealed that some of Japan's best and brightest young people were members of the cult and long profiles of the young senior leaders ran in Japan's leading newspapers. TV coverage rivaled or exceeded America's addiction to obsessional coverage of the O. J. Simpson trial.

The cult's headquarters is in a place called Kamikuishiki, a dairy farming community high on the slopes of Mount Fuji. It is now a huge tourist attraction and Shoko Asahara has become a household name. Even little children know who he is. On the day of his arrest, the major television stations each assigned several hundred people (yes, several hundred each) to the story. More than fifty newspapers printed special editions about the cult and the events now associated with it.

One of the most curious phenomena is the obsession of teenage girls with Fumihiro Joyu, who at a very young-looking thirty-two was the spokesman for Aum Shinrikyo, and who overnight became Japan's number-one media star. Young women and girls all over Japan fell in love with this articulate, good-looking graduate of one of the country's best schools, Waseda University, where he earned a degree in engineering. Even though he was described in the press as "a doe-eyed monk who says he shuns wine, women and sex," they showered him with love letters and flowers, and cut pictures of him out of all the newspapers and magazines. The onetime head of the cult's office in Moscow and fluent in English, Joyu received far more TV exposure than the government, especially during the early stages of the police investigation of the cult.

Cult leader Shoko Asahara, a half-blind forty-year-old with very long hair and an unkempt beard, and more than one hundred Aum senior leaders were arrested in connection with the subway gas attacks. Asahara is the sixth of seven children of an impoverished tatami mat maker. His young aides hold degrees from prestigious Japanese universities (Tokyo, Keio and Waseda, among them). And it was shocking and embarrassing to the Japanese government to discover that thirty Self-Defense Forces (Japan's army) soldiers were members of the Aum Shinrikyo cult.

Just as disturbing was the fact that Asahara attracted many affluent young Japanese to his cult. His message is that with persistent training, members can gain spiritual powers not defined by science. "In the past people who have joined 'outlaw' organizations like the *Yakuza* or *Bosozoku* [motorcycle gangs] have been education dropouts or people who somehow failed to cash in on the affluent society," says a retired government official. "The truly frightening thing about Aum is that it attracted affluent young people from top universities. The movement looks like a protest to our whole way of doing things, not just against the individual's failure to make good in society."

To rule Japan after a vaguely planned coup, Aum established a shadow government, a political structure that mirrors Japan's ministries. In this structure, Shoko Asahara is the "Divine Emperor." There is a Home Affairs Ministry, a Defense Ministry, a Science and Technology Ministry (which is in charge of fortune-telling by the stars and the development of personal computers), a Health and Welfare Ministry, and so on—a network of twenty-two ministries and agencies.

Aum had become a powerful business conglomerate (from noodle shops to personal computer makers), with assets of more than $1 billion. Members lived together in the sect's commune and donated all their possessions to the cult. However, since the bombing about two-thirds of the followers who lived in the Aum compound have quit the cult. Shoko Asahara, on trial for murder, may face the death penalty.

The Country That Can't Say "I'm Sorry"

In the spring of 1995, Japan's then Prime Minister Tomiichi Murayama pushed hard for a parliamentary resolution of remorse and apology for Japanese acts before and during World War II, as part of the fiftieth anniversary of the end of that war. But most in the Diet opposed or were lukewarm to the idea of apologizing for Japan's actions.

In the middle of the bickering over whether to apologize, Michio Watanabe, a leader of the powerful Liberal Democratic Party, said at a political rally that Japan's thirty-five-year military rule in Korea was the result of "a treaty of peaceful merger signed under the auspices of international law." In Korea, where anti-Japanese feeling runs high, the reaction was quick and furious. (During its brutal colonization of Korea the Japanese banned the Korean language—everyone had to learn Japanese—and made all Koreans take Japanese names.)

In the end, the Japanese parliament could not bring itself to apologize and issued a bland, meaningless statement of remorse that there had to have been a war. That was followed by an apology of sorts by the lame-duck prime minister—who dropped it out of subsequent speeches—which did not, in any case, satisfy very many Asians. It is not a Japan that can say "no." It is a Japan that can't say "I'm sorry." The whole enterprise leaves one to judge Japan as a country that has no moral compass or backbone, no real sense of who it is or what it has done.

In a world where economic considerations will increasingly overwhelm political ones, future success will rest to a great extent on economic performance, but not that alone. With a decline of political power taking place all over the world, a country's moral balance and stability will stand in its place. On both economic and moral grounds, Japan's rise has peaked, not soon to be regained.

There is a serious spiritual gap in Japan. Today it is a very tender, vulnerable country. And while Japan has one of the world's most successful economies—in many ways, the most successful—it may have reached a stage where new social and political ideas are needed.

At this juncture, for example, Japan does not know if it wants to be identified with the East or the West. Should Japan rejoin Asia? Although it really does not need to choose between East and West, Japan has already decided. As one of the G-7, all Western nations with the exception of Japan, it is identified with the West.

Today, Southeast Asia is certainly more important to Japan than the West. I have heard this wherever I go in the region and my suggestion (which I made in a speech in Tokyo) to Japan is: pull out of the G-7. Make the G-7 the G-6. Show you identify with both East and West by ceasing to be a member. It would send a strong message to Asia that Japan wants to be part of Asia. The G-7 is irrelevant anyway, though highly symbolic. Pulling out of the G-7 would also demonstrate that Japan can make a decision.

Find a Gateway to Asia

Western companies that fail to participate in the great Asian boom will not only lose opportunities, but may also undermine the competitiveness of Western corporations. The fact is the maturing economies of the West *need* external stimulus. Western technologies and sophisticated goods must find wider application and new markets, and it is in Asia that these technologies and goods will find the greatest potential.

Like accessing the Internet, the West must find a gateway to Asia.

That gateway is the Chinese Overseas. Having lived, worked and dealt with the West from Southeast Asia and in the West—in Canada, the United States and Europe—the Chinese understand the market economy and how to operate in it. To bring the rest of Asia into the free-market club, the Chinese Overseas are the ticket of admission.

The Chinese Overseas are the most global among all the players, and are paving the way for the emergence of a truly global operating model. Before Westerners appreciated the value of offshore havens, the Chinese Overseas were already there. Enormous amounts of the world's money are sheltered in offshore havens, much of it belonging to Chinese. The Chinese seek out the most attractive operating base, and governments looking for foreign investments should court them. For now, the Chinese are developing Vancouver (where 20 percent of the population is Chinese) as the operating base for the Dragon Century. Many of the really big players in Hong Kong, like Li Ka-shing and Stanley Ho, are already there. British Columbia won favor because it does not tax income earned offshore, which is perfect for the Chinese. After depositing their families in beautiful Vancouver, and serving out an "immigrant sentence"—the residency period required to qualify for citizenship—they themselves fly back and forth to Asia, or control empires of business enterprises spread all over the Pacific Rim through cyberspace. The Chinese Overseas seem to think national identity is only relevant when it comes to tax rates and mobility.

Ethnic Chinese capital represents a good source of capital for the West. Chinese entrepreneurs are increasingly making inroads into the economies of the West, providing healthy stimuli to many parts of the world. As Asian-Americans, the ethnic Chinese are already reshaping the economic and cultural landscape of some parts of the United States, especially California.

While the world moves from nation-states to networks, the Chinese are creating the first truly global, tribal network.

Indian counterparts of the Chinese Overseas are usually referred to as nonresident Indians. Numbering about 10 million with a combined income of an astonishing $340 billion, equivalent to India's entire income with its 940 million people, they have been highly successful in Britain, South Africa, Hong Kong and Southeast Asia, and the United States. As economic reforms settle in place in India, these émigrés are working with entrepreneurs in India, much as the Chinese Overseas have worked in China, and will become a powerful force in the ever-so-promising economic development of India. Stay tuned to the Indian network.

The world is moving from a collection of nation-states to a collection of networks. As borders are erased, paradoxically, national identity becomes more important. As we yield a little of our identity by becoming so economically interdependent, we seek a stronger cultural identity. Our roots, our nationality become more important.

Ethnic networks will be only part of the emerging global network of networks. Business sector networks have begun to form: architecture/construction networks; a fashion network of designers, textile providers and clothing manufacturers; automobile, travel, medical and, of course, financial networks are being formed in an endless process as the importance of political nation-states yields to the economics of global networks.

Still Trapped in the Old Paradigm

Meanwhile the political West, and especially the United States, continues to be the prisoner of the vocabulary and concepts of the nation-state, Cold War period. The U.S. government with its bilateralism in trade tags behind an ever-changing world. The whole planet is moving beyond multilateralism to borderless trade, and the United States hasn't even got to multilateralism yet. It says it supports the multinational World Trade Organization, and indeed played a crucial role in its creation, but its actions are all based on the old paradigm.

The United States and other Western governments continue to be obsessed with the government of China. Both politicians and the media hype the growing military threat of China at a time when half of China's military is engaged in commerce, with very little interest in performing military duties.

Governments do not trade. Governments do not create the world's added value. People do. Entrepreneurs do. Economic considerations have long since overwhelmed political ones. The role of government ought to be to stay out of the way so entrepreneurs and corporations can continue to create the global economy.

Because the Chinese Overseas network is so decentralized, it does not matter what the point of entry is; everything is connected to everything else. So choose a partner who is in the same business or who is directly connected with the part of China or Malaysia or Indonesia that interests you.

Many in the West know a lot about Japan and something about China. Now Japan is in decline and not really part of the New Asia. Many of the Chinese Overseas operate out of the young dynamic economies of the region. If you are serious about doing business in Asia, you have to know more about the huge countries of India and Indonesia, about the much smaller but dynamic economies of Taiwan, Malaysia, Thailand, South Korea, Singapore, Hong Kong and, increasingly, Vietnam and the Philippines.

I think Europe especially is badly in need of an Asian wake-up call. Europeans and the European media are squandering their time and energy on issues that pale in comparison to the impact the developments in Asia will have on Europe. Europe is preoccupied if not obsessed with monetary union and other Maastricht matters, which in the long run will not even be implemented, let alone count for very much. Some of that time and energy should go into understanding the developments and the opportunities in Asia. What happens in Russia and Eastern Europe will not begin to measure up to the importance of the changes in Asia.

CHAPTER TWO

From Traditions to Options

Asia's newfound wealth has provoked major shifts in Asian thinking and attitudes. Economic restructuring, which grabs most of the headlines, has set in motion a profound psychological revolution involving Asia's self-image, culture and heritage. The changes happening today in Asian values are complex and paradoxical, yet it is important to sort them out in order to comprehend their far-reaching effects.

The most fundamental truth to grasp is that today's revolutionary changes are taking place against a backdrop of history and heritage encompassing thousands of years. Ancient norms and practices, and long-established hierarchies resulting in predetermined behavior and social status. In tradition-laden Confucian societies, for example, women were subservient to men, not only in rights and status but also in their opportunities for self-expression. The ancient iron-clad caste system of Indian societies made upward mobility almost impossible. The same was true for Confucian societies, which ranked scholar, farmer, artisan and merchant in that order. Even today, under the communist regimes, the party determines what you do for a living and where, and how many children you may have. For centuries men or women trapped in unfulfilling marriages might have considered themselves unlucky, but were compelled to endure in the interest of honor and family. Strong social stigma awaited any recalcitrant. In the collective memory, social behavior equaled conformity. Period.

Politically, Asian countries have been subjected to varying degrees of domination. All except Thailand have, at one time or other, been under colonial rule. Japan dominated the region by conquest until it was defeated in World War II. After being ruled by England, India was for years on a socialist path. After the war, however, beginning with Japan itself, Asian countries began undergoing various forms of political transformation. Communist governments won control of Vietnam, China and North Korea. The colonial powers withdrew and nationalistic movements led to self-rule and independence, then to the establishment of representative government or an evolution from dominant one-party rule to participatory democracy. Decades later these gradual changes were further transformed by a rise in people power, notably in the overthrow of the Marcos dictatorship in the Philippines and the pro-democracy riots of 1992 in Thailand. All these movements heralded the end of domination and the beginning of new experiments in multiple political options.

Adding to the structural upheaval has been the empowerment of the individual through information and technology. Jimmy Lai, founder of *Next,* a pro-democracy, pro-market Chinese magazine in Hong Kong, says, "Information offers choice; choice motivates interaction; and people's interactions form the network of society. This new society . . . extends far beyond local physical boundaries."

The more Asian values are challenged by change, the more Asians are learning about what those values are and what they mean. In the process, Asia is moving from traditions to options.

Wealth, political change, technology and the market economy, as well as the enlightenment and empowerment of people through travel and business, are the key factors behind these new options. As Asia expands economically, as Asian societies move toward greater political openness, individuals, companies and institutions will experience more and more options. New models and structures, new ways of organizing relationships are emerging between women and men, employers and employees, government and the people.

This huge wave of change is rolling across Asia with unprecedented speed. Individuals, society and governments are now confronted with the challenge of not only managing the changes presented by these new options, but also the speed with which they are taking place. In some countries, the radical changes are creating turmoil and chaos in the social fabric, increasing stress and producing undesirable consequences. Both the advantages and the ills of progress and prosperity are most apparent in urban Asia, but are also increasingly felt in rural areas.

Do all these new options offer a better quality of life than the life of tradition and predestination? That is the question Asia is grappling with. One thing is certain. These new options are available for the first time in the lives of many people. As Chen Li, the sixty-nine-year-old retired editor at large of the *China Daily* in Beijing, announced euphorically, "For the first time in history, we have control over our destiny."

How Do Eastern Values Differ from Western Values?

The two recent lightning rods that brought the East-West debate about values to the forefront were America's linking of human rights with the extension of Most Favored Nation status to China and the caning in Singapore of teenager Michael Fay. Which, then, should take precedence: the rights of the individual or the rights of society?

"The expansion of the right of the individual to behave or misbehave has come at the expense of orderly society," says Singapore's senior minister, Lee Kuan Yew. "I would hazard a guess that it has a lot to do with the erosion of the moral underpinnings of a society and the diminution of personal responsibility. . . . The fundamental difference between Western concepts of society and government and East Asian concepts . . . is that Eastern societies believe the individual exists in the context of his family."

First of all, the big debate currently raging in Asia is *not* about the relative superiority of the values of East or West. **It is a rebellion against domination; it is Asia standing up to its former masters.** Whether Asian or American values, some values are universal.

One of the main conclusions of David I. Hitchcock in *Asian Values and the United States, How Much Conflict?* is that "the common threads developing between East and West across the Pacific are far more significant than the differing values each holds dear. . . . And that most of the strains of development evident in East Asia today stem from modernization, rather than Westernization."

Hitchcock, of the Center for Strategic and International Studies, a thinktank in Washington, D.C., interviewed 100 people from different professions in Singapore, Kuala Lumpur, Jakarta, Bangkok, Shanghai, Beijing, Seoul and Tokyo. The majority were academics and most "would be considered quite influential in their own country," he states. He asked these individuals to rank what values they believed were "critically important" to their fellow countrymen. Interestingly enough, when compared to American responses to a similar question, many values appear to be fairly universal, not specifically Eastern or Western, but they differ in priority.

Top Asian Personal Values	*Top American Personal Values*
Hard work	**Self-reliance**
Respect for learning	**Hard work**
Honesty	Achieving success in life
Self-discipline	Personal achievement
Self-reliance	Helping others
	Honesty

Top Asian Societal Values	*Top American Societal Values*
Orderly society	**Freedom of expression**
Harmony	Personal freedom
Accountability of public officials	Rights of the individual
Openness to new ideas	Resolution of conflicting political views through open debate
Freedom of expression	Thinking for oneself
Respect for authority	**Accountability of public officials**

Asia Chooses Its Own Values

Asia has come of age. It seeks to determine its own agenda, to do things in the Asian way. Throughout the continent, the voices of Asia are saying good-bye to Western domination, politically, culturally and economically. Asia will only join the world as an equal partner. It will make its own decisions, decide for itself what role to play on the world stage. Any policymakers, government or private, who fail to see this fundamental change in mindset will be greatly disadvantaged in their dealings with Asia and Asians. Recognizing and appreciating this change is basic to building a meaningful or successful East-West relationship.

To Modernize Was to Westernize

Historically, Asia has accorded the West a sort of "superior" status. Because of its advanced material progress and overpowering military and political might, the West was rarely challenged or questioned. For decades, modernization was almost synonymous with Westernization. In Japan beginning in the Meiji era (starting in 1855), modernization has been a process of Westernization. Traditions handed down through the earlier Edo period were systematically expelled, affecting the government's cultural policy, university system and legal institutions. Banished subjects ranged from Chinese medicine and literature to the study of national classics and Buddhism. The Western way was best. Those subjects that managed to survive did so by being recategorized as Western disciplines. The society gradually assimilated the essence of Western culture. It should be noted, however, that the Japanese have possessed a great ability, over the years, to "Japanize" all things foreign, possibly in part because of their limited usage of English and other foreign languages and their very tight and closed feudal society. So Japan embraced a sort of *Japanized* Western way.

In English-speaking Southeast and South Asia, however, Western influence has had a later but much greater impact. When colonies, like Malaysia under the British or Vietnam under the French, became independent nations, there was no immediate return to precolonial cultures. Things Western were still considered superior and desired. In Southeast Asia, for example, it was prestigious to send children to English-language rather than to native-language schools, to work at the offices of multinational companies and in some places (e.g., Hong Kong and Malaysia), for women to marry Caucasians. For many years Chinese-school-educated Singaporeans were considered an underclass compared to their English-language-educated counterparts. Postcolonial Asia embraced Western ways unconditionally. The brain drain to the West in the 1960s and 1970s was inspired by the pursuit of possibilities abroad and driven by lack of opportunities at home and abhorrence of repressive, suffocating regimes.

New Asian Assertiveness

All that has changed and there is an upsurge in confidence throughout Asia today. As I traveled around, without fail, in my many conversations with government officials, academics, business leaders and journalists in Singapore, Bombay, Shanghai, Kuala Lumpur, Jakarta, Tokyo, Taipei, Manila, Hong Kong, Bangkok and elsewhere, I found overwhelming self-confidence, even assertiveness. A collective consciousness of being Asian is emerging.

Malaysia's young deputy prime minister, Anwar Ibrahim, who himself is at the forefront of a movement toward an Asian renaissance, describes the phenomenon: "Since the nineteenth century, Asian nations have been overawed by the wealth and power of the West. Under the yoke of colonialism, Asian nations had no choice but to examine themselves critically vis-à-vis their masters, not their neighbors. Even after having gained independence, they were unable to exorcise the ghost of their erstwhile superiors. Thus all their energies and efforts went towards the quest for parity with the West, brought about by a deep-rooted sense of inferiority and the need to restore their self-esteem. This was the fundamental cause of the crisis in the Asian consciousness, manifested by a profound sense of helplessness in the face of Western military and political onslaught."

Now that Asia rivals the West economically, Ibrahim continues, "the Asian mind has finally broken free from intellectual morass." That is it. Asians are coming to grips with themselves. There is emerging, in Ibrahim's words, ". . . a more positive attitude towards our own traditions, and a genuine interest in the traditions of our fellow Asians. What we are about to embark on is a voyage of self-discovery, a journey through the myriad Asian traditions in order to understand and know each better."

Noordin Sopiee, director general of one of the most influential think tanks in Asia, the Institute of Strategic and International Studies (ISIS) in Kuala Lumpur, Malaysia, is another enthusiast for this new Asian renaissance. Dr. Noordin is spearheading the Commission for a New Asia, a group of eminent intellectuals from all over Asia, coming together to draw up a blueprint for modernization. "A great deal of Asia has started to rediscover Asia," he says, "to begin to have faith in Asia, to begin to be proud of being Asian."

This faith in Asia, that it can develop its own models, the Asian way, is now shared by many. Dr. Chandra Muzaffar, director of Just World Trust, a human rights group in Malaysia, says, "We want a more holistic approach to development, one that addresses in totality the various human realms of existence, material and spiritual." Professor Sang-Woo Rhee of Sogang University talks about Korea's national vision for the twenty-first century: "that progress is not quantity, but also quality. We want to create harmony in our societies."

East to West: Stop Lecturing Us

The intellectual discourse between East and West has intensified the values debate. When trade issues are linked with human rights, for example, Asia is increasingly impatient with, even aggravated by, what it views as the West's patronizing "big brother" attitude. Kishore Mahbubani, permanent secretary in Singapore's Foreign Ministry, calls for the West to "stop lecturing Asians." He says the West does not have the *moral standing* to tell others what to do. He sees Western societies in great disarray.

Mahbubani, who is also the dean of the Singapore Civil Service College, recently wrote in *Far Eastern Economic Review* that it is the breakdown of the family in the West that is leading to its social decay.

"Since 1960," he notes, "the U.S. population has grown by 41 percent. In the same period, there has been a 560 percent increase in violent crimes, a 419 percent increase in illegitimate births, a 400 percent increase in divorce rates, a 300 percent increase in children living in single-parent homes, a more than 200 percent increase in teenage suicide rates, and a drop of almost 80 points in Scholastic Aptitude Test scores."

So What Are Asian Values?

For many, the term "Asian values" is a rallying cry against the perceived evils of Westernization, a desire to reinstate the best of the old ways in the face of rapid, stunning modernization. Changes that transpired over centuries in the West have occurred in the space of a few decades in Asia. The question now is how best to preserve the old culture and traditions even as life changes at an incredible speed.

While the West cannot expect to impose its own social order on Asia, at the same time it cannot be blamed for all the problems inherent to modernization. Though it is popular to criticize the West, Asia must come to terms with its own struggle to modernize and accept the responsibility that comes with it. It must figure out how to hang on to cultural traditions while adapting to the modern world, a challenging contradiction for any culture.

The problem is that Asian values connote different things to different people. Asia is a region of great diversity, and there is no agreement on the virtues of Asian values, even by Asians themselves.

"If We Like It, It's Modern; If We Don't, It's Western"

This mocking quote is heard often in Asia. "You will find people unreceptive to the idea that they be Westernized," says Singapore's Lee Kuan Yew. "Modernized, yes, in the sense that they have accepted the inevitability of science and technology and the change in the lifestyles they bring." Lee is a very vocal representative of Asia, yet many Asians dislike the fact that he tries to speak for all Asians. All Asians are not of one mind and one thought.

For three decades Lee has ruled Singapore, most of that time modernizing and, yes, Westernizing this city-state. (Go there; it's as Western as Kansas City.) And once Singapore became a celebrated success story, Senior Minister Lee himself became a celebrated spokesman, much of the time as the only voice of Asia. With the shifts in the tides, Singapore has now returned to emphasizing Asian values, and Lee is an eager spokesperson for the Asian way. But, again, can he speak for all of Asia?

A Region of Diverse Values

The collection of countries and cultures that make up Asia did not undergo any systematic integration until recently, when free-market mechanisms began to be embraced. The cultural, religious and linguistic diversities of the region made harmonization otherwise impossible. Historically, there has been no movement to blend Asia together, except the activities of traders and political conquests. In precolonial and colonial days, strong imperial powers dominated separate states, which remained isolated. Since the rise of nationalism, Asian states have been preoccupied with the struggle to gain sovereignty, and after independence, to build and strengthen their own states. These national preoccupations have until now prevented solidarity with neighbors and the forging of common systems.

David Hitchcock, whose report on values was mentioned earlier, found that "on no other point was there more unanimity among those interviewed in seven countries than on the question of an 'Asian way' and Asian 'kinship' or affinity. Most respondents found little significant kinship between their own country and their neighbors in the region."

• One response was from a Singaporean researcher who said, "I find it difficult to say there is a kinship. . . . Singapore wants to be able to rely on China as a heavyweight vis-à-vis the rest of the world. . . . 'Asianness' is largely a reaction to the lack of Western sensitivity."

• Another scholar said, "Our only common heritage is Asian. . . . Some of us are not very Chinese. . . . We are trying to define ourselves."

• A journalist from Bangkok stated that while an "Asian way" could be seen in business dealings among the country's Chinese population, "we do not feel any special affinity for other countries in the region."

Asian Values Reexamined

When Asian societies talk about Asian values, says Dr. Chandra Muzaffar, "this is a very selective approach. They pick up the values that suit them as far as the elites are concerned, that these values will not challenge them." He points specifically to Singapore. "They talked of Confucian values, they talked about loyalty to the state, the attribute of hard work, but no one talks about profit from the Confucian ethical point of view."

Dr. Muzaffar is not excited about what he views as "another grand cycle of capitalism," which, he argues, "betrays the fundamental values embodied in the Asian religions. Asian values do not mean recycling of some values practiced elsewhere. If we are to produce something new, our notion of Asian values must go beyond hard work, family, etc., and deal with more fundamental values."

Muzaffar promotes a holistic approach. Malaysian Deputy Prime Minister Anwar Ibrahim goes for balance. "If we in Asia want to speak credibly for Asian values, we must be prepared to also champion those ideals which are universal and which belong to humanity as a whole," he says. He refutes the notion that Confucianism and Asian traditions advocate suppressing the individual for the benefit of society. "It is altogether shameful, if ingenious, to cite Asian values as an excuse for autocratic practices and denial of basic rights and civil liberties."

What Does Reverend Sage Confucius Say?

Is it the Confucian way of family and community over individualism that has catapulted Asia's economic success? Some say it is.

Others disagree. Nobel laureate Dr. Lee Yuen Tseh, president of Academia Sinica in Taipei, says, "In fact, Confucianism was never given that much attention in our society, apart from being promoted as a guide to right living. The success of the East Asian economies has given Confucianism a good name."

Many in Asia believe that Asia's phenomenal growth is a result of the embrace of Western science, technology and management. "Confucianism of any version . . . was not the spiritual or ideological source of inspiration or impetus for . . . capitalist development in the initial stage of East Asian modernization. It was the impact of Western modernization that provided the impetus for change," says Korean scholar Kim Kyong-Dong.

But what, then, has Confucianism contributed? It instills the value of hard work, but so does the Protestant ethic. Just what are Confucian values?

Professor Tu Wei-ming, world authority on Confucianism who teaches at Harvard University, provides the explanation. Confucianism embraces two mainstreams of philosophy, politics and personal ethics. "Political Confucianism," he says, "legitimates a hierarchical political system culminating in the emperor . . . [while] 'Confucian personal ethic' . . . regulates day to day life." Some Asian governments are employing political Confucianism as an umbrella to legitimize their mode of governance, whereas Professor Tu argues that "the more important legacy of traditional Confucianism is not its political teaching, but rather the personal ethic that regulates attitudes towards family, work, education and other elements of daily life that are valued in Chinese society."

Many Westerners do not understand that in the Asian concept of hierarchy, responsibility flows in two directions: Confucianism is not just, "Listen to thy father." The father must also be accountable to the son. **"Confucianism is not simply the advocacy of obedience to government, but also the accountability of government,"** explains Professor Tu. He adds that student activists and radicals who protest the policies of the governments in Taiwan and South Korea are responding to Confucian teachings.

"Under the Confucian tradition, leaders must meet certain minimum conditions in order to claim moral authority, and that is highly problematic for the current leadership in China," observes Tu. He believes that Confucian tradition would prosper more in a democracy that promotes individual rights than in a totalitarian atmosphere. "If they really want to learn from Confucian humanism, they have to open up to more enlightened values, such as freedom of expression, the dignity of the individual and other human rights."

So it is not individualism or liberalism that is the problem when Confucianism is being promoted as incompatible with Western-style democracy. The problem lies in the relationship between individual families and the state. Francis Fukuyama, author of *The End of History and the Last Man*, says, "The essence of traditional Chinese Confucianism was never political Confucianism at all, but rather an intense familism that took precedence over all other social relations, including relations with political authorities. That is, Confucianism builds a well-ordered society from the ground up rather than the top down, stressing moral obligations of family life as the basic building block of society. The bonds within the family take precedence over higher sorts of ties, including obligations to the political authorities."

Traditionally, Chinese families are suspicious of the state and avoid dealings with government. Settling disputes through the courts did not guarantee delivery of justice because of corrupt court officials, who represented the government. But ironically, it is their deference to authority that, at times, has created the need for an authoritarian government. Historically, the Chinese people have experienced continuous social and political instability, as well as devastating natural disasters. They fear chaos, which undermines development and progress, and will do anything to preserve stability. Fukuyama suspects that "the emphasis on political authoritarianism in Singapore and other Southeast Asian states is less a reflection of those societies' self-discipline—as they would have others believe—than of their rather low levels of spontaneous citizenship and a corresponding fear of coming apart in the absence of coercive political authority."

The resurgence of Confucian values, both on the part of Asian governments and the academic community, represents a campaign to ward off the social decay that stems from "Westernization"—the weakening of work ethics, hedonistic consumption, excesses of individualism and agitation for participation in government. Confucianism is seen as the way to prevent the decline of the family unit in Singapore, the only East Asian country to "explicitly" stress it in values education. "China is looking for something to take the place of failed Marxism," says W. Theodore de Bary, a Confucian scholar at Columbia University. The state is trying to advance a Confucian socialism to take the place of a Marxist one.

In 1994, China celebrated the 2,545th anniversary of the birth of Confucius. While Mao would be quite disturbed by the state's support of Confucianism, as de Bary suggests, it fills the void left by the downfall of Marxism. The celebration also marked the founding of the International Confucian Association, whose goal is to "spread Confucian studies throughout the world." De Bary believes that East Asian societies are trying to establish a cultural bond against Western decadence as they see it. China hopes its plans to instill Confucian values will inspire people to care about others, not just themselves.

Senior Minister Lee, honorary chairman of the International Confucian Association, said,

It is my business to tell people not to foist their system indiscriminately on societies in which it will not work. As an East Asian looking at America, I find attractive and unattractive features. I like, for example, the free, easy and open relations between people regardless of social status, ethnicity or religion. And the things that I have always admired about America, as against the communist system, I still do: a certain openness in argument about what is good or bad for society; the accountability of public officials; none of the secrecy and terror that's part and parcel of communist government.

But as a total system, I find parts of it totally unacceptable: guns, drugs, violent crime, vagrancy, unbecoming behavior in public—in sum, the breakdown of civil society. . . . In the East, the main object is to have a well-ordered society so that everybody can have maximum enjoyment of his freedoms. This freedom can only exist in an ordered state and not in a natural state of contention and anarchy.

Why I Love America

As the debate about the evils of Westernization grew more intense, Tommy Koh, director of the Institute of Policy Studies in Singapore and a former ambassador to the United States, became a defender of the United States. Writing for the *International Herald Tribune,* he said that reports of America's sorry demise may just be a bit exaggerated. "America's problems are real. But they should be seen in proper perspective. The United States has many strengths and virtues." He went on to list the many strengths and virtues he had experienced in his nineteen years in the United States. Among them:

• In Singapore, only about one person in ten does volunteer work. More than 80 million Americans donate to a cause.

• There is a strong tradition in the United States of giving money to schools, colleges, universities, hospitals, libraries, churches, museums and to supporting the arts. In 1993, Americans contributed $126.2 billion to educational and charitable institutions, $9.6 billion to artistic, cultural and humanitarian organizations, most from individuals.

• American culture nurtures original thinking and pioneering research. More Nobel prizes are awarded to Americans than to scientists from any other nation. Asian scientists who have won Nobel prizes have been based in America.

• Since the end of the Vietnam War in 1975, 850,000 refugees from the region have been taken in by America—no nation has welcomed so many immigrants and refugees, and none has assimilated them so well, as the United States.

• Today, Asian-Americans are the fastest-growing community in the United States, made possible by the relative absence of racial or class barriers.

• No other nation has been as generous as the United States in sharing its technology with others.

The Way Forward

Most of Asia does not blame the West's influence for its problems, and acknowledges the West for its economic development and higher standard of living. Still, Asia's intelligentsia are concerned with what they see as the impending social decay brought about by Asia's new prosperity. Dr. Mahathir Mohamad, prime minister of Malaysia, who volunteers friendly advice to the West from time to time, sums up this concern: "We can easily achieve material progress by physical planning and development. But the stark truth is that all the material wealth that we have accumulated can be completely wiped out if we do not have the morally right set of values among the people who manage it."

Changing Lifestyles

The intelligentsia, especially in industrialized and urban Asia where social problems are most acute, will continue to debate and agonize over causes, effects and remedies. Meanwhile, the vast majority of common people, especially the young, are adopting Western, mainly American ways. Teenagers around the world often have more in common with one another than they do with their parents. Right or wrong, it's reality and there's no going back. It is the globalization of lifestyles. Too bad ideas about American lifestyles come from the entertainment media. Led by Hollywood and TV, the media are responsible for the distorted image of American life that is spread all over Asia. Asian governments, in turn, are keen to censor negative signals that glorify violence and sexual wantonness.

But the major shifts in the social and cultural landscape that are beginning to take place in Asia run deeper than changing lifestyles. They have to do with the changing role of the individual within the system, regardless of whether the outcome is positive or negative. But paradoxically, I think the widely perceived onslaught against Asian values brought about by galloping materialism will strengthen them. The more the threat is experienced, the more Asian intellectuals will become aware of their basic values and the more they will want to shore them up. And the more economically interdependent all Asians become (thereby losing at least a part of their individual identities), the more interested they will be in their identity, and the more they will want to defend it. This translates into renewed interest in who they are as expressed by their language, arts and literature, and history. The Thais will become more Thai, the Koreans more Korean and the Malaysians more Malay.

A New Family Style

Increased divorce rates are no longer a unique Western phenomenon. All of urban Asia has them. They're everywhere. Korea's divorce rate is up threefold since 1970. Taiwan's and Singapore's have doubled since the early 1980s. China's has tripled since 1990. In Hong Kong, the divorce rate increased tenfold from 1972 to 1992.

Even in Singapore, where the family is so emphasized, the juvenile crime rate increased 27 percent between 1992 and 1993. Single-parent households are also increasing. In an effort to stop the rise in the number of unwed mothers, they are punished by having certain privileges revoked. Legislation was introduced to allow parents to sue their children for support.

In Hong Kong, the number of single-family households is estimated at nearly twice what census figures report. The suicide rate of those under nineteen years of age in Hong Kong has increased substantially. Between 1993 and 1994 police figures show an eightfold increase in the number of drug arrests of sixteen- to twenty-year-olds. "Families in Hong Kong are very geared towards making money; they don't spend enough time together any more and crime is just one part of a youngster's maladjustment," says C. C. Lu, senior clinical psychologist for Hong Kong's Correctional Services.

The phenomena of divorce, unwed motherhood and juvenile crime may indeed be the downside of greater individualism and openness. And while some opt to let individual fulfillment prevail, whatever the consequences, most Asians still prefer to stick with the emphasis on building families. Some successful women in Asia, when asked to choose between family and individual career aspirations, chose family.

Sexuality: It's O.K. to Look at Me

In Japan, PDA—Public Display of Affection—i.e., kissing in public, has become increasingly common. Some call it "evil behavior from overseas"; others complain the kids have "absolutely no manners." But while some find kissing in public offensive, posters of nude women are plastered all over the newspapers and on TV.

"Nowadays it's perfectly fine to directly project your sexuality," says Japanese psychologist Nobue Nakamura. Why? Because, she explains, the "self-restraint" of the Japanese culture is changing to allow people to become more "individualistic." Or to have the option of becoming more individualistic.

The Chinese cities of Tianjin, Shanghai, Guangzhou and Jilin air call-in shows that discuss dating, sex, sexual diseases and other questions. The program *Secret Whispers* airs in Shanghai after midnight. "Sex" and "banking" top the list of caller questions on Shanghai's "information radio line." Magazines and papers feature stories on contraception and sex.

The place to express one's sexuality is at a disco, where an ordinary office girl can shine like a glamorous diva. "Most OL's [office ladies] have to wear terrible uniforms all day and make copies and serve tea," says Ken Lyle, manager of Juliana's, a British-based company that opened a huge disco in Tokyo a few years ago. "This is their 15 minutes of fame, the chance to wear sexy clothes and say to men, 'I'm a good-looking woman, and now you're looking at me.' "

More than 50,000 women recently flocked to the Tokyo Dome for a contest of "dancing, waving feather fans and boas." But, some wonder, "Is it women's liberation or exploitation?" At the Ronde Club in Tokyo's Akasaka area, women wear feathers, G-strings and other tiny items of clothing on stage. "It's wonderful," says Misao Kawaii, who at age sixty-seven went to Juliana's to see what "dirty dancing" was all about. "My, the young women's legs today are so pretty and well-shaped! So different from our generation. I was really impressed."

In Japan, unmarried women over age twenty-five are called "Christmas Cakes." Increasingly, however, Japanese women refuse to get married well beyond twenty-five and no longer worry about being called a stale "Christmas Cake" or becoming a (much older) "New Year Cake." "We are living in a very different culture to that of a decade ago," says Hong Kong psychologist C. C. Lu.

Honor Thy Father

In Japan, "how to" books on caring for senior family members rank on the best-seller lists, including what to look for in a retirement home. In China, the ancient contract stipulating that children will support aged parents is being renegotiated. While 97 percent of Beijingers surveyed by the China Academy of Social Sciences said children should take care of their parents, 20 percent said they would put their parents in "old-age homes" to do this. Seventy-five percent said they were "reluctant to live with their parents." The nursing home is an innovation for Asia. Modern ones have the pluses of medical facilities and recreational programs for residents. Still, many Asians are very uncomfortable with the idea of an "old age home," says Indonesia's Wahid Supriyadi. "Sending a grandparent to a nursing home is regarded as inhuman in most Asian society."

Although many new ways of family and economic life have begun to appear all over Asia, there will not be a total shift from "communitarianism to individualism," maintains Lam Peng Er of the Department of Political Science, National University of Singapore. The trends, he says, "will co-exist side by side."

"[It] may not necessarily mean that by going towards individualism one is leaving behind communitarianism," affirms Marzuki Darusman, vice chairman of the Human Rights Commission and a former member of the Indonesian House of Representatives. "It's a question of balance."

No Yesterdays, No Tomorrow

The influx of a new individualism is most evident in the younger generation. New Delhi sociologist Atiya Singh says of the young,

"They work hard, play hard, and think only of themselves. Tradition and idealism are out. Casual sex and mobile phones are in vogue. They call it maximization. The idea is to squeeze the most out of the time without jeopardizing the future." Yet it is the future that might be in jeopardy. A young Taiwanese remarked to a colleague of mine, "Why save? If I need money, I just go out and earn it."

"There is a sense of craziness here," said one of about 1,500 people crowded into Shanghai's JJ's disco. "That's why so many young people want to come here. After I go home, I think about how coming here costs a lot of money. But then the next day, I want to come again." What was surprising about JJ's was that there seemed to be almost no one over the age of thirty, and they had cash. Plenty of it, reports Hong Kong *Advertising and Marketing.* They pay an entrance fee of $9.40. "It is like a Cultural Revolution all over again," quips a visitor from Hong Kong, "except this time they're not trying to destroy it—they can't get enough of it."

JJ's was started by Andy Ma, an American from Taiwan who formed the venture with China's People's Liberation Army. JJ's was ordered to close by China's Public Security Bureau in 1995, but it will be back.

Asians have always worked hard and saved hard. Purchases are postponed for decades to enable capital to accumulate, to save for old age, to finance children's education and to support the obligations of the extended family. The forty- and fifty-somethings knew, in a Chinese expression, the hardships of working "no day and no night" (always working), but today's young seem to be practicing another tenet, no yesterdays and no tomorrow. The mantra for today's Asian youth is "Let's have fun." In some liberal households it is often remarked that suitable parental advice to a teenager has changed from "Come home early" to "Don't forget your condoms." The new generation of Japanese workers will not work at the jobs their parents did, even more so now as they see their elders ending up on the scrap heap.

But against the face of growing conspicuous consumption and hedonism, it would be erroneous to assume that Asia is playing too much and not working hard enough. While some choose to smell the roses now, others are working feverishly to build global empires. A glance at the senior managers of Asian companies, entrepreneurs and professionals reveals a stunning picture of young, aggressive and ambitious thirty- and forty-somethings who are working very hard indeed.

Chen Cheng-chung, age forty, one of the most successful entrepreneurs in Taiwan, started working when he was very young and labors tirelessly to expand his empire. His flagship company, with assets worth $173 million, is preparing for a listing on the local stock exchange. Catherine Yan, thirty-eight, heads a thousand-strong cleaning service company and decided to stay single so that she can focus on her business. There are millions of Chens and Yans throughout Asia.

Confucius Will Understand the Need to Make Money

Qufu, the birthplace of Confucius, is becoming a giant enterprise to cash in on the legacy of the "First Teacher of Sagely Accomplishments," according to the *Asian Wall Street Journal.* Kong Qingx, a seventy-third generation relative of Confucius, helped found San Kong beer, named for the three most famous Confucian memorials in Qufu. Kong said that "San Kong has the potential to make the Qufu name famous world-wide." Elsewhere in town, near the Confucius temple, "another Confucius-inspired" liquor was born. Called the Kong Fu Jia Jiu, or Confucius Family Liquor, the company claims that it "became China's best selling white liquor."

The commercialization of the "brand equity" of Confucius might appear to be in contradiction with the sage's admonition against drunkenness and his warning that "wealth and rank can be as insubstantial as floating clouds," but his disciples have an explanation. Professor Luo Chenglie of the Qufu Normal University, the center for the study of Confucian thought, actually encourages the trend. In the few years since the local government licensed companies to use the name of Confucius in promoting their products, Professor Luo counts twenty-nine drinks and eight foodstuffs that use Confucius's name. "Confucius was a very broad-minded and understanding man," he says. "He would not have been bothered if someone borrowed his spirit to make money." In any event, the companies will doubtlessly respect Confucius's dictum to students: "If you have wine, you must offer some to your parents and teachers."

Moral Bearings

In a fast-changing world, especially one in which the media so influence lifestyles, many Asians believe that moral grounding is needed. "We are all groping towards a destination which we hope will be identifiable with our past," says Lee Kuan Yew. "We have left the past behind and there is an underlying unease that there will be nothing left of us which is part of the old."

There is also increasing concern that the next generation is going to hell. Moral education programs in Asia have been around since Confucius; they are now being created to teach and protect Asian values.

• A 1994 Values Education in ASEAN seminar discussed how to insert Asian values into school curricula—at the beginning of a child's education.

• In Singapore, the one class *not* taught in English is moral education.

• South Korean children spend two hours a week studying the "26 virtues" dealing with the individual, family and country. A "national ethics" class is taught in secondary school.

• Taiwan students receive forty minutes per week of "moral education." During 1995 and 1996 about 1,000 private schools opened in Taiwan to teach the Chinese Classics.

• Members of Hong Kong's Community Youth Club are taught to "learn, be concerned and serve."

Choosing Governance

With its sleek modern skyscrapers, well-manicured lawns and gardens, impeccable public housing, ultra-efficient Singapore is in some ways the envy of Asia and the world. Delegations from developing countries have flocked to learn about the Singapore model, carefully designed programs of social engineering which seek to manage the conduct of the lives of its citizens.

Secretary José T. Almonte, presidential security advisor in the Philippines, says that Singaporeans joke about their situation. "Everything here in Singapore is 'fine.' " It's "fine," all right. You get a *fine* if you fail to flush the toilet in a public lavatory, a *fine* if you throw a cigarette butt on the street, a *fine* if you are caught selling chewing gum. While proud of the prosperity they enjoy, some Singaporeans wish for greater room for self-expression. As Liak Teng Kiat, a researcher at a Singapore think tank, writes in the *Far Eastern Economic Review*, "The second generation leaders have tried to appease younger voters by adopting a more accommodating style than the Old Guard. But the voting record since the 1984 election, when the People's Action Party (PAP) share fell 12.7 points to 62.9 percent, shows that it is not enough—even with the booming economy. Singaporeans seem to want some more fundamental changes in the PAP approach to governance before they will fully return to its ranks."

Senior Minister Lee Kuan Yew still has a dominating, if not the dominant, influence in government. When it was suggested that a referendum be held on the government's initiative to peg the salaries of top politicians to private sector wages, Lee said, "The people at large . . . are they in a position to judge? Is it within their range of experience?"

Meanwhile, in China, the *China Daily*, introducing a new edition of Deng Xiaoping's selected works, commented, "The point of departure and ultimate consideration for formulating various goals and policies are whether the people support them, whether they agree with and are happy with them, and whether they have given them the nod." In this case the rhetoric for democracy is stronger in China than in Singapore.

Is Democracy Incompatible with Asian Culture?

The debate between West and East seems to suggest that some believe democracy is foreign to Asian values. But Kim Dae Jung, a leading champion of democracy and human rights in Korea, argues that democratic ideas are fundamental to Asian culture. "Almost two millennia before [John] Locke, Chinese philosopher Meng-tzu preached similar ideas," Kim says. If a king did not "govern righteously, the people had the right to rise up and overthrow his government in the name of heaven.... The ancient Chinese philosophy of *Minben Zhengchi,* or 'people-based politics,' teaches that 'the will of the people is the will of heaven' and that one should 'respect the people as heaven' itself.... There are no ideas more fundamental to democracy than the teachings of Confucianism, Buddhism, and Tonghak [a native religion of Korea]. Clearly, Asia has democratic philosophies as profound as those of the West.... Confucian scholars were taught that remonstration against an erring monarch was a paramount duty."

"The argument that it took many years for the first democratic governments to develop in the West is not a valid excuse for Asian and African countries to drag their feet over democratic reform," says Nobel Peace Prize winner Aung San Suu Kyi, released in July 1995 from six years of house arrest in Burma.

History shows that peoples and societies do not have to pass through a fixed series of stages in the course of development.... It is often in the name of cultural integrity as well as social stability and national security that democratic reforms based on human rights are resisted by authoritarian governments. It is insinuated that some of the worst ills of Western society are the results of democracy, which is seen as the progenitor of unbridled freedom and selfish individualism. It is claimed that democratic values and human rights run counter to the national culture ... [yet] many of the worst ills of American society are increasingly to be found in other developed countries. They can be traced not to the democratic legacy but to the demands of modern materialism.

In each country, the democratic system will develop a character that accords with its social, cultural and economic needs. But the basic requirement of a genuine democracy is that people should be sufficiently empowered to be able to participate significantly in the governance of their country.

Singapore's Lee Kuan Yew, however, sees democracy from another viewpoint. "I do not believe that democracy necessarily leads to development," he says. "I believe that what a country needs to develop is discipline more than democracy. The exuberance of democracy leads to undiscipline and disorderly conduct which are inimical to development."

Malaysia's Prime Minister Dr. Mahathir Mohamad disagrees. "When Malaysia became independent in 1957, our per capita income was lower than that of Haiti," he said in a speech at Cambridge University. "Haiti did not take the path to democracy. We did. Now Haiti is the poorest country in the Americas. We could not have achieved what we have achieved without democracy."

Several studies clearly demonstrate the economic benefits of democracy. *The Political Economy of Policy Reform*, edited by John Williamson of the Institute for International Economics, considered thirteen countries and concluded that democratic countries get "high marks for effectiveness in economic reform."

The Economist reports that "nearly all of the world's richest countries are free (meaning, among other things, democratic) and nearly all of the poorest countries are not . . . it is absurd to conclude from East Asia's success, and from that fact alone, that non-democratic government is best for development. . . . If dictators made countries rich, Africa would be an economic colossus."

Is Open Debate Un-Asian?

In January 1995, Singapore found five defendants guilty of contempt of court because of an article by Christopher Lingle in the *International Herald Tribune*. The defendants were fined. Lingle had earlier fled the country. The article referred to an unnamed Asian country where the government "bankrupt[ed] opposition politicians." Interestingly enough, between 1971 and 1993 the Singapore government sued and bankrupted eleven opposition politicians. Lee Kuan Yew took offense at Lingle's piece and filed a libel suit against the five defendants and the paper. Will he now try to bankrupt the *International Herald Tribune*? Lee also sued the *Herald Tribune* for calling his political grooming of his son an example of "dynastic politics."

Singapore enforces a strict code of conduct for the press. In recent years, *The Economist,* the *Asian Wall Street Journal,* the *Far Eastern Economic Review,* the *International Herald Tribune, Time* and *Asiaweek* have all had their local circulation restricted, accused by the government of interfering in domestic politics. An editor and a reporter from Singapore's *Business Times* were fined for prematurely reporting a government estimate of the country's quarterly GNP growth.

If outsiders find it difficult to justify such censorship, the government does not. "Singapore is not America," Prime Minister Goh Chok Tong's press secretary, Chan Heng Wing, said on the front pages of Singapore's newspapers. "It is small and fragile and needs a strong and fair government to survive. If its government is continually criticized, vilified and ridiculed in the media, and pressured by lobbyists as in America, then the government will lose control. The result will not be more freedom, but confusion, and decline.... Singapore will expand its political and artistic space pragmatically and gradually, not in accordance with any formula urged upon Singapore by the Western media, which have pushed for and praised American-style democratization in Taiwan and South Korea. In 10 to 20 years, the results in Taiwan, South Korea and Singapore will speak for themselves."

What Do Other Asians Think?

Media censorship is not limited to Singapore. Thailand, Taiwan, Malaysia, Indonesia and China all require the media to comply with government guidelines. But authorities have grown more liberal of the media in recent times. Newspapers and private radio and television stations enjoy greater latitude in reflecting various voices, even though any pronounced deviation from a code of conduct set by the government might cost them their permits or licenses.

The media in Taiwan, the Philippines and Hong Kong voice criticism of their governments and view this freedom of expression as a necessary condition for a democratic system and survival in the marketplace. "A well-educated and well-informed community will not allow itself to be cheated and maliciously misled for long," said Louis Cha, the widely respected founder and former chairman of *Ming Pao,* a leading Chinese newspaper in Hong Kong, in a public lecture at Hong Kong

University on freedom of the press. "That is the essential merit of the open society, and the mass media have a role in helping to create, promote and preserve this quality of openness in a society. In an open society readers have freedom of choice. . . . To survive in this highly competitive market, the media must have the support of their audience. . . . In other words, ethical journalism is dictated in Hong Kong not only by a moral imperative, but by the realities of the market."

Now How Do You Deal with Cyberspace?

"Technology such as Internet will make it increasingly difficult to suppress information," states Cheong Yip Seng, group editor in chief of Singapore's *New Straits Times.* "What one newspaper suppresses will re-emerge in another. The process will be accelerated by economic development and mass education."

There is, in fact, no stopping the spread of information and cultural exchange. Taiwan plans to spend $114 million on computers for its schools by 1998. South Korean students study in sixty countries. Hong Kong sent 86 percent more students abroad to study in 1990 than in 1985. China sends 40,000 students to the United States to study; Japan sends 45,000. And getting on the Internet is the latest Asian craze.

The Internet is an important gateway of access to information, ideas, knowledge and networking with the world. It will do society much good if this access is facilitated, especially in developing countries, to help to expand the infrastructure for learning. A young generation of cybernauts, comfortable with technology and receptive to new ideas, is indeed a strategic asset to society, serving as agents of change.

One Man One Vote, Some Men Two Votes

"Never before in Asia have so many people had the right to choose their leaders through the ballot box," reports *Asiaweek.* "For many, voting has become a routine part of life." Elections were held in Malaysia, the Philippines, Japan and Hong Kong in 1995, in Thailand and

Taiwan in 1996. Pakistan recently held its freest and fairest elections in decades. "Unpredictability is a certainty in the democratic system," says Thailand's former Prime Minister Chuan Leekpai. "You used to ask about coups; now you no longer ask. It means you yourselves have more confidence."

"No single formula [of democracy] has been adhered to by the Western countries, no single model can be adhered to by the societies of Asia," reports the Commission for a New Asia, a group of eighteen intellectuals from twelve Asian countries. "There is a trend towards greater political openness, younger electorate, greater accountability and transparency," says former Ambassador Tommy Koh. "The process towards democracy is evolving."

There is yet another trend going on. Concerned with stability, Senior Minister Lee proposed the idea of giving citizens of a certain age group two votes instead of one. The argument was based on the fact that people with family responsibilities will make decisions in the interest of the stability of society. The proposal has not yet been adopted.

The "new economic world order requires guaranteed freedom of information and creativity," says Kim Dae Jung. "These things are possible only in a democratic society. Thus **Asia has no practical alternative to democracy; it is a matter of survival in an age of intensifying global economic competition."**

In time, I think all Asian countries will be democracies. What is resisted in Asia is the presumption by the West that the West gets to say what democracy is and is not. But democracy is not a neat, tidy product. It is a continuing process. We all get to say what we think democracy is. As I emphasize throughout this book, Asians will participate in the process in an Asian way, not in a Western way.

Choosing Your Human Rights

Although some have tried to label human rights as specifically Western—or even a Western ideal being imposed on the East—it is increasingly being acknowledged that human rights are basic. They apply to everyone.

"Human rights are not conferred by society or state; rather it is a right by virtue of birth," writes Indonesia's Tommy Thomas in Malaysia's *New Straits Times.* "It is futile to examine the issue of human rights from an East-West vantage point or in North-South terms. Instead, it is far more productive to consider the universality of human rights." Human rights are "universal in the sense that one either accepts or rejects the whole idea and concepts."

A contrary view is stated by Chinese Premier Li Peng: "It is not fair to impose the human-rights concepts of a developed country on a developing country. For a developing country, human rights are first and foremost, the rights to survival and development. . . . A person must first survive before talking about rights."

To some Asians it is now clear that economic ascendancy goes through stages, and human rights is a luxury item on the priority list of development. But is development really the issue? In wealthy Singapore, the government believes excessive individual rights lead to social chaos. Yet all members of the United Nations have signed on to uphold Article 55, which provides for human rights. In Asia, only Singapore, Vietnam, China, North Korea and Burma do not have human rights organizations.

Are human rights something the West is forcing on Asia? Not exactly. Buddhism puts forth that "nothing is nobler than self in the whole universe," meaning that each person has "certain inalienable rights." Tonghak, a native Korean religion, says that "man is heaven," meaning man should be served "as we do heaven." Consider this admonition from Korean scholar-statesman Yi Yul Gok of the five-hundred-year-long Yi dynasty at the end of the fourteenth century: "The rise or fall of a society depends on whether or not a way is open for free speech."

There is also the question of workers' rights. U.S. President Bill Clinton has called for a code of human rights principles that American firms overseas would pledge to abide by. Among the voluntary principles are provisions for "a corporate culture that respects free expression consistent with legitimate business concerns." The code also calls for the right of workers to bargain collectively, which is perhaps even more controversial. Some human rights groups call the code "too vague." "Wages are only a small part of it," says a trade unionist in Jakarta. "What's important is that the workers have their dignity, and they'll only have that if they have the right to organize."

Some Asians complain that American companies are trying to impose Western human rights requirements in an attempt to make Asian products less competitive. "I don't buy it," responds Deborah Leipziger of New York's Council on Economic Priorities, "because there are universal standards of human rights."

Choosing a Religion

A spiritual vacuum is sometimes the by-product of material success. That does not appear to be the case in Asia. Rapid economic changes are undermining the support system provided by the extended family, and the quest for something to replace it is on the rise. Spirituality is on the increase and religious faith is flourishing.

In Asia, Christianity is emerging as one somewhat surprising religious option. David Barrett, editor of the *World Christian Encyclopedia*, estimates that around 8 percent of Asia's population is Christian. Each day some 25,000 Chinese join the Protestant faith. Three new churches open every two days.

Between 2 million and 5 million people attended Pope John Paul II's mass in Manila in January 1995, considered the largest mass of his papacy. The Philippines, where about 85 percent of the people are Catholic, is Asia's only predominantly Catholic country.

There are as many as 18 million Christians in South Korea, up from 1.2 million in 1957. About 41 percent of South Koreans are Christian. Christianity is just a little less celebrated than Buddhism. South Korea's Reverend David Yonggi Cho claims 700,000 members at his church in Seoul. He calls it the "largest Christian congregation in the world." Each Sunday seven services are held. Twenty overflow chapels and thirteen satellite churches with television monitors hold those who don't fit in the church.

Japan is witnessing increased interest in New Age spiritualism. Bookstores have added New Age sections that include books on reincarnation and channeling. The Cosmo Space New Age Center in Harajuku, Tokyo, rings up sales of $2 million a year. The store's top-selling items include "power stones that are said to help people meditate or regain their stability."

Religion in China

As guests of the Guangdong Christian Council in southern China, Todd Crowell, a senior writer for *Asiaweek*, and members of his church in Hong Kong were allowed to visit and worship with a church there. They were shown the Baiwan village school—the first instance of the state giving a religious school, turned state school, back to the church. The Baiwan church has 350 members. Open worship is allowed at 12,000 "registered" Protestant and Catholic churches in China, and there are thousands of meeting places where actual buildings have not yet been built. However, most worship in unofficial house churches.

The estimated number of Protestants in China ranges from 20 million to 100 million. However, official estimates put the number of Protestants at just 6 million. The China Patriotic Catholic Association, the state Catholic Church that has no association with the Vatican, counts 4 million members. The number of underground, Vatican-affiliated Roman Catholics is estimated at around 6 million.

The change in China is extraordinary. A country that tried to ban Christianity is now promoting it. China's Bureau of Religious Affairs is said to be "actively helping churches." A church in Qingyuan was rebuilt with state funds. And a seminary in Guangdong, allowed to reopen in 1986, has graduated two hundred students, all of whom are greatly needed. The average Protestant minister in China is seventy-five years old.

Elsewhere in China, Buddhist temples are being rebuilt, followers are allowed to leave food for Taoist monks, and Muslims are allowed to worship in mosques. Religious tolerance, however, is not freedom of religion. The number of house churches and the fact that Bibles are still smuggled into China show that the government is not totally comfortable with the religious revival.

The Marketing of Buddhism

"Buddhism booms," reports the *Far Eastern Economic Review*, "as monks ride the wave of Thai middle-class prosperity." Ninety-five percent of Thailand's population is Buddhist. Donations are so high, the *Review* concluded, that "the wats are, in a sense, among the largest corporate concerns in the kingdom." Wats are those striking green and red temples one sees all over Thailand.

Luang Poh Koon, who reputedly holds "the supernatural power to make followers rich and healthy . . . is a superstar among Thai Buddhists. . . . Hordes of believers, including top politicians and military men," have contributed generously to his temple. Exactly how much he collects is unknown, but in 1994 he gave $2.55 million to charities, according to ledgers kept by the abbot. And in January 1995 he gave almost $3 million to King Bhumibol Adulyadej for use in his charities and plans to give almost $10 million more to build schools and hospitals. Thailand's 30,000 temples, or wats, have prospered with Thailand's increased prosperity, collecting revenues that run to many millions annually.

The way to the Dharma has gone high-tech as well. Besides innovations in marketing to help devotees embrace the faith, some Buddhist groups use laptop computers to assist in writing and translating the mantras, and record them on videocassettes to be played on karaoke. This approach caught on rapidly and is spreading like wildfire all over Asia.

The behavior of individual monks is more controversial. Some have earned a reputation for conspicuous consumption, traveling in expensive luxurious cars. A recent scandal that many dubbed a "crisis of faith" involved a charismatic Thai monk named Yantra Ammaro Bhikku, who "allegedly used credit cards provided by a follower to pay for illicit sex while he was travelling overseas." Yantra was stripped of his status in the monastery, disrobed as it were.

Wat Phra Dhammakaya, a temple in Phathum Thani, which is north of Bangkok, was so successful at attracting followers that it received a marketing award from Thammasat University in 1989. The temple uses a "million-name computerized database for direct mail publicity drives. The campaign promoted Buddhism with glossy brochures promising followers wealth and prosperity . . . personal beauty, radiance . . . career success, strong health, and long life . . . [and] forthrightness and steadfastness in Dharma practice."

Rising Interest in Islam

Asia's Islamic countries—Indonesia, Pakistan, Bangladesh and Malaysia—are also experiencing heightened religious interest. And the revival of Islam, like the increase in other religions, is in part a reaction to modernization and outside influence. The past twenty-five years have seen incredible growth in Islamic fundamentalism. While there appears to be a clash between Western Christianity and Islam, a recent special report on Islam in *The Economist* notes that they "have more in common with each other than either has with the Confucian world or the Hindu one. . . . Both have their origins in religions that believe in a single God. . . . Few westerners believe that God dictated the Koran, and no Muslim believes that Jesus was the son of God. Those are important disagreements, but they sit alongside a large number of shared convictions. A Muslim and a westerner both believe, more clearly than most other people, in the idea of individual responsibility. They can exchange opinions about the nature of good and evil, or property rights, or the preservation of the environment, in something like a spirit of brotherhood." To say that the West is evil and materialistic, in comparison to Islamic belief, is incorrect. "Both the Koran and Muhammad himself assumed a system based on individual enterprise and individual reward."

"Islamic movements today are driven more by appalling local social conditions than by some all-pervasive ideology," reports the *Far Eastern Economic Review*. Khalid Ahmed, a Pakistani writer on Islam, goes even further in saying that "in the Islamic world, by and large, the ruling elites have failed to deliver the goods to the people, and the end of the cold war has only stripped off the veil [that obscured that fact]. The growing gap between rich and poor, runaway inflation, unemployment, massive corruption, and widespread disillusionment with the mainstream parties and their leaders are the core issues in the Islamic world."

Young people are embracing the religion with greater intensity, and the number of people making the Haj, the pilgrimage to Mecca, the holy land, is on the rise. Traditionally, for economic reasons, the Haj could be made only once in the lifetime of a Muslim; but with increased affluence, many people are making frequent trips. Derivatives of the mainstream religion are being developed, too. The Islamic sect of Al alqum attracted more than a million followers and grew into a sprawling business enterprise. The Malaysian government subsequently banned the movement, closing it down totally.

Choosing Family Help or Help from Institutions

In Asia, the family unit has long been the foundation of society. The family system, instead of the government, provides social, economic and emotional support to the individual as well as the family itself. Self-reliance and personal responsibility are nurtured within the family. But with the increased urbanization and industrialization of Asia the family unit is in danger of breaking down. If the family is weakened beyond recognition, what social structure could possibly take its place? Will Asia, like the West, turn to the government for help? Most Asians cringe at the very thought.

How much government do Asians want in their lives? Should the government assume a bigger role? Many think that the government's role should be confined to providing basic infrastructure to nurture an environment that encourages enterprise. As for comparative tax rates between the East and West, "When you give half of what you earn to the government, that's a Western philosophy," says Mohammed Sadli, a former minister under Indonesia's New Order administration.

Lee Kuan Yew, not surprisingly, is against the government assuming responsibility for the individual. The difference between East and West, he argues, "is that Eastern societies believe that the individual exists in the context of his family. . . . In the West, especially after World War II, the government came to be seen as so successful that it could fulfill all the obligations that in less modern societies are fulfilled by the family. This approach encouraged alternative families, single mothers, for instance, believing that government could provide the support to make up for the absent father."

The challenge for Asia is managing the transition to modernization. Can the family be preserved in the process, thus ensuring Asia's competitiveness?

The traditional family system has served Asia well in the past. The system provided support to the young and cared for the old. Asia's population is young today, but graying rapidly. The World Bank estimates that by 2030, about 22 percent of China's population will be over sixty. "By 2030, Hong Kong, Macau, Singapore, South Korea, Taiwan, Sri Lanka and Thailand will all have a greater percentage of people over 60 than the United States had in 1990."

Is there a welfare system in place to provide a safety net? The answer is no. Asia cannot boast of a well-structured social security system. Two schemes, however, are widely practiced. Japan, South Korea and Taiwan have a defined benefit system that guarantees a certain level of pension. In Singapore and Malaysia, there is a defined contribution plan by both employer and employee. At the end of a stipulated period and subject to specific rules, the employees get back what they paid in, plus investment return. In Singapore, employers contribute 18.5 percent of an employee's salary and the employee 21.5 percent. In Malaysia, employers put in 12 percent, employees 10 percent.

The World Bank dislikes both schemes. First, investment decisions are made solely by the governments involved. Second, rates of return are too low. "The authorities claim the returns have been high, but the claims cannot be corroborated, since audited, published data are not available," states the 1994 World Bank report, "Averting the Old Age Crisis." In any case, it adds, "the relatively low interest rate paid to the fund could thus be viewed as a hidden tax on workers to finance government expenditures and reserves."

Jimmy Lai, a great promoter of personal responsibility and self-reliance, believes that the solution to the problem lies with the market.

Referring to the low tax rate in Hong Kong, he says, "If you only give so little to the government, you don't care a damn what they do with that money. The government can facilitate a lot of self-reliance by allowing the market to take over. When the government only takes 9 percent of our income [in taxes], and leaves 91 percent to the market for us to take care of ourselves, we are only allowing the government to intervene in a very small part of our lives."

Sue Your Son and Farewell My Concubine

Lawmakers in Singapore and Hong Kong are trying to legislate solutions to social problems. One prominent example is Singapore's "Sue Your Son" law, which allows parents to sue children for support. The Hong Kong legislature also debated a law that would have forbidden Hong Kong men to take concubines (it was especially aimed at those commuting to southern China). It was a big issue among women, but the male-dominated legislature did not "get it" and the legislation did not pass.

Toward Shared Values

The ethnic and cultural diversities within Asian nations present challenges to national unity and cohesiveness. But Asian countries are exploring solutions to forge national identities. In the quest to build modern nations, the leaders of Singapore and Malaysia sought to "unify" the diverse cultures within their boundaries with the vision of a single national identity. In Singapore, "One People, One Nation, One Singapore" was the theme of the twenty-fifth independence anniversary in 1990. But now, after years of promoting integration, the leadership has abandoned the quest for a singular identity and come to terms with diversity. Officials speak of a mosaic of cultures, a successful blend of immigrant peoples and "shared values."

Malaysia has come a long way in trying to integrate the major racial groups within its national boundaries. Although mainly driven by economics, the country is now more tolerant, accepting diversity. Commenting on the showing of a multiracial front in the general election of 1995, Dr. Noordin Sopiee expressed optimism on the shift. "Some people have gone so far as to celebrate the end of racial politics in Malaysia. I think it is more like the beginning of an end." There has been a clear shift in mindset from "one country, one people" to "one country, shared values." As for the relationship between Taiwan and the mainland, many people are advocating a postponement of closure. As Taiwan legislator Yung Wei puts it, "no solutions," just hang on with one country (China) and multiple systems.

Greater economic integration, cultural exchange through travel and the mobility of people will, however, bring about the blending of Asia's diverse cultures. This fits my conception of a global paradox in which the more universal we become, the more tribal we act—the more we become the same in things economic, the more we become different in those things that represent our unique identities, including our language and our cultural history.

Perhaps the frantic alarms sounded by Asian intellectuals on family values can inspire Western societies to reclaim their traditional values. As Francis Fukuyama writes in *The End of History and the Last Man*, "Families don't really work if they are based on liberal principles, that is, if their members regard them as they would a joint stock company, formed for their utility rather than being based on ties of duty and love." Asia is moving into the future in its own way.

CHAPTER THREE

From Export-Led to Consumer-Driven

The driving force behind investment in Southeast Asia is the region's growing urban middle class.

A new middle class, the size of which the world has never before seen, is being created in Asia. In February 1995 the Gallup Organization released the results of the first ever scientific national poll of China—the world's most populous country. Its conclusion: a billion Chinese want to become rich and buy millions of TVs, washing machines, refrigerators and videocassette recorders. That news might shock some Westerners, but it comes as no surprise to the 84 percent of Chinese households that already own a TV, the 25 percent that spent their hard-earned money on refrigerators or the 35 percent that purchased a washing machine in the last few years. Some 68 percent of the Chinese polled desired to "work hard and get rich." Just 4 percent subscribed to the philosophy of the late Chairman Mao: "Never think of yourself, give everything in service to society."

"This is a society with strong material aspirations, not all of which are currently being met," said Richard Burkholder Jr., Gallup director of worldwide operations. The trick, of course, is to find out where this new urban class will be, and to discover something about its generational composition.

The rise of the middle class is revamping Asia's economic structure. Once dependent on exports for economic expansion, Asia can now also rely on domestic demand to fuel growth. In Thailand, for example, consumer spending now contributes 54 percent to its gross domestic product, while exports contribute 30 percent. That means a bigger economic pie and a more sophisticated, well-rounded economic picture.

That said, however, one caveat must be offered. The gap in wealth between urban and rural is still so significant that averaged nationwide income levels and other demographic data are almost meaningless. When a businessperson or well-heeled tourist stays in a five-star hotel in Jakarta or Shanghai and shops in the nearby boutiques, it might *feel* just like Chicago or London. That's how extraordinarily sophisticated Asia's urban centers have become. But let me tell you, ten or twenty miles out into the countryside, it is clear you are visiting a developing country.

In unchartered waters, there is no formula for successful market penetration, no sure predictors of consumer response.

Nevertheless, the fundamental economic shift in Asia today has profound implications for domestic companies and foreign investors alike. Learning to read this new market can result in enormous profits. Failing to do so could mean lost opportunity, even bankruptcy.

From Survival to Middle Class

What is happening in China, as reflected in that Gallup poll, is happening throughout Asia. The average Asian's living standard is bursting out of "survival" into consumption. Incomes are rising dramatically. In the United States, 45 to 50 percent of household income goes to rent, health, education and transportation. In China, where the government still subsidizes food and housing, the comparable number is an incredible 5 percent. In time, China's cost of living will rise as subsidies are cut. But income will grow, too. Meanwhile Chinese households have money to spend on products that enhance their quality of life.

For twenty-five years, Asian countries needed exports to grow. And producing low-cost consumer products for world markets, they climbed toward economic prosperity. Later, when Japan and then the "Four Tigers" diversified into telecommunications, computers, and financial and professional services, education levels increased and employment skills improved. That brought higher labor costs. Manufacturers then sought lower cost alternatives in neighboring countries. Economies grew in a "flying geese" formation, with the more developed countries leading the less developed countries along the path to prosperity. Trade within Asia then became a more important piece of the region's overall economy. Companies invested in one another, and there has been a dramatic increase in intracorporate trade. Standards of living throughout the continent increased.

If Asian economies continue their 6 to 10 percent annual expansion rate of the last decade, their middle classes will double or triple in the next decade. The Asian middle class, not counting Japan, could number between 800 million and 1 billion people by 2010, resulting in a stunning $8 trillion to $10 trillion in spending power. That's in the neighborhood of 50 percent more than today's U.S. economy. It took Britain's middle class nearly a century to evolve. In Asia today, that process is being accomplished in little more than a decade.

A Billion Consumers

But you don't have to be middle class to *buy* something. Hong Kong Bank chairman John Gray estimates there will be "a billion people in Asia with some consumer spending power" by the year 2000.

• Already in *South Korea*, 70 percent of those who describe themselves as "middle class" are home owners, and 60 percent are worth at least $62,200.

• In *India*, between 1990 and 1991 consumer activity increased 14 percent to $122.6 billion—four times 1981 levels.

• Almost two thirds of households in Petaling Jaya, near Kuala Lumpur, *Malaysia*, earn more than $800 a month; over a third make more than $1,200.

• In *Thailand*, the number of Bangkok households earning $10,000 a year has jumped from just 160,000 in 1986 to one million today.

Similar rises in income and consumer activity are recorded elsewhere in the region and will gather momentum over the next five to ten years.

Young and Eager Consumers

Asia's young population is in its consumer-spending prime. Each of the Little Dragon nations—Hong Kong, Singapore, Taiwan and South Korea—has more than 65 percent of its population between fifteen and sixty-five years of age. The percentages are also high for countries in developing Asia. Thailand, Indonesia, Malaysia, China, India and the Philippines range between 59 and 66 percent. Malaysia, averaging more than 8 percent of economic growth for each of the last nine years, has 59 percent of its 20 million people in this age group and is set to launch a retail boom. The country's retail sector expected 30 percent growth in 1995.

Asia's middle classes are changing the economic, social and political landscape of the region. They are better educated, marrying later, having fewer children. The young, urban middle class of Asia is as sophisticated as any in the world. They lead sophisticated lives and want sophisticated products and services. They are looking for quality as part of a self-conscious search for a quality-of-life lifestyle.

This new middle class represents tremendous purchasing power, which ultimately will result in tremendous political power. We will see the *Asianization* of democracy as governments become responsive to an increasingly vocal middle class. In 1992 in Thailand, for example, the middle class took to the streets for the first time and toppled the government, ending military rule.

In the meantime, however, purveyors of consumer products and personal services, and peddlers of convenience and quality will profit handsomely if they can read the market and respond appropriately. "American hucksters are taking this part of the world seriously," says Mike Ferrier, the Hong Kong–based regional director of U.S. advertising giant McCann-Erickson. "It shows that Asia has turned from a production market into a consumption market. Asia used to only manufacture goods for the West. Now the West is sending things here."

Purchasing Power Parity

In many ways, I believe household income is a poor gauge of economic status, not only between rural and urban classes, but among countries as well. A middle-class family in Taipei might well have an annual income of $40,000, while a family in New Delhi could qualify as middle class with an annual income of $7,000. In China, families are still subsidized by the government, resulting in their having more spending power than their incomes would lead a Westerner to believe.

As I point out in my book *Global Paradox*, "Traditionally, a country's economy is measured by determining a per capita income which is calculated by converting the value of its gross domestic product into U.S. dollars at the official exchange rate. A big problem with this method is that if a country's currency weakens against the dollar, its economy automatically shrinks, which can be very misleading. But that is precisely what happened in the case of China. Between 1978 and 1992, the Yuan (China's currency) fell from 1.7 to the dollar to 5.5 to the dollar. But to use this traditional measurement effectively negates China's real economic growth during the same period. By this calculation, China's economy is the 10th largest, and its people among the poorest."

Even keepers of the world's ledger know those numbers make no sense. So in 1993 the International Monetary Fund (IMF) tried a new methodology, the purchasing power parity (PPP), and came up with dramatically different results. The IMF calculated how much, for example, a loaf of bread, bicycle or soft drink cost in one country's currency, then figured out how much the same commodities cost in other countries' currencies. Then calculating each country's national output based on the PPP method, the IMF found that China had produced $1.7 trillion in goods and services in 1992, far greater than the $400 billion previously estimated, and that in 1992 its per capita income was $1,600, not $370.

Using UN data and a different analysis, the IMF calculated that in 1990 China's per capita income was even higher, somewhere around $2,600. Other economists insisted it was much higher, even as high as

$4,000, which historically in other countries had, in effect, opened the floodgates of consumer spending, exactly what China is experiencing now.

Using China as an example, the arithmetic is straightforward. If its real per capita income were $4,000, China would have a $4.8-trillion economy (1.2 billion × $4,000). Furthermore, if China continues to grow about 8 percent annually (it has averaged nearly 10 percent growth for fifteen years), then in five years, per capita income will be closer to $6,000 and the economy $7.2 trillion, equal to today's U.S. economy. That's a formula for a new economic order.

To no one's surprise, global corporate giants and entrepreneurs alike have gone into overdrive in an effort to capture a share of this very attractive market. Those most likely to be successful are the ones who take the time to understand the unique nature of each Asian market as well as the new collective consciousness emerging in the region.

Asia Is a Collection of Markets

Certainly, what constitutes middle class differs from country to country, and within countries. In some parts of some Asian countries, education and social standing can be as important as economic status and achievement. Owning a car or home, or both, often distinguishes people as middle class. There is a kind of hierarchy of ownership that tracks middle classdom: television sets and refrigerators and air conditioners, succeeded by cars and homes and vacations. Across the board in most parts of Asia, people's disposable incomes are increasing. The fact is Asians are getting richer day by day. And they are hopeful for the future.

Companies wanting to sell in Asia should not look at the region country by country. They should look at Asia as market centers, operating and selling to urban Singapore, Hong Kong, Taipei, Seoul and Kuala Lumpur using a similar marketing approach. But selling to urban and rural populations within the same country can be very different. Marketing should not revolve around countries but examine common profiles in different market centers.

Top of the Class

This growing new middle class, by and large, is a more sophisticated consumer. Value sells. But, at the top, so does luxury. Joseph Kanoui, chairman and chief executive of Vendôme Luxury Group, anticipates that Asia will be the group's largest market by the year 2000. Vendôme owns some of the world's leading luxury brands, including Cartier, Dunhill men's clothing, Piaget and Baume & Mercier watches. Asia is already Vendôme's second-largest market. Sales of Mercedes-Benz cars in Asia increased 3.5 times between 1991 and 1994. Sales of BMWs increased almost 50 percent.

Brand consciousness is on the rise. Those with the means, especially young women in Hong Kong, Singapore or Taipei, will not settle for anything less than their favorite designer labels. Single Asian women who live with their families have large disposable incomes and are eager to embrace styles of the very best. Many would not blink an eyelash to spend a month's salary on a Chanel bag or a Fendi wristwatch. Even little kids insist on wearing outfits with Mickey's label. Disney is expecting to reap a bumper harvest in Asia as Mickey becomes a pal to millions of Asia's children.

Just Charge It!

Asia, where buying on credit was once considered imprudent at best and shameful at worst, is ushering in a whole new era—the age of the credit card. Asia's middle class is increasingly comfortable buying on credit. Citibank alone has 5 million credit cards in circulation in Asia. Seven million new cardholders are expected by 2000.

- In Japan, there are 215 million credit cards in circulation, two for each citizen over the age of twenty.
- MasterCard International recently became the first to issue credit cards in Vietnam, and plans to issue 500,000 cards.
- Citibank, one of the region's biggest issuers, has seen its credit

card revenues in the Asia Pacific region increase from $400 million in 1994 to $1 billion in 1996. Revenues of $2 billion are expected by 2000.

- Credit card holders in India now number 1.75 million.
- In China, the number reached 8.4 million by the end of 1994, an increase of 110 percent over the previous years. The People's Bank of China, the central bank, has set a goal of 200 million credit card holders by the year 2000.
- With 120 different types of plastic, Thailand might hold Asia's title to "the greatest variety of credit card options"; yet many card issuers believe the Thai market is not saturated yet.
- In the Philippines, if you have an income of $300 a month, you can get a card.

In 1994 regional spending with a MasterCard or Visa totaled more than $220 billion, "more than the economic output of Singapore and Hong Kong combined." And yet only around one percent of consumer spending in Asia is done on credit cards, compared to 20 percent in the U.S.

Shopping in Asia's urban centers feels a lot like shopping in America's urban centers.

Shopping Is Asia's Favorite Pastime

From the days when a refrigerator was placed prominently in a corner of the living room as a symbol of affluence to now having the means to furnish an entire living room, Asians are on a buying spree. Coupling that with the lack of recreational facilities in crowded Asian cities, shopping malls and department store complexes have become favorite weekend hangouts. Asians delight in strolling and looking at window displays, either on their own after a day at the office or as family activity.

Savoring this trend, the world's retailers are wasting no time establishing a foothold in Asia. Asia's version of the Mall of America, which opened in August 1994 in Bangkok, caters to affluent urban households. Bangkok's Seacon Square Mall has miles and miles of shops, a fourteen-screen movie theater and even an amusement park with roller coasters. It is just one of four malls anchored by a department store in the Bangkok area. The Megamall in the Philippines is the largest shopping mall in Asia. The mall's owner is now planning to build the world's largest mall on reclaimed land in the Manila Bay.

In the meantime:

• Nike's Shanghai store is open daily from 10 a.m. to 10 p.m. Shoppers want only the more expensive shoes. According to the store manager, no one wants the cheaper sneakers because they think they might be fake.

• There were already 258 7-Eleven shops in Thailand in 1993, with growth projected to reach 1,000 by 1997.

• Kmart is opening a store in Singapore. Wal-Mart is looking at several locations in Asia.

• Orchard Road in Singapore has been named Singapore's equivalent of London's Bond Street. It is really more a mix of Bond, Oxford and Regent streets, with "going out of business" sales as well as luxury boutiques. It boasts a global array of stores from Marks and Spencer (Britain), Toys 'R' Us (United States), and Takashimaya and Isetan (Japan).

• Japanese giant retailer Yaohan, headquartered in Hong Kong, is planning to build and operate 1,000 stores in major urban centers in China.

The Auto Industry as Metaphor

Emerging economies first create a national airline, which every Asian country now has or will soon have. Next they will all want their own car company.

It is easy to see why Asia has attracted the entire global community. Paying closest attention of all are the world's car makers. Within the world's mature economies, car ownership reached saturation years ago. Worldwide demand for new automobiles has dropped almost 3 percent since 1991. There will be some increase, but demand is expected to stall out at 2 percent around the year 2000.

"The developed world just can't carry the load anymore," says Wayne Brooker, Ford's Asia-Pacific vice president. "The future of the industry will depend on new markets." Asia offers new markets of extraordinary potential. Not only are increasingly well-off consumers eager to buy—cars are a universal success symbol—but governments seek to bolster their fledgling auto industries, which are metaphors for economic growth and prosperity.

Throughout the developed world, car ownership brings the individual a sense of independence and freedom. At the same time, the existence of an automotive industry suggests that a country has achieved a certain level of industrial development. Supplying citizens with affordable vehicles is a hallmark of economic progress.

That status symbol, however, does not come without sizable attendant costs such as strain on an already inadequate transportation infrastructure and outpourings of carbon monoxide in smog-congested Asian cities. Countries throughout the region face a unique set of logistical and environmental challenges. Nevertheless, the pursuit of "progress" through development of an automotive industry continues, as the world's car makers queue up to capture their share of the prize.

The People's Car

China is at work developing what it calls "the people's car," described as "an affordable compact sedan for the masses in the world's largest untapped car market."

"The car is the focus of an ambitious effort by leaders of China's Communist Party to double the country's annual production, to 3 million vehicles, half of them automobiles, by the end of the decade," reports the *International Herald Tribune.* "The plan calls for the cars to increasingly go to individual consumers; in the past the emphasis had been on larger vehicles such as minivans that could move groups of people."

What's more, the government intends to provide incentives to encourage widespread car ownership. "The official *China Daily* newspaper reported officials responsible for the automotive sector as saying that to 'increase sales the state will introduce incentives to car buyers to boost market demand,' " informs the *Financial Times.* Though *China Daily* offered no specifics, it implied bank loans and other financing would be available.

China invited the world's top car makers to submit their concept of the Chinese family car. Even Germany's Porsche and Daimler-Benz, hardly known for their affordability, responded.

"Japan's Mitsubishi Motors Corp. offered a so-called X concept car," reports the *Asian Wall Street Journal,* "a minivan that doubles as a cargo vehicle, for China's entrepreneurial families. Toyota Motor Corporation indirectly pooh-poohed the whole idea, and asked China to consider a larger Toyota model, the two- to three-liter Crown, as a first step. . . . General Motors Corporation and Ford Motor Corporation [*sic*] urged China to anoint one of their current models as the new family car. Ford recommended its Fiesta line and GM pushed its Corsa model, both from their European operations, as the least expensive and most flexible alternative."

"China is such a potentially huge market that if one percent of Chinese people could afford cars, that would be 12 million," says Michael G. Meyerand, a GM spokesman. "That's roughly our market size of Europe."

Meanwhile, Chinese and Western analysts question the wisdom of encouraging automobile transportation when the country's infrastructure is inadequate to support the 7 million to 9 million cars already on the road, and when cities like Beijing are choking on smog. Says Vaclav Smil, a Canadian scientist studying China's growth, "Forty percent of United States energy consumption goes into private cars, and the United States is importing half of its crude oil. If the Chinese try to model themselves on the United States, or Japan or South Korea, there is simply not enough crude oil on the planet for them to import and, of course, it will speed up the arrival of the third oil crisis."

Will China pioneer what the world has so far ignored—energy alternatives? Perhaps the electric car will finally get some serious consideration. Energy and environmental concerns, in any event, are unlikely to inhibit the growth of China's fledgling auto industry. There is too much at stake. A profitable auto industry signals China's arrival as an industrial power. For its people, it means freedom and status. China's economic boom is expected to continue. Soon car ownership will lie within the grasp of millions. Currently, there are some 7 million to 9 million cars on the roads, depending on which statistic you trust. But China's population exceeds one billion. What car manufacturer wouldn't want a slice of that pie? And what government would spurn economic growth and the creation of 15 million or so new jobs?

World's Auto Makers Are Welcome

Although China is the most dramatic example, car sales are booming throughout the region. By 2000 Asians are expected to buy 16 million cars a year.

"Hardly a week passes without an announcement of plans to invest in the manufacture of cars or trucks somewhere in Southeast Asia," reports the *Financial Times*. Thailand is home to 17 car makers including Honda, Ford, Mazda, Chrysler and Volvo. There are also 350 parts suppliers and 12 major assembly plants. General Motors is spending $750 million to produce the Opel in Thailand.

Meanwhile, the Proton, Malaysia's "national car," recently agreed to build a Proton manufacturing plant near Manila—its first outside the country. At the same time, Mrs. Rafidah Aziz, Malaysia's minister for trade and industry, was in Brussels for the inauguration of Proton's first left-hand-drive models in Europe. For some, Proton has become a symbol of the country's recent economic growth. While the Protons seem a little small by American standards, my rides in them have been comfortable and entirely satisfactory.

Proton sees itself as the next Hyundai. The company is committed to play in the big leagues. That means prosper, perish or form a partnership. The same goes for any U.S. manufacturer moving into Asia. Ford Motor Company, the world's second-largest vehicle maker, announced it would invest $50 million for a 7 percent stake in the Indian car maker Mahindra & Mahindra. In doing so, Ford is following in the footsteps of General Motors, Volkswagen, Daewoo and Mercedes-Benz, all of which anticipate big profits from the growing middle class in India, where annual car sales are expected to double to nearly 500,000 by 2000. Hyundai is building a factory near New Delhi.

Still many in Asia today question whether Asia should start filling itself with millions of polluting vehicles. Dr. Lee Yuen Tseh, the Nobel laureate who is president of Academia Sinica in Taipei, says the West should "help us with the technology and know-how to build subway and train systems, not sell us cars." He has sounded the alarm. In the years ahead there will be a big debate on the relative merits of the introduction of massive numbers of automobiles in Asia.

Travel and Tourism Get a Tailwind

"The seven day getaway was called California Fantasy, and it sold like a dream," reports the *Asian Wall Street Journal Weekly*. "A promotional flyer, issued jointly by a Thai travel agency and a credit card company, invited a group of Bangkok cardholders to sign up for a tour featuring Disneyland, Sea World and other California attractions for the equivalent of $1,200 to $1,500 per person. Within three hours, all 2,000 packages were sold."

The world's newest middle class is eager to see what lies beyond the boundaries of their village, town or city. They travel by automobile to neighboring communities, by train to nearby cities and by plane to distant countries. Travel and tourism, the world's largest industry, will by the year 2005 employ an estimated 338 million workers—one in five of those workers will be in the Asia-Pacific region, and as likely as not serving other Asians. Interregional travel is growing faster than intercontinental travel as individuals traveling on business extend their trips for pleasure, or as families long separated seek one another out.

Suddenly, people in Asia can afford to travel, and exposure to satellite television has piqued their curiosity about faraway places—and not so faraway places. Comments Peter Sutch, chairman of Cathay Pacific Airways, "Cathay Pacific used to be an English expat airline. No more. Today, Asians dominate the passenger list on the 795 weekly flights." Adds managing director Rod Eddington, "Now 75 percent of our passengers are Asian, compared with less than 70 percent just five years ago—40 percent are ethnic Chinese." On some of my Intra-Asian flights, I have been the only non-Asian.

- Taiwan and South Korea have relaxed restrictions on exit permits and currency exchange. Result: a surge in travel activity.
- Fifty percent of visitors to the Philippines are from Asia; 75 percent to Indonesia are. In 1995, 3.3 million Asians traveled to Japan, more than 60 percent of Japan's tourist arrivals.
- Vietnam plans to increase earnings from tourism from 3.5 percent of GDP in 1994 to 27 percent in 2010.

At the first annual International Travel Expo '94—the combination of Hong Kong's eight-year-old InterTour and China's four-year-old National Travel Fair—fifty-one countries exhibited, including Japan, Malaysia, Singapore and Thailand. Hong Kong promoted itself as the gateway to the Pearl River delta, Macau and Guangdong. For some time, tourism has ranked as one of Hong Kong's top-earning industries. It is almost certain this trend will continue. Tourism will become the top-earning industry in a growing number of Asian countries.

Throughout the region travel has become a middle-class rite of passage.

The Boeing Company estimates 40 percent of world passenger growth in the next fifteen years will be from the Asia Pacific. The International Air Travel Association predicts Asian traffic will grow 7 percent a year from 1991 to 2010. Asia will represent 39.2 percent of world traffic in 2000. By 2010, it will surge to over half.

Airports Signal Economic Arrival

"A new airport is more than the sum of its numbers. It can be a catalyst of development. In Osaka and Seoul, the airport complex is accompanied by massive infrastructural undertakings—from business centre, seaport facilities to entire communities supporting the aviation industry," writes Jay Khosla in Singapore's *Business Times*.

"It is also a product of national image building—a manifestation of political clout," Khosla continues. "It signals that as a nation you've arrived. Kuala Lumpur's new airport, for instance, is scheduled for full capacity of 60 million passengers by 2020—the target year by which Malaysia aims to achieve developed nation status. The Hong Kong project has been a symbol of the political tug-of-war between China and Britain that underscores their ideological differences."

Whatever the impetus, Asia is abuzz with airport construction, all with the hopes of achieving the same level of excellence as Singapore's Changi Airport—voted "Best in the World" seven years in a row. "What makes a good airport?" asks the *Business Times*, which concludes the question must obsess planners all across Asia, given the number of great airports newly opened and planned in the region. The article lists Osaka's $15-billion Kansai Airport, along with airports planned in Nanjing, Guangzhou, Shanghai and Fuzhou. By 1997, Hong Kong's new Chek Lap Kok Airport will replace Kai Tak. Kuala Lumpur, Manila, Macau, Bangkok and Seoul will have spent billions on new facilities by 2000.

In Singapore, Terminal 3 is scheduled to open by 2002 at a cost of $1 billion. There is already talk of a third runway and a fourth terminal at Changi. If airports are a measure of importance and affluence, and I think they are, New Asia has arrived.

Hoteliers Hustling to Meet Demand

Everywhere in the region, as airports expand, upgrade or undergo construction, hotel chains are renovating or building anew, while at the same time reassessing their customer base. Everyone, it seems, wants to ride the tailwind of growth in travel and tourism.

Ten years ago executive-class cabins and lobbies of five-star hotels were the domain of Caucasians on holiday and Western business travelers working for multinationals in Asia. Frugal Asians who used to fly coach for business and stay in midprice hotels are increasingly taking those executive-class seats and checking into the region's upscale hotels. And hoteliers are upgrading accordingly. The regular Hyatt Regency has been transformed into a chain of Grand Hyatts throughout Asia, while the Holiday Inns are building their upscale range of Crown Plazas.

A new generation of middle-class Asians intent on visiting friends and family is creating extraordinary opportunity for the midprice hotels. Most growth is from Asians traveling to other Asian countries. For example, more tourists from China visited Malaysia in 1993 than did tourists from the United States. "I've never seen anything like it," says Brendan Ebbs, senior vice president of Choice Hotels of the United States, the world's largest midrange chain. "We're seeing our hotels mushroom in all of these countries. Over the next 10 years, there is virtually unlimited growth for us in Asia."

Hotels in India are operating at full capacity. There are only about two thousand international-standard budget hotel rooms (fewer than in Singapore or Bangkok) in a nation of 940 million. Compare that with 3.5 million midmarket rooms in the United States. No wonder the world's hoteliers are flocking to India, despite the bureaucratic red tape. Holiday Inn, a unit of Britain's Bass PLC, and Choice Hotels International each plan eighty hotels in India.

Accor SA of France intends to build 123 hotels throughout the Asia-Pacific region, including forty in Australia and twenty in Vietnam. The group's most profitable Asian hotel is Hanoi's Sofitel Metropole Hotel. Accor is eyeing five sites in Malaysia and already owns four Ibis hotels in Indonesia. China already boasts 36 five-star hotels, 87 four-star hotels and more than 400 three-star hotels. It began to use the "star" designation in 1987, endeavoring to relate its facilities to global standards. And Hilton International will focus primarily on new properties in China, Japan, Korea, Malaysia, Indonesia and the Philippines. It is also considering Vietnam and India.

Gerald Pelisson, co-chairman of Accor SA of France, explains the surge in hotel, leisure and travel: "In this part of the world, there are tens of millions of people in the middle class starting to travel for leisure and business. Our objective is to build hotels to tap this clientele."

Slow Boat to (and from) China

Twenty years ago the average Asian would reject the idea of vacationing on a boat. "Boats were uncomfortable vessels only to be endured because they took you somewhere," explains the *Far Eastern Economic Review.* "You only lived on one if you couldn't afford a 'proper home.' And the Asian experience of larger vessels has been limited largely to ferries, those uncomfortable floating platforms inevitably over-burdened with people and lorries."

No more. The world's cruise lines have taken an active interest in Asia. Today, local firms are offering services that meet international standards. Western companies with reputations for quality and service are forming joint ventures in Asia to bring the pleasures of cruising to adventurous, upscale young Asians eager for new experiences.

The *East King,* a $10-million luxury river cruiser which has "bars, a gymnasium, a sauna and a telephone in each of its 78 rooms," travels down the Yangtze River. It is owned by Hubei Orient Royal Cruise and run by Holiday Inn. China's Dalian Marine Transport Group ordered two vessels from a Dutch company to carry a thousand passengers, plus cars and other items, between China and South Korea. Singapore's Star Cruise Company spent $250 million on the *Langkapuri Star Aquarius* and the *Star Pisces* during 1994.

Less Is More

Wherever there are people with disposable incomes, there will be amusement parks, restaurants and shops to help them spend their money. But that is only part of the story. Not only do Asians have money to spend, they have more time in which to spend it. In Japan, the average workweek has shrunk. Japanese workers now work an average of 1,800 hours a year, less than the 2,058-hour average of U.S. workers.

Attitudes toward work and leisure also are changing. In a survey conducted by the *Far Eastern Economic Review,* when working men and women were asked "which of a number of factors would improve their enjoyment of life, 60 percent of respondents opted for more leisure—that is, spending less time at work. Significantly more of those with high incomes—Singaporeans and Hong Kong Chinese—chose more time off than those from still developing countries such as the Philippines and Thailand. This could signal a change in Asian values."

Eat, Drink and Be Merry

According to Hong Kong businessman Gordon Wu, there are a succession of expenditures, mostly dictated by affordability, that can be used to measure the economic growth of developing countries. The first is that people start to eat out. If the number and variety of fast-food restaurants in Asia is any indication, then Gordon Wu is right. Twenty-six years "have passed since the epoch-launching Osaka International Exposition, when Asians were first beguiled by such exotic phenomena as McDonald's and Kentucky Fried Chicken units, a Western-style cafeteria, a newfangled sushi-to-go operation and a host of never-before-seen foreign restaurants" reports *Nation's Restaurant News.* "Although numerous U.S.-based dining concepts went on to glut the now-sluggish Japanese marketplace, Yankee food service innovations are still debuting in Asia as American chains tackle start-up or expansion challenges in countries throughout the region."

Kentucky Fried Chicken, a division of PepsiCo, is so certain of the company's future in Asia that it plans to open twenty-five company-owned restaurants in Thailand and Hong Kong. This is a dramatic departure from the company's traditional foreign expansion plan of joint ventures and limited partnerships.

- There are 107 McDonald's in China, including five of the ten busiest McDonald's in the world. McDonald's opened four restaurants in Beijing in one weekend in August, 1995. The city now has 30. The company plans to have one hundred outlets in Beijing by 2003, and more than six hundred nationwide.
- T.G.I. Friday's is the darling of the Korean dining-out crowd.
- Starbucks Coffee Co. plans to have 12 coffee stores in Japan by 1997.
- Baskin Robbins, now in forty-nine countries, including China, will set up shop in India.
- Kenny Rogers Roasters is expanding throughout Asia.

The path has not been smooth for these purveyors of food for people on the go. In many Asian cities, prime locations are in short supply and, when available, very expensive. Cumbersome distribution channels pose enormous challenges, and satisfying Asian palates is not as simple as putting soy sauce on hamburger meat. But the promise of access to billions of mouths hungry for new taste sensations is enough to motivate any businessperson to find a way to work around the obstacles.

One of my favorite quotes regarding the compelling arithmetic of the size of the consumer market in China is from the chicken industry in the United States. It has to do with the fact that Chinese love chicken feet, which are not eaten much in the West. Bill Roenigk, the senior vice president of America's National Broiler Council, lamented, "We could sell a lot more but there are only 7 billion chickens in the U.S., and each has only two feet."

The Economist reports that Chinese consumers also are "wooed by Cadbury's chocolate, biscuits from United Biscuits, Maxwell House coffee from Kraft General Foods, and Knorr bouillon cubes from America's CPC. Smokers are tempted by advertisements for Marlboro, Salem and Lucky Strike cigarettes. Drinkers are invited to open a can of beer from Australia's Fosters, Denmark's Carlsberg or the Philippines' San Miguel. Department stores offer Estee Lauder cosmetics, shoes from London's Gieves & Hawkes and Louis Vuitton handbags."

AB Electrolux, the Swedish vacuum cleaner maker, plans to double sales in Asian markets over the next five years. Unilever, the Anglo-Dutch personal hygiene company, is entering China to take on Procter & Gamble, which "washes more heads of hair in China than any other foreign shampoo maker." Unilever will invest $100 million annually through the year 2000 to increase production.

Just hours after the lifting of Vietnam's trade embargo, PepsiCo sent truckloads of its soda into the streets of Ho Chi Minh City. Coke cut its price from 60 cents to 20 cents and put two 30-foot Coke bottles in front of the Hanoi Opera House. The cola kingpins are going head-to-head in China, too. Pepsi's investment in China has already hit $600 million, but the company says it "will invest whatever it takes to build the China market." Although Coca-Cola is the market leader in Asia, Coke and Pepsi are running "neck and neck" in Thailand. Pepsi introduced its Pepsi Max to Thailand with a three-month, $2-million ad campaign in the race for market share there.

Persuading Asians

Fast on the heels of this avalanche are the advertising agencies seeing to it that their clients' products get their share of consumer attention. The list of agencies with offices in China reads like a who's who in big-ticket advertising: McCann-Erickson, D'Arcy Masius Benton & Bowles, Saatchi & Saatchi Advertising, Bates Worldwide, Ogilvy & Mather, J. Walter Thompson, Grey China Advertising, Leo Burnett, Batey Ads Pte Ltd., Dentsu Young & Rubicam Partners, Dentsu, Euro RSCG Ball, DDB Needham Worldwide, BBDO, Lintas, Bozwell Worldwide Inc., Lee David Ayer, Fortune and Compu-Ad.

Advertising expenditures in 1993 reached $14 billion in nine East Asian countries, including China, reports Zenith Media Worldwide/ Saatchi & Saatchi Advertising. Add Japan and the figure rises to $47 billion. China's advertising market quadrupled to $3 billion between 1993 and 1995 and is expected to increase to $22 billion by 2000. Taiwan and the Philippines have also had significant increases.

Sums like that show that Asia, and especially China, will become one of the world's top advertising markets in the next two decades, predicts the *Asian Wall Street Journal Weekly*. *Advertising Age* already considers China the fastest growing media market in the world. In 1995 advertising expenditures in South Korea increased 18.7 percent, to $5.7 billion. South Korea, the world's tenth largest advertising market in 1994, jumped to sixth place in 1995.

This surge of Asian advertising speaks volumes about the changing political environment. Advertising depends on the media. Ten, even five years ago, advertisers were limited to state-owned media, print or broadcast. Closely monitored and carefully censored, procurers of airtime or ad space could never be certain if their material would run, or if it did, whether it would bear any resemblance to its original form. But now a combination of deteriorating state media monopolies and the advent of commercial television is creating huge opportunities.

Even Katmandu Has Cable

In the past few years Asia has plugged into the worldwide web of television broadcasting. **Four hundred million Asian homes have television.** In Taiwan, South Korea, Singapore and Japan, at least 99 percent of the households own televisions; in Hong Kong it's 98 percent. India has 50,000 private cable operators. By mid-1995 there were thirty cable channels—and that was expected to double in 1996. With one million cable subscribers, Shanghai has the highest cable penetration in the world, says the *International Herald Tribune.*

• For $23 a month, South Koreans can tap into twenty-five cable channels.

• Every citizen in Singapore will soon have access to a hundred cable stations.

• There are four hundred cable operators in Taiwan.

Even Katmandu has cable. At the beginning of 1995, about a thousand homes could choose among sixteen different channels. Prazwol Pradhan, who brought cable there, intends to grow the industry into a satellite broadcasting hub rivaling Hong Kong and Singapore.

"Every household in Thailand now has a receiver for home entertainment—whether a TV, a radio, VCR, stereo or CD player," says Thai entertainment entrepreneur Paiboon Damrongchaitam, founder and majority owner of Grammy Entertainment Public Company Ltd., a $400-million entertainment conglomerate launched in 1983. "Up country everybody has a radio, a cassette player and a water buffalo."

Print media are also proliferating as governments relax their stranglehold on all information. India offers 369 daily newspapers in eighteen different languages. Indonesians can choose from 247 newspapers and 117 magazines. There, as elsewhere, the potential for a crackdown still exists. So "safe-style" reporting is generally the guiding principle.

Nonetheless, Asians have access to more information than at any other time in their history, and the media push the envelope of government restrictions daily. Jimmy Lai's magazine, *Next*, described China's Premier Li Peng as the "son of a turtle's egg with a zero IQ." A recent article in Malaysia's *Men's Review* carried the subheading "Booze, bars and babes." Other lead stories include "Sex on your first date." "We are testing new ground," says founder and publisher Faridah Stephens. "We are writing for a younger set—many of whom are used to reading magazines from abroad . . . people are becoming more liberal."

Straight Talk Is on the Air

Estimates put the number of talk radio fans in Shanghai at one million. Listeners of the call-in show *Citizens and Society* question city officials about infrastructure problems, such as why the phones aren't working. *No Appointments Tonight* is devoted to relationships, love and marriage. "The people have needs, and the time has come to let the authorities know what these needs are," says Yuan Hu of Radio Shanghai. "That's the primary purpose of the talk shows."

"Taiwan is seeing a radio revolution," reports the *Far Eastern Economic Review*. "Despite periodic crackdowns by the government, underground stations have mushroomed." In 1994, Taiwan witnessed the growth of twenty new pirate radio stations, whose topics range from literature and homework advice to sex and drugs. "Never before have so many people in Taiwan listened to radio as now," says Chen Chengteh, manager of Voice of Taiwan in Taipei. "For more than 40 years we haven't had a voice of the people like this. For only NT$1 [4 cents, the cost of a local telephone call], everyone can express their opinions in public."

Regularly raided by the government, Taiwan's pirate stations are usually back on the air in hours. People are hungry for information and increasingly bold about free speech. When Voice of Taiwan was raided in 1994, riots erupted in Taipei. Having sampled the information explosion, people are unwilling to return to the silent days of government-controlled media. Furthermore, the economy of Asia cannot afford to return to those bygone days. Advertising—particularly in print, but increasingly on television and radio—is already a multibillion-dollar business. What government is going to turn its back on that kind of revenue?

Access to worldwide satellite broadcasting, movies, print and radio gives the emerging middle class a clear picture of "the international good life"—albeit a somewhat skewed one if it's *Dynasty* and *Dallas* that are shaping their vision. In any event, the closer the good life comes to being within their reach, the more eager they are to grasp it.

An explosion in broadcast and print media brings Asia more and better entertainment choices. In 1990, Star TV became the first Pan-Asian satellite television network. Reaching more than half the world's population, Star TV sparked a cultural revolution. Rupert Murdoch's News Corporation bought control of Star TV to capture the hearts, minds and pocketbooks of Asian consumers. Star TV's joint venture, Phoenix Satellite Television, hopes to enter China's market.

For the past year or so, global media moguls have been engaged in a power struggle to determine who would dominate the Asian market. CNN, NBC, the BBC, Star TV and Hong Kong's Television Broadcasts (TVB) all were scrambling for a toehold. Not one has made a profit—or even broken even. What is becoming apparent, however, is the likelihood of two or three alliances among the major players, with CNN as a "wild card."

Media moguls have learned one important lesson: as much as Asians initially are drawn to all things Western, in the final analysis they want to be entertained in their own language. Part of the joy of being a couch potato is expending no energy whatsoever. Struggling to interpret English-language programming just isn't fun.

Entertaining Asia's Middle Class

Middle-class economic status opens the door to the big world of entertainment. *Jurassic Park* was the first major Hollywood movie to be dubbed into Hindi since *Gandhi.* In April 1994 the movie opened in 110 Indian theaters. Chinafilm just recently started importing ten "outstanding" movies a year. Before only outdated, cheap foreign films were bought.

B. B. King performed at the Hard Rock Cafe's opening in Beijing. The 16,000-square-foot restaurant is almost exactly like the one in Dallas. There are also Hard Rock franchises in Singapore, Bangkok, Bali, Taipei, Jakarta and Kuala Lumpur. Planet Hollywood has the rights for restaurants in sixteen Asian countries. Audiences of Asia's glitterati have seen *The Phantom of the Opera* and *Les Misérables*. Even Luciano Pavarotti has performed. Michael Jackson's Dangerous Tour was a sellout in Singapore.

T. Ananda Krishnan—Asia's Answer to Rupert Murdoch

Not content to let Western media moguls walk off with the prize, Asian entrepreneurs and established business tycoons are vying for the lion's share of the market. Malaysian businessman T. Ananda Krishnan fully expects to convince the governments of Malaysia and Singapore to team up to capture the regional media market. He very likely will achieve that goal. Involved in everything from oil trading to property development—including the sky-scraping Kuala Lumpur City Centre —Krishnan's passion is media. With the launching of Malaysia East Asia Satellite (Measat), his next goal is to "become a state-of-the-art provider of multimedia services—the full array from POTS (plain old telephone services) to entertainment by exploiting the synergies in telecommunications, satellites and broadcasting."

Few doubt Krishnan's ability to become Asia's answer to Rupert Murdoch. He will achieve that in part because he understands an important paradox: to be truly successful he must appeal to the broadest possible audience within a segmented market, yet without creating one-size-fits-all broadcasting. Somehow one has to do both. It is a lesson that all who hope to market to the new Asian middle class will have to learn. Asia is not a single, homogeneous market, but a collection of countries, a collection of markets. As in other aspects of their economic development, Asians are influenced by Western ideas, styles and attitudes—as seen through international broadcasts—but they are not becoming Western as such. *They are modernizing in the Asian way.*

Cultural Norms and Consumer Markets

Part of that modernization is the changing construct of Asian households. With Mom, Dad and two children, they are beginning to look more like Western households. Grandma and Grandpa live elsewhere. More Asian children are now being cared for by nannies, housekeepers and au pairs from other Asian countries. "In Singapore, Hong Kong, Malaysia and other affluent parts of Asia, many mothers are increasingly willing to leave their children in the care of helpers. The domestics—from the Philippines, Indonesia, Thailand, Sri Lanka—are often well-educated and hard-working."

As in the West, the widespread exodus of women from household to workplace has engendered endless worry about children's mental and emotional development. The pursuit of their education, always highly valued, is sometimes a status symbol. In India, for example, children as young as three take rigorous entrance exams to get into the "right" preschools.

"In India, where the world's fastest-growing middle class is undergoing profound changes . . . toddler stress has become the latest manifestation of the frenetic race to get ahead," says a story in the *Washington Post.* "Overachieving parents now begin grooming children as young as two and a half for the battery of entrance interviews for admission to the city's most elite private nursery schools. Once in school, the stress only increases."

Similarly, in China and elsewhere in Asia, private kindergartens are springing up in major cities in a mad frenzy to prepare children to live proper middle-class lives. "Zhu Xiaoying, a village woman in southern China's Guangdong province, wants only the best for her son," reports a *Korea Times* article. For her that means paying $21,350 up front, the equivalent of twenty-five years of an average worker's wages in nearby Guangzhou, to send her six-year-old son, Chen Juhui, to the private Guangdong Country Garden School just south of the city.

Why are the parents in the new middle class in China willing to spend extraordinary sums to finance, not university, but early childhood education? First, it is in part a reaction to their own sense of loss. For many, the hope of education was all but eradicated by the Cultural Revolution. Its victims are increasingly aware of the deficit that loss has created. Second, it is a function of the "six-pocket syndrome." Strict population controls created a generation of single-child households, many of which have six income-earning adults—two parents and two sets of grandparents—indulging the child's every whim.

The children of the middle class are themselves a significant economic force. "The sheer numbers of these teens are fuelling a global consumer revolution with youth culture as its raison d'etre," reports the *Business Times* of Singapore. "Demographically, Singapore's teens have yet to overtake the 30-somethings here . . . but what teens lack in numbers they make up for by sheer spending power. These teenagers are out there spending close to $250 million a year (or an estimated $100 a month)—and that's just pocket money. Throw in what their indulgent parents buy them and what they earn in part-time jobs to pay for extra luxuries and you have a formidable force in the marketplace."

Heavily influenced by Western television, marketers are discovering that teenage consumers nonetheless reflect local tastes and conform to some traditions and cultural norms. "If you take a typical Indian teenager in Bombay, Delhi or Calcutta, you would find that tangibly he has moved toward the West," says Jagdeep Kapoor, director of Parle Agro, a Bombay-based marketer of Frooty, a boxed fruit drink, and Bailley's mineral water. "He'd be wearing a Lacoste shirt, Wrangler jeans, Nike shoes and maybe a pair of Ray-Ban glasses." Still he is very much an Indian in his values, says Kapoor. He respects his parents, lives together in a family and removes his Nike shoes and Ray-Bans before entering a place of religion.

"This is the land of karma, where everything is worked out for you, your destiny, your kismet," says Alyque Padamsee, a well-known Bombay adman. "But the new generation feels 'The hell with waiting for reincarnation!' and they are breaking the karma handcuffs. They're deciding that what they want is a better life, now, and if they have any money, they want to spend it now."

Savings, Investment and Retirement

Asian countries have high savings rates, averaging around 30 percent. But with the rise in consumer spending, will the savings rate go down? If it does, more investment capital will have to be raised outside the region.

From Export-Led ──▶ Consumer-Driven

It is reported that urban Chinese have about $200 billion outside the nation's banking system "in their hands or under their beds." Per capita income in China is $2,600 (using the purchasing power parity method). There are more than 80 million Chinese earning between $10,000 and $40,000 a year. We also know that there are more than a million millionaires in China. To channel savings into productive capital and let money make money for the Asians, tremendous opportunities are opening up in the field of personal finance. The region's major financial institutions are launching unit trusts and mutual funds to mobilize domestic savings and help its citizens hedge against inflation.

"In terms of life insurance, China represents the end of all roads," says Andres Kabel, National Mutual Asia's chief executive of finance. A new era is dawning in the region's life insurance industry, with local players revitalized by the newfound wealth and foreign players keenly eyeing the market. With markets in the West nearing the saturation point, U.S. and European insurers are looking to Asia to underwrite their future growth. *Asia Inc.* reports: "In 1992, according to Swiss Reinsurance Co., 35 percent of the world's 1.47 trillion insurance business was written in the U.S., 31 percent in Europe and 22 percent in Japan. The rest of Asia represented just 5 percent of the global market so far. But within 10 years, China will be the world's single biggest insurance market, predicts Mick Newmatch, chairman of Prudential Corp. Asia Ltd." Veteran American player American International Assurance (AIA), a wholly owned subsidiary of American International Group, is already writing new policies at the rate of 55,000 a month. Its Chinese sales force already numbers 5,400 agents.

It is not only China that has attracted the interest of the world's insurers. Except for Japan and South Korea, all other Asian countries have insurance premiums totaling less than 5 percent of their GDP. (Japan has 8.6 percent, totaling $320 billion, while South Korea has 12.3 percent, totaling $36 billion a year.) Besides China, the wealthy individuals in Singapore, Taiwan, Hong Kong and Malaysia, along with the rising middle class in Indonesia and India, offer great untapped potential.

The Renaissance in Asian Art

The next stage of human gratification after material needs are satisfied is the quest for aesthetics and artifacts of the past. Asia has been a source of art objects for centuries. The richness of Asian civilizations, its people, culture, religions and a long, and sometimes glorious, past have produced a steady supply of art to the world's discerning connoisseurs, who, until recently, were mainly in the West. Collectors and art lovers from Europe and America have long been fascinated with Oriental art and have created the greatest demand, thus setting standards and prices. But the balance of interest and buying power are now shifting to the East.

In an auction held in Singapore in March 1995, Singaporean artist Tan Swie Hian sold his *Sound of Sutra* painting for $90,800, the highest price ever paid for a living local artist. At a Christie's auction in the same city in the same month, a painting by the famous Indonesian artist Raden Saleh Bastaman Saleh (1807–80) sold for $640,000, a record high for the artist.

Art appreciation is a function of affluence, and the rising economic tides in Asia will lift the fortunes of the Asian art market. From Shanghai to Singapore, Bombay to Bangkok, Hanoi to Hong Kong, Tokyo to Taipei, the art scene is becoming increasingly vibrant and holds great promise. Galleries are opening and cultural promotions are receiving heightened attention from governments, all driven by a growing middle class. The Korean government is expending tremendous energy on a national cultural program it calls "New Renaissance," aimed at reshaping the cultural climate of the country. Demands in the Indian art market are so great that artists sell their works as fast as they are finished.

The assertiveness of being Asian is rippling through the world of art. Money has a liberating influence on the soul, and as Asians begin to display greater confidence in themselves they will focus on and appreciate their indigenous cultures. Contemporary Asian art is set to flourish. The antique and craft markets will also boom as Asians celebrate their success and reassert their pride in the past.

Asians are collecting one another's art. Chinese art has been the most prized and popular. Now there is interest in a wide range of contemporary art on the part of the increasingly affluent middle class. In Southeast Asia, the Singapore Art Museum is on a buying spree to put together a collection of the best from the region.

Masanori Fukuoka, the owner of a food processing company and founder of the Glenbarra Art Museum in Himeji, Japan, has a collection of three thousand works of contemporary Indian art. He has said of his interest in Indian art that while "European art may be very beautiful, it is less provocative to the modern audience. Given that India, which contains about 15 percent of the world's population, faces daily many problems plaguing much of the world, contemporary Indian artists often address and/or reflect the circumstances of the modern world. To the extent that these issues are global, the art can touch the Japanese mind and can affect a Japanese more profoundly than the older European works, which are of a wholly different time and world than ours today."

Given the dynamics of the entire region, the world may soon see exciting contemporary creations from Asia.

$39 Million for a Van Gogh Sunflower, Anyone?

When rich Asians begin to buy art, will they do for the art market what the Japanese did in the 1980s? And who in Asia would have so much interest in Western art as to outbid everyone at all costs—the Chinese, Indians, Indonesians, Thais or Koreans?

The answer is, none of the above. Asians have long traditions and they are very centered in a universe of their own values. Unlike the Japanese, whose culture is largely derivative and highly insular, the Indians and Chinese particularly take great pride in their civilization and greatly value their past. Interest in Western art is not likely to rise. At most, it will be confined to the well-traveled and Western-educated Asians, and may center on Western contemporary and modern art.

A Boom in Classic Chinese Art

While all of Asia is prospering, the greatest impact on the art market is expected to come from the Chinese, especially the Chinese Overseas. Their wealth is growing dramatically as a result of Asia's economic explosion. The implications of this are enormous for the world art market, even greater than the rise of the Japanese in the 1980s. But one important point must be noted: the Chinese are very culture-bound. The 57 million Chinese Overseas, wherever they are in the world, remain culturally Chinese. They hold on strongly to their cultural identity and manifest it in all aspects of their lives. It is this "Chineseness" that is creating the excitement in the classical Chinese art market.

In auctions of Chinese art in and around Asia, the Chinese are the most interested buyers, and they are prepared to outbid one another. For example, at a Christie's auction in 1995 in Hong Kong, an anonymous Chinese buyer—rumored to be from the mainland—paid $1.5 million for a jade bangle. Auction houses dealing with Chinese art in Asia are reporting breathtakingly high prices. Given their scarcity and the heightened interest in classical objects of art, prices are expected to go through the roof when the Chinese return to reclaim the trophies of their civilization. Collectors and dealers of the art world, fasten your seat belts.

The boom will not only be fueled by some few rich individuals buying art. Millions of middle-class Asians are coming to appreciate the finer things of life. And when preoccupation with the GNP and stock market performance gives way to greater refinements, the middle class will be buying art. A new generation of buyers has already emerged with an interest in midprice antiques, preferring them to classic ceramics. Ten years ago only 5 percent of buyers at Hong Kong's Atfield Galleries were Asians; today the figure has risen to 40 percent. The demand for art, not just fine art but everything from architecture and home furnishings to fashion and entertainment, will follow in the wake of Asia's booming economy.

Eastman Kodak CEO George Fisher likes to say that "Half the people in the world have yet to take their first picture." And the majority of them are in Asia, where most of the region's 3 billion people have yet to own a wristwatch, a suitcase, sunglasses, a Wonderbra or a radio, not to mention a computer, a motorcycle, a refrigerator, a microwave oven, a television, an apartment or a house, a Ming dynasty ceramic, or take a trip abroad. But the progression has begun and it will just go on and on. That's Asia.

Catching Moving Targets

By now, it should be beyond doubt that for the West, Asia is the site of a new gold rush, like the one in California that drew so many early Asian migrants to America. But the Asian gold rush is not as easy to mine. It takes great skill and tenacity to find and study before you can reap rewards. In marketing to Asians, you have to address the mosaic of varying levels of purchasing power, as well as the varieties of cultures and religious sensitivities. And you have to persuade in several different languages. But the rewards are there for those with patience, for those who are looking at Asia as a twenty- to fifty-year project.

Today's new urban Asia is just as sophisticated and in many ways more exciting than Western cities. Urban Asian consumers are knowledgeable, modern and keen to embrace the global lifestyle. Young urban Asians have grown up accustomed to many things that originated in the West. They have, for example, completely embraced pizza, some even claiming that it is part of their heritage. The story is told about a young Singaporean boy who was taken by his father to Rome. "Hey, look, Dad," the little boy exclaimed. "They have pizza here, too." On sampling the product, the boy decided that it was not as good as the original back home.

Nury Vitachi, who writes for the *South China Post* and the *Far Eastern Economic Review*, describes the Asian middle-class phenomenon: "Executives in Asia have become rich at warp speed by taking full control of their own lives. They invest a great deal of time in their work, they use strategy to scramble up the corporate ladder, and they demand payment in cash—so that they can make their money work as hard as they do."

Signs of affluence are everywhere, but don't get carried away. Traveling around Asia, no matter how rich the Asians become, signs of their frugal nature are still apparent. And they are very cost-conscious. Shopkeepers in many Asian cities, most notably in Hong Kong, demand payment for discounted merchandise in cash instead of plastic, and many Asians are accustomed to that. Most people save the increases in their income, and many prefer to put it into fixed or other income-generating assets. Stock, land and property are their favorites.

Many affluent Asians still regard financial security as the most important form of security, and they are confident that Asia is the place to be to achieve that. While many have begun to savor the good life, they are not letting go of their top priority of education for their children. Education is looked upon as the most important contributing factor to success in life. And in many of Asia's competitive urban centers, there is a rush to acquire a second degree and other forms of professional qualification to ensure personal competitiveness in the workplace. There are extraordinary opportunities in Asia for education and training programs from language to software programming.

Despite the rise in their assertiveness, Asians still look to the United States and not so much to Europe for ideas and trends. In general, except for those in Hong Kong and Japan, they are not particularly concerned with being fashionable. For today's Asia, Japan and Hong Kong are the sources of Asian fashion ideas, but as Asia becomes more affluent, there is a great opportunity to develop an indigenous fashion industry. For example, a huge market potential exists in introducing new materials and simplified but fashionable designs for countries in tropical Asia with a hot humid climate throughout the year.

The population density and lack of space in urban areas has prohibited Asians from exercising frequently and few indulge in outdoor activities. This is changing. Most Asians consider themselves in good health. Compared with Americans, few are overweight—largely as a result of the Asian diet. But now health clubs are becoming popular among younger Asians. Potential for indoor exercise equipment holds great promise. It is also important to dress for the gym, and younger Asians are serious about looking good, complete with makeup, sunglasses, designer exercise shoes and outfits, and a gym bag.

In trying to hit Asia's moving targets, regardless of what you are selling, it is a good idea to stick with market density—not country by country but, mostly, city by city. Asian markets can be a marketer's dream in that their densities are among the highest in the world. Java, Indonesia's main island, has 115 million people. On Nanjing Road, Shanghai's busiest street, businesses are open twelve hours a day almost every day of the year. More than 1.5 million people visit the shops there and spend more than $50 million every day.

Someone said that you can only become rich if you sell to the rich. I would add that you can become richer faster if you sell to the new rich. For investors in the West, watch for Western companies that are preparing a big push in Asia. The world has not seen anything like it before, and you can reap handsome dividends if you back those stocks that are going eastward.

One measure of the incredible spread of consumerism in Asia is the growing celebration of Christmas. In December in downtown Tokyo, Kuala Lumpur, Hong Kong, Singapore and, of course, (Catholic) Manila, there are wall-to-wall Christmas decorations. I was startled to learn that in Japan, Christmas is a verb: "Christmas your best girl." Retailers all over Asia have adopted Santa Claus as a helper to escalate gift-giving. Asians are great gift-givers. It will be a stupendous market.

Sales of new cars in Malaysia in the first half of 1995 were up 50.6 percent over the same period in 1994. In Bangkok, five hundred new cars a day are added to the absurdly heavy traffic where speeds average less than a mile an hour during peak hours. "They come with briefcases full of cash," says Anthony McDonald, who sells Rover cars in Bangkok. Range Rovers sell for about $160,000. Sales increased from 1,206 in 1994 to 2,000 in 1995 and are expected to increase 30 percent in 1996. Sales of new cars in Indonesia increased more than 30 percent in 1995.

Singapore has made it very expensive to put a new car on the road. It imposes very high import duties and taxes, and the new owner must also purchase a certificate in order to operate a vehicle in the city. Consequently, even a little, cheap Proton from Malaysia costs $65,000 to put on the road. A Mercedes can cost $300,000. Yet, sales remain high and waiting lists long. Tommy Ng, a car dealer in the state of Johor in Malaysia, who sells luxury imports, says, "The more expensive the car, the longer the waiting list," adding, "We keep thinking that it is going to slow down, but it never does."

Credit cards are issued by banks in China, but the banks are so outmoded they are the main obstacle to developing a nationwide system. Nonetheless progress is being made. At the end of 1994, there were about 8.4 million credit cards in use in China, double the year before. The People's Bank of China, the central bank, has made a goal of 200 million credit card holders by the year 2000—nice round numbers.

In this exploding Asian market, it will pay to Asianize Western efforts as much as possible. Do not open branches. A company's operations should take on an Asian identity—and a local identity as well. Asia's leading computer company, Taiwan's Acer, is going all out to become a truly local operation in each Asian country.

In a multipolar world, sharing ownership and leadership is much desired, and it fits well with Asians' need to have individual ownership in the companies they work for. Acer, for example, is launching a program that will create local shareholder majorities in each of its key markets. The idea is that in each country the Acer brand would be perceived as domestic. The company is restructuring itself into twenty-one companies to keep each unit focused and create an entrepreneurial environment. And each of these company subsidiaries is planning to go public in local stock markets to allow employees and customers to own a stake in the operation—a very Asian communitarian approach. If one of Asia's most successful companies takes this approach, it should be instructive for Western companies who want to do business in Asia.

CHAPTER FOUR

From Government-Controlled to Market-Driven

IT has been just nine years since Taiwan was a one-party state under martial law. It was a command economy run by the government, which overwhelmingly dominated economic and social decisions. In 1995 Taiwan's 21 million people elected a provincial governor and mayors of its two largest cities. In 1996 Lee Teng Hui became Taiwan's first elected president.

As Asia moves to a market economy, politics becomes dramatically less important, almost irrelevant. With a 7 percent annual growth rate, quipped one journalist, nobody wants revolution. In fact, Asian annual growth rates routinely hit 10 percent. Politics irrelevant? In India, university graduates traditionally entered the civil service. Now they want jobs in private enterprise. In teeming urban centers, Asian yuppies, dressed for success, walk with cellular phones glued to their ears and the latest stock quotes clutched in their hands. Revolution? It would not be good for business. It might interrupt the fruits of prosperity. Everywhere there is talk of the Asian Dream: making money, having the "good life."

Throughout Asia, ideology is giving way to economic and political reality.

To ensure their survival, governments are abandoning all but the pretense of maintaining command economies and betting their future on the vagaries of the marketplace. There is fierce competition among countries to attract foreign investment. Asians have tasted economic freedom; any reversal now would bring disastrous political upheaval. Governments must get out of the way and let the marketplace manage growth.

From Ideology to Pragmatism

This quote from the *Asian Wall Street Journal* makes the case: "What China's Communists consider truly threatening is creeping irrelevance. Ironically, that irrelevance is exacerbated by their greatest success: the reforms the Communists themselves unleashed 16 years ago have produced an economic frenzy.

"The economic opportunities since the party unfettered the economy in December 1978 have made money a rival to the party for people's attention. Nowhere does the party's marginalization show up more clearly than with China's youth, especially in booming coastal cities. Top university graduates used to consider party membership a career-gliding rite of passage required for advancement through the ranks. Now, they scorn party recruiters."

All over Asia, economic considerations dominate.

Development in the "Asian Way"

Tales of the success of Asia's "Four Tigers" are legendary. The world watched in awe as Hong Kong, Singapore, South Korea and Taiwan leapfrogged over the industrial stage and pushed full force into the information age. Singapore, for example, has the world's most sophisticated telecommunications infrastructure and is an operations center for multinational computer firms. Hong Kong's role in global finance equals London's or New York's. South Korea is a world leader in manufacturing sophisticated, high-tech, quality products.

Flush with success, the Four Tigers have invested in the region's less developed countries with unprecedented confidence. By 1995, Asia's newly industrializing economies and Japan contributed 74 percent of Vietnam's total foreign direct investment. The Asia-Pacific region accounted for 80 percent of Vietnam's exports and 75 percent of imports in 1992.

Gearing Up to Join the Big League

On March 24, 1978, the Vietnamese government closed all private businesses. Restrictions remained in place until 1986. But what is happening today in Vietnam's private sector is a dramatic illustration of the shift from government-controlled to market-driven Asian economies:

- Between 1989 and 1993 private businesses created 4.7 million new jobs.
- The number of entrepreneurs applying for business licenses increased from 76 in 1991 to 4,403 in January 1993.
- Entrepreneurs are now responsible for 90 percent of the agricultural output, 70 percent of domestic trade and 60 percent of transport services.
- Just seven years ago there were only 22 registered private companies in Ho Chi Minh City. Today there are 2,600, plus tens of thousands of small shops.
- In the first part of 1994 alone, the Ho Chi Minh City government gave out more than 100,000 small retail business licenses.

In 1994, BMW began assembling cars in Vietnam, which has 75 million people, a 95 percent literacy rate and a strong work ethic. In Germany, BMW pays auto workers $30 an hour, 50 percent of which goes to the government to fund welfare programs. In Vietnam, BMW pays workers $1—a day.

"If we wait to gain experience, we won't be able to do anything," says Huynh Thanh Chung, a twenty-eight-year-old millionaire who dropped out of college and developed Hai Vuong Company into a $50-million business with dealings in construction, beer and clothing.

In 1993 he invested in a $3-million seafood processing plant, 70 percent of whose sales are to Japan.

Vietnam's sizzling economy is growing at 9 percent or more a year. Once out of control, inflation is now comfortably under 10 percent annually. Historically an importer of rice, the country is now a major exporter. Rubber, coffee and seafood exports are increasing. A natural hub between Northeast and Southeast Asia, Vietnam holds an enviable geographic location. Furthermore, it has an educated population, a stable currency, a huge domestic market and a government intent on economic reform. Political reform will follow. Lastly, the 2 million overseas Vietnamese—in Europe, North America and Australia—provide a reservoir of capital and skills for their former home.

Although Vietnam struggles with the same infrastructure problems as other Asian nations, and has further to go than most, there is a long line of foreign companies eager to invest. While the United States was deterred by the MIA issue, others walked through the doors just as soon as they were opened. Now that the U.S. government has formally recognized Vietnam, total pledged American investment in the country is $1.1 billion.

"Caterpillar wants to supply equipment for a $2 billion highway project. Some 50 other U.S. companies, including Morrison Knudsen, plan to submit bids for the first stage. Mobil has teamed up with three Japanese partners to begin drilling offshore. Exxon, Amoco, Conoco, Unocal and Arco are negotiating production-sharing contracts with Petro Vietnam," reports *BusinessWeek*.

GE, AT&T, Coca-Cola, Citibank, Boeing, Motorola—a who's who of American multinationals—are queuing up to invest in, and profit from, improved relationships between Washington and Hanoi. Despite the late start, U.S. companies almost certainly will garner their share of the Vietnamese market. For one, many consumer products like Coke, Pepsi, Marlboro and Colgate toothpaste already enjoy widespread brand awareness as holdovers from the Vietnam War. And secondly, having experienced domination by Asian neighbors, Vietnam is keen to maintain a strong U.S. presence to counterbalance the influence in their markets of Japan and Taiwan, particularly.

The World Bank is at a loss to explain Vietnam's recent rise to economic prominence. By most economic yardsticks, the country simply does not measure up:

- Incomes are unevenly distributed.
- Public administration is still ineffective.
- The legal framework is unreliable.
- The banking business is shaky.
- And personal savings levels are considerably lower than in other Asian countries.

Perhaps most important, Vietnam does not have the infrastructure to support current growth, much less the anticipated acceleration in growth. But the switch to a market economy is very popular in Vietnam, and given the intelligence, ingenuity and determination of the Vietnamese people, the country will become an important economic player in the region.

Privatization and the People's Liberation Army

Like many armed forces across the globe, China's People's Liberation Army (PLA) was hit with painful budget cuts. Its response, however, has proved more entrepreneurial than most—especially considering the short history of Chinese capitalism. Since 1984 the PLA has set up more than 20,000 companies with profits of about $5 billion (yes, $5 billion). That makes the PLA the largest and most profitable commercial empire in China. By some estimates, as many as half of China's military personnel are engaged in nonmilitary, commercial activities.

Citicorp has invested in the 999 Pharmaceutical Company, which is part of the PLA's San Jiu Enterprise Group, one of Shenzhen's fastest-growing companies. Baskin Robbins works with a military-run firm to sell its ice cream. Other successful PLA businesses include Guangzhou's three-star hotels, the best karaoke bars, the best bus routes between Guangzhou and Shenzhen, and Shenzhen's fastest-growing securities companies. The PLA even owned JJ's, Shanghai's largest nightclub, until it was closed down.

The PLA has figured out the concept of Strategic Market Advantage. "Civilian airports aren't everywhere," says Ge Bulei, an executive of China United Airlines, which is owned by the PLA. "Military airports are. We use this special advantage to fly places civilian planes can't." It is as if a bunch of U.S. Air Force officers decided to use some of their military planes to fly civilians around to various parts of the country in order to make a few extra bucks.

The People's Liberation Army is now the largest privatization project in the world.

Vietnam's military is following the PLA's lead: military-run companies in Vietnam had revenues of $360 million in 1995. The military owns 300 major state companies and by mid-1996 was involved in 49 joint ventures with foreigners valued at $445 million.

Privatization

Would that the rest of China's institutions were faring as well. Or that the pace of privatization were faster. About 50 percent of state enterprises are in the red. Though they contribute a decreasing share of industrial output—48 percent today versus 80 percent in the late 1970s—they still employ three in four urban workers. Some 340 million Chinese, dependents included, owe their livelihood to state firms. No wonder many argue in favor of maintaining state enterprises. But inefficient state-owned enterprises are in many countries employment programs for the chronically unemployable.

"Yuan Mu may not have a prize in economics, but we'll say this for him: He has his fundamentals down," reports the *Far Eastern Economic Review*. "In a recent article in *Economics Daily*, the head of China's most powerful think tank opposed privatization on the grounds that it denies the 'basis of socialism in China.' That, of course, is the very reason to support it. The color of the cat shouldn't matter so long as the cat catches mice, runs Deng Xiaoping's famous aphorism, and the socialist cat hasn't caught any mice lately." In August 1995, China announced it would retain only about 1,000 state companies and leave 99,000 others to sink or swim in the market.

In India, the return on assets of the three hundred central and seven hundred state government enterprises dropped to below 2 percent. More than 40 percent of central government operations are losing money. If not for the profitable oil and telecom sectors, the public sector would be drowning in red ink. "In total these public sector enterprises manage about 55 percent of India's capital stock (excluding households) and account for one quarter of non-farm GDP. As a result, their inefficiency means a serious drag on the economy, knocking two or three percentage points off GDP growth," reports the *Far Eastern Economic Review*.

The original idea behind state ownership was not jobs. It was to eliminate "useless competition." The defenders of state firms fail to realize that the value of privately owned, profit-making companies is not that they create jobs, although they do, but that they are designed with the goal of keeping fixed costs low to earn the highest possible profit. That is what leads to efficiencies, which create profits, which make for robust economies. And that's the important lesson being learned in Asia.

The Privatization of Malaysia

Arguably, Malaysia has learned that lesson better than the rest. The country now saves about $24 billion annually as a direct result of privatization, savings that are not the result of scaling down development or of raising taxes. Some 120 businesses have been privatized since 1983.

"To say that Malaysia is a model to developing countries is an understatement," says Khoo Eng Choo, the managing partner of Price Waterhouse in Kuala Lumpur. "Compared with the developing countries, privatization in Malaysia is more advanced and more widely applied." Jeffrey Sachs, the Harvard economist, also applauds the country's twelve-year-old program: "Malaysia has proved that privatization works."

The 120 privatized businesses have raised $4.2 billion in one-time payments alone, while the government is also trailblazing "an international path as a privatization consultant; economists and officials of multilateral-lending agencies tout Malaysia's programme as one of the most successful in the world," reports the *Far Eastern Economic Review.* The government also saves $2 billion annually in salaries and pensions.

What's more, the country's drive to turn the reins of state-run enterprises over to the private sector has fueled growth and efficiency and resulted in almost no unemployment. While some complain that privatization has enriched some of the prime minister's political cronies, no one denies that it has upgraded the efficiency of many services now in private hands.

At the Kelang Container Terminal, it takes less than three days to clear cargo; it used to take eight. There are wider choices in TV and radio programs, and a huge reduction in power outages means both can be enjoyed. There is steady telephone service. And the privately built North-South Highway shaved ninety minutes from the six-hour drive from Kuala Lumpur to Singapore.

The architect of Malaysia's privatization program, Prime Minister Mahathir Mohamad, continues to be its most ardent supporter. It was for Malaysia like catapulting across the great divide. Mahathir's predecessors believed that national economic interests, particularly those of ethnic Malays, could only be properly supervised by the state. Mahathir proved them wrong by including in his economic strategy an affirmative action plan to ensure that a significant share of the privatization opportunities went to *bumiputras* (indigenous Malays).

Malaysia's privatization schemes differ from most by carving out a continuing role for government as either shareholder or regulator, to protect the interests of the state. Raising capital has never been the goal of Malaysia's privatization program. "It's never been a fundraising exercise," says Anwar Ibrahim, the finance minister. "We let the private sector take the lead and the government acts as a check and balance. If we make some money in the process, that's the bonus."

Mahathir chose to do things not just in the "Asian way," but in the "Malaysian way." Similarly, Philippine President "Steady Soldier" Fidel Ramos is charting his own course there.

The "Sick Man of Asia" Is Recovering

The Philippines has long been famous for crippling electrical brown-outs, but not any more. More than $1 billion has been spent in the power sector since 1992, and electricity supplies increased 18 percent during 1994. Once considered one of the most backward countries in Asia, the Philippines has become a leader in the privatization of its infrastructure.

Much of the credit for this remarkable turnaround is given to the country's president, Fidel Ramos. To maintain momentum, the general-turned-politician continues to compel Filipinos to pass reforms to make the country competitive. He paved the way for foreign companies to come in and get the country powered up, removed barriers to foreign investment and broke up monopolies. That forced the Philippines's mostly family-owned megacorporations to retool and reinvest. In 1993, President Ramos opened the telephone industry to competition. Foreign companies are coming. During the fall of 1994, Nynex agreed to buy 25 percent of a local telephone company and spend $175 million by 1998.

There are many indications that the Philippines is on an economic development fast track. Philippine companies raised some $670 million on international capital markets in 1993, and many companies are expanding. Intel Philippines Manufacturing Inc. plans to invest $200 million by 1999 to increase the capacity of its memory chip and micro-processor plant. Avon has its manufacturing hub in the Philippines, and Procter & Gamble expects to build a $100-million detergent plant.

Although the Philippines has a long way to go before being considered a roaring tiger, it is certainly beginning to flex its muscle. Signs of the times are everywhere as buildings rise up to fill the capital city's skyline, and as former military installations are turned into a resort and an industrial park.

Clark and Subic Bay

The Philippine government's refusal to extend the life of U.S. military bases has turned into a win-win situation. With the end of the

Cold War, the United States doesn't need them—and entrepreneurs see them as commercial bonanzas. "Tourism will be our cash cow," says José Antonio Gonzalez, who invested $65 million into developing Clark, the former U.S. air base, into a resort. The Mimosa resort is scheduled to be finished in 1997 and will include a golf course, a theme park, vacation homes, hotels and restaurants, and a retirement community. And, if the government allows it, a casino. "Clark is going to be Asia's playground," adds Gonzalez. "It can be a major tourist attraction."

Just forty-two miles northeast of Clark is Subic Bay, the former U.S. naval base, which some hope will be "Asia's next economic miracle city." "It's perfect," says Jeffrey Koo, a Taiwanese billionaire. "The harbor, the airport, the infrastructure—it's all there."

As a result of Koo's lobbying, the Taiwanese government helped form an industrial park on Subic Bay. Reebok, AT&T, Enron and Acer are just a few of the companies that operate at Subic Bay. FedEx invested $100 million in Subic and uses it as its Asian hub. Subic Bay's airport can handle 18 planes at any one time. Shipments out of Subic Bay have grown from $19 million in 1994 to $182 million in 1995 and $158 million in just the first half of 1996. Subic Bay had already created 22,000 jobs by mid-1996. (President Ramos told me that President Bill Clinton made it a point to speak to him personally about the importance of a FedEx hub at Subic Bay.) Malaysian billionaire Lim Goh Tong is part of a venture investing in resort facilities.

In 1993, Subic Bay attracted more than $300 million in foreign direct investment, compared with $250 million in 1992 for the country as a whole. By the end of 1995, investment in Subic Bay totaled $1 billion.

Business confidence in the country's prospects for continued growth and stability is apparent in a comment by Thomas J. Leber, vice president and general manager of Wyeth Philippines, a U.S. pharmaceutical company: "When Ramos promised no brown-outs by December 1993, most people laughed. In fact, he delivered."

India Opens Its Doors a Little Wider

Ramos delivers. These days many other Asian leaders are also delivering. In 1991, India's then prime minister, P. V. Narasimha Rao, faced limited choices. He could open his country's doors to foreign trade and capital or let the Asia miracle pass his country by. He opened the doors. "Today, despite poverty, financial scandals and political violence, India's growth is accelerating, and it's attracting money from abroad," reports Singapore's *Business Times.* "American companies invested more in India in 1992 and 1993 alone than they had in the previous 40 years. Ford, which now sells no cars in India . . . [in late 1994] announced a joint venture with Mahindra & Mahindra and will begin manufacturing soon."

Although the government recently suffered some political setbacks, slowly but surely India is implementing the necessary reforms that will allow it to engage in activities with the rest of the global economic village. Included in its efforts are some tentative steps toward privatization. Most of the licensing controls that prevented private enterprises from competing with state firms are now gone. Consumers can fly in private airlines or bank with private banks. Faced with additional capacity and more choices from competitors, state enterprises like Indian Airlines have had to improve their services. And the government has eliminated those barriers that made companies dependent upon indifferent government suppliers for capital goods. In state-run enterprises that play a strategic role in the economy, management has been given greater autonomy and the authority to run the business like a business, not a welfare program.

India has the third-largest economy in Asia. Among its 940 million people, 150 million to 200 million are middle class and well educated. More than 25 million Indians own stock. Importantly, entrepreneurship has a long history. Robert Lloyd George, a Hong Kong investor, maintains that India is the most promising of the large emerging markets, more promising than China. That belief is based on the maturity of India's stock market—it's been around for more than a century—and that the rule of law is entrenched, even if somewhat difficult to navigate. Not so, argues an editorial in the *Far Eastern Economic Review.*

"The problem is that India has embraced capitalism with only one arm."

Both have missed the point. It isn't either/or, either China grows or India grows. It is not a win-lose situation. It's a win-win, and while no two Asian countries are going about the business of economic development in quite the same way, collectively they are creating the world's third great regional economy.

The New Asia: Leveraging for the Future

To the world and to Asians, the great landmass stretching east from Iran to Japan and from China to Indonesia is a collection of economies and cultures of extreme diversity. In the past, no one could fathom the idea of looking at Asia as one. That view is now changed. The market forces at work are now reshaping the economic landscape of the region.

There was no grand scheme coming from lofty government summits. Asian countries are competitive with one another for direct foreign investment, and their primary commodities and services compete on the world market. But conditions at home and external competition, potentially from Latin America and Eastern Europe, are creating the necessary impetus for Asian countries to close ranks. They are discarding their nationalistic preoccupation and reaching out to one another. The prime minister of Malaysia, Dr. Mahathir Mohamad, said at the Pacific Dialogue held in Penang, Malaysia, in November 1994, "It is time for us all to adopt prosper-thy-neighbor policies. . . . I most earnestly believe that we must work together and for the first time in human history for a single global commonwealth founded on the principle of cooperative prosperity. . . . We must seek to establish a new world order securely grounded not only in the idea of common prosperity but also in mutual understanding and mutual regard."

Malaysia's Renong Group has a proposal to build a 6,000-mile highway network that will wind the length of the Indian subcontinent, linking the major cities. It will also lay fiber optics along the highway. If it materializes, reports *Asia Inc.*, "it will be the single biggest infrastructure project of its kind in the world, at an estimated cost of $35 billion to be built over a 20 year period. The fiber optic will integrate

India electronically, an achievement as significant as the railroad network the British built in the 1850's."

A willingness to cooperate and work together in Asia is emerging. A decade ago alliances and cooperation among governments and businesses were unheard of and unthinkable. Much of the integration in Asia today happened in the marketplace. It did not happen by design, but as a direct consequence of demand and supply. The governments helped, by not standing in the way.

"The economies in East Asia are integrating faster than anyone had imagined a few years ago," says Andrew Freris, chief regional economist at Salomon Brothers. Already, he says, one third of East Asia's shipments go to Asia, and that number will increase to almost one half by 2000. Asian countries make up 70 percent of foreign direct investment in Asia.

"In Asia Pacific, one has much more of an impression of business networks, complex and sophisticated, and infinitely flexible in reacting to the needs of their markets," says John Jennings, group managing director of the Royal Dutch/Shell Group of Companies.

- South Korea's Daewoo is the largest foreign investor in Vietnam, with $2 billion in current and planned business ventures.
- Malaysia's Perusahaan Otomobil Nasional, which produces the Proton, opened its first foreign assembly plant in the Philippines. As described in *Asiaweek*, Proton is a car of "Japanese and Malaysian design, capital and technology and Filipino manpower, marketing and management—a marriage unthinkable two decades ago." Proton will also open a plant in Vietnam.
- Mitsubishi Motors has factories in Malaysia, the Philippines and Indonesia in order to sell in each country. With trade liberalization, one factory could serve all the countries.
- While all of Singapore-based Liang Court Holdings's properties were in the country in 1993, by 1995 more than half of its hotels and property developments were outside Singapore—including in China, Vietnam, Thailand, Malaysia, Indonesia and Australia.
- Thailand's largest construction company expects to spend $3 billion transforming the former American Clark Air Base in the Philip-

pines into an international airport. A rail system will link Clark to metropolitan Manila.

• Nissan expects to come out with an "Asian truck" that will be sold throughout Southeast Asia. Toyota has plans for an "Asian car."

• Japan's NEC and South Korea's Samsung, rivals for many years, are now teaming up to jointly produce chips for the European market. "The Korean-Japanese alliances are designed to take advantage of each other's strength for their mutual benefit," says Han Il-suk, electronics analyst for BZW Securities in Seoul. "The Japanese are strong in chip design, while the Koreans excel in the production processes."

• A provincial Chinese carrier, Yunan Airlines, will buy a 60 percent stake in Laos Aviation for $15 million.

Trade and investment dominate government-to-government agendas in Asia. Visits of heads of state are accompanied by a legion of corporate chieftains eager to seal deals with their local counterparts, and heads of state give their blessing to these joint ventures.

ASEAN

The Association of South East Asian Nations, whose members are Indonesia, Thailand, the Philippines, Malaysia, Singapore, Brunei and Vietnam, encompasses a population of 450 million people. Cambodia has applied for observer status, and Laos and Burma are candidates for future membership. Malaysian investment in Indonesia reached more than $600 million in 1994, over ten times the amount invested in 1993. Thai companies led by telecommunications giant Shinawatra, agri-industrial conglomerate Charoen Pokphand and the government petroleum authority are starting various projects in the Indochina states of Laos, Cambodia and Vietnam.

The Go South Initiative

Two-way China-Malaysia trade was an estimated $2.5 billion in 1994, 40 percent more than in 1993. Around 134 Chinese companies have invested more than $200 million in Malaysia. Taiwan, one of the largest foreign investors in Malaysia, increased its investment in Malaysia by 215 percent to $1.02 billion in the first ten months of 1994. There are more than 30,000 Taiwanese in Malaysia. Taiwanese, Hong Kong and Japanese companies were the leading investors in Vietnam before the rest of the world started to pay attention to this emerging market.

Asia to the Japanese

Japan has dominated Asia economically since the 1970s, but integration is slow, if at all. Asia is becoming more important to Japan than to the rest of the world. Consider:

- In 1985, Japan exported a third more to the United States than to Asia. Now Asia buys 25 percent more than the United States and almost three times as much as Europe.
- Japanese imports from Asia increased 150 percent between 1985 and 1995. In 1996, Japan's trade with Asia topped its trade with the U.S. and the EU combined.
- Japan invested $7.7 billion in Asia during the 1993–94 fiscal year. A study by Japan's Export-Import Bank estimates that during the next few years 75 percent of new Japanese direct investment will be in Asia.
- China is now the primary investment place for Japanese companies. Japanese direct investment in China increased 78 percent in 1995. The country's direct investment in China totaled $349 million in 1990 and is estimated to be ten times that now.
- Close to half of Japan's offshore direct investment now goes to East Asia, up from 12 percent in 1985.
- Thailand expects new Japanese investment to reach $8 billion between 1995 and 1998. Japan already controls 90 percent of Thailand's auto market.
- Matsushita Electric Industrial Company's fifteen Malaysian affiliates make up 4 percent of Malaysia's exports while 5,000 of Aiwa Japan's 8,000 employees live outside Japan in Singapore, Malaysia and Wales.

• "[Japan's] shift to Asia is driven by the higher profits that the region's growth generates," says Kenneth Courtis, an economist at Deutsche Bank Capitals Markets in Tokyo.

People Know No Borders

Cathay Pacific Airways, based in Hong Kong, has recently repositioned itself to be the airline at "the heart of Asia." The airline has more than 650 flights a week in and out of Hong Kong. In four hours or less, Cathay Pacific can fly you from Hong Kong to within reach of one half of humanity.

Each year 1.75 million Taiwanese travel to Hong Kong, most passing through on their way to China. In 1995, Hong Kong residents traveled to China 26.4 million times.

Thailand is now the home to nearly 100,000 people of Indian descent, many of them concentrated in Bangkok's Pahurat, the area known as Bangkok's Indiatown.

Mobility of Talent

Rapid economic growth has created an acute shortage of skilled and unskilled labor in urban Asia. In a region known to the West as the largest labor pool in the world, the varying levels of growth of Asia's "terrace economies" (uneven in levels of progress just like the terraces on which rice is grown) have produced a new phenomenon: cross-border movement of labor. While some countries and regions are exporting labor, the rapidly industrializing centers of growth are welcoming immigrants, though not always with open arms. But they are accepting them into their fold to sustain growth. Asian nations are racing to build and expand existing infrastructures in order to maintain their competitiveness. Roads, airports, ports, power plants and telecommunications infrastructures are being built as rapidly as possible. As a result, an enormous number of workers with a wide range of skills are needed. In the last five years there has been very heavy traffic in cross-border labor throughout Asia. In 1995 more than one million workers went to work outside their home countries.

The cross-border movement is not confined to unskilled labor. It also occurs in the professional and managerial classes:

• In Hong Kong, the number of expatriate workers, ranging from domestic help to senior corporate executives, increased by 45,500 in just the first nine months of 1993.

• In Singapore, government estimates put the number of foreign employees between 150,000 and 200,000, some 20 percent of the country's 1.1 million workforce, the second-highest proportion of foreign to local workers in Asia after the Sultanate of Brunei.

• In Indonesia, some 1,000 Malaysian managers and professionals are serving two- to three-year contracts. About 75 percent of the approximately 600 Filipinos in senior managerial positions in Indonesian banks have been in those positions five years or less. There are about 5,000 Indians in technical and managerial positions in private Indonesian businesses.

• More than 4.3 million Filipinos work in various parts of the world, exporting human resources to earn foreign revenues.

Muscle for the Building Boom

In most of the sizzling economies of East and Southeast Asia, armies of migrant workers are building the skyscrapers, expressways, airports and transit systems. In Malaysia's capital city, Kuala Lumpur, as many as 30,000 Indonesian and Bangladeshi workers labored day and night to put up the tallest building in the world, the Petronas Twin Towers. Elsewhere the statistics are just as stunning. Japan has between 160,000 and 200,000 foreign construction workers, Malaysia 475,000 and Taiwan 270,000.

While the home country faces a tremendous shortage of labor and is forced to take in foreigners, the more adventurous are leaving home to find greener lands with higher wages. The talk in Asia is not of the shortage of labor, but the shortage of cheap labor, and companies are forced to import. For example, during the recession of the mid-1980s, some 200,000 skilled construction workers left

Malaysian shores for Japan, Taiwan and Singapore. Officially Malaysia has about 1 million foreign workers, but other estimates put the number at closer to 3 million. Most are from Bangladesh, Burma, Indonesia, Thailand and the Philippines. In 1995, 400,000 workers left Thailand to work on the building sites in Singapore, Hong Kong, Malaysia and Taiwan.

The Way to the Future: Growth Triangles

The diversity of Asia and the varying levels of its economies are prompting Asian governments and businesses to explore new ways to cooperate, to create opportunities in employment and investment for the less developed, and to maintain competitiveness for the industrially advanced. The way of the future is the creation of growth centers, be they formal or informal. Some areas designated as growth triangles or quadrangles enjoy political commitment from national leaders, while some where border trade flourishes are merely renewing their regional links and exploiting geographical advantages as trade intensifies with the rising prosperity of the region.

For the first time, a new regionalism is emerging. Growth triangles are a convenient solution to cooperation. President Fidel Ramos of the Philippines writes in the *International Herald Tribune:* "The growth triangles concept has taken hold because it is a controlled experiment in regional cooperation whose adverse effects, if any, can be limited to the triangle, but whose beneficial results can subsequently be applied to the national economy as a whole. It offers the benefits of regional integration without great loss of economic sovereignty."

The growth triangles began as export zones with "the synergy that comes from mixing various corporate cultures and resource endowments," Ramos continues. "The exchange is straightforward. Investing countries provide capital, technology and management skills. Receiving countries provide land, other natural resources and labor, both skilled and unskilled," and businesspeople on the ground cement the ties. Some of the informal growth triangles are expected to be more successful because they are not driven by politicians or administered by bureaucrats, but run by the free market.

Growth triangles are win-win propositions. "The greatest benefits necessarily accrue to the most industrially mature partner," Ramos writes. "But even the poorest partner gains in practical terms as a result of job generation, skills development, technology transfer and the infusion of industrial discipline in the local workforce. Radiations from the growth pole catalyze development in other sectors of the larger national economy."

For the industrially advanced, "growth triangles are a way of sustaining the competitiveness of their exports despite rising wages and increasing shortages of land and workers," Ramos adds. "For Indonesia, Thailand and the Philippines, and eventually for Vietnam, they are a means of speeding up development, creating jobs and importing technology. [They are] flexible, low cost, fast track, uncomplicated and well-focused. They can be started quickly with little fuss. Formal trading blocs need gestation periods stretching over many years."

The region's businesspeople are excited at the potential, while carefully assessing its risks. *Asia Inc.* magazine and experts in Asia have identified more than ten such formal and informal growth circles and triangles. While some run into one another and are sometimes known by different names, the growth triangles herald the dawning of the first phase of a movement toward a borderless Asia.

The growth triangles listed by *Asia Inc.* are:

• The "Golden Quadrangle," which includes southwest China, Burma, Thailand and Laos.

• The Japan Sea economic zone, which includes Japan, the two Koreas, northeast China and the Russian Far East.

• The Yellow Sea economic zone, which includes maritime China from Zhenjiang in the south to Liaoning Province in the north, the two Koreas and Japan.

• A Yangtze River–based growth circle, which includes Wuhan and Shanghai in China backed by investment from Taiwan and Hong Kong.

• Taiwan and the neighboring Chinese province of Fujian.

• Hong Kong, Guangdong Province and Macau.

• South China, Vietnam, Cambodia, Laos and northeastern Thailand.

- The Straits growth triangle, which includes Singapore, Malaysia's Johor State and Indonesia's Riau Province.
- The Northern Growth Triangle, which includes northern Malaysia, southern Thailand and northern Sumatra in Indonesia.
- A Sulu Sea–based growth circle, which includes the Malaysian and Indonesian-governed parts of Borneo, the southern Philippines and northern Sulawesi.
- A growth circle linking Indonesia's southern Sulawesi Province with Australia's Northern Territory.

The growth triangle experiment, a unique Asian way of development, is creating regional integration. Commenting on the market-led integration in Asia, John Jennings, group managing director of Shell, said, "Seen from within the European Union, I have to tell you that we greatly admire the success of the Asia Pacific countries and wish we had our own secret formula to replicate it."

While governments are still busy sorting out the legal and regulatory infrastructure, "business is going to flow according to its own rules—like water," said Noordin Sopiee, director general of the Institute of Strategic and International Studies in Kuala Lumpur.

Building Bridges to Tomorrow: Asia's Infrastructure Challenge

"It cost a fortune, was way over budget and took far too long to build," writes the *Asian Wall Street Journal*. "It didn't meet specifications. And it helped bankrupt a dynasty. About the only good thing that can be said about the Great Wall of China as an infrastructure project is that the Chinese paid for it themselves, sparing foreign investors from taking a bath. Nevertheless, the wall serves as a cautionary tale for today's planners of grand public works projects. It was one of the largest construction projects in history, snaking the length of one twentieth of the earth's circumference, according to one estimate, from the Yellow Sea to Central Asia. Yet no one even knows for certain how much it cost or exactly when it was started."

All the world is titillated by stories of plans gone awry. There is some bleak satisfaction in knowing that great plans encounter great obstacles everywhere, not just in one's hometown, country or century. And opportunity for disaster is ripe indeed as Asia attempts to build an infrastructure for both the industrial and information eras. If Asia relies on government action alone, it might end up littered with projects far less successful than the Great Wall. Instead, infrastructure development is moving forward at breakneck speed mostly because the private sector is on the case.

"A billion here, a billion there and pretty soon you're talking real money." That could be Asia's new motto when it comes to infrastructure. In addition to Gordon Wu's billion-dollar, six-lane superhighway from the Hong Kong border to Guangzhou, *BusinessWeek* reports the following infrastructure projects in Asia:

- **China** is putting $6 billion in roads, a port and telecom links for Shanghai's new Pudong district. Three billion dollars is going into the 1,500-mile railway linking Beijing to Kowloon. Then, of course, there is the $20-billion hydroelectric dam at Three Gorges.
- **South Korea** is investing $13.4 billion in a high-speed train link between Seoul and Pusan, and another $50 billion will be spent on thirty new power plants, including seven nuclear plants, by the year 2000. Seoul is getting a new $5-billion airport.
- In **Thailand,** TelecomAsia is building more than 2 million telephone lines costing $3 billion. Another $11 billion is going into 3,800 megawatts of electricity projects in 1995. The first phase of Bangkok's second airport will cost $3.3 billion.
- **Malaysia** plans to spend $9.1 billion on infrastructure, **Indonesia** $11.8 billion and the **Philippines** some $4.5 billion. Some countries manage the infrastructure challenge better than others. Malaysia has pulled ahead of Indonesia, claims *BusinessWeek,* which credits "the quality of the government's decision-making, combined with a competitive private sector." Taiwan trails Singapore, Hong Kong and South Korea. Taiwan, *BusinessWeek* says, "has made such a mess of its infrastructure" that it attracts much less foreign investment.

Well managed or not, these sums are utterly mind boggling. The Asian Development Bank figures that Asia will spend $1 trillion by the year 2000 mainly on energy, telecommunications and transportation. John Reed, chairman of Citicorp, insists that China alone needs to spend $55 trillion to build an infrastructure to support a developed economy—three times the world's current annual gross domestic product and more than fifty times the Asian Development Bank's estimate.

Of course, no one knows really what the final cost will be or exactly where the funds will come from. Historically, Asia's high individual savings rates meant large cash reserves would be available from that source. But some say the 30 percent savings rate is artificial, that real domestic cash reserves are considerably lower. In any event, we are talking $55 trillion here. That's a lot of passbook accounts. Enter Gordon Wu and his pioneering BOT scheme, an exciting but stunningly simple financial model for public/private enterprise and a win-win-win situation for the entrepreneur, the government and the public.

BOT—*The Wu Factor*

Gordon Wu pioneered the BOTs (build-operate-transfer) project concept through his Hong Kong–based Hopewell Holdings Ltd. Basically, it works like this. A private firm agrees to build a highway or power plant. The company then collects tolls (in the case of a highway) or operates the plant for a fixed period of time at a previously agreed upon price. When the private firm earns back its investment, plus a profit, the project is turned over to the government at no cost. The country gets a public utility at little or no cost. The private firm makes a good return on its investment—a very good return if the project is completed early. And the people get a public utility managed like a private enterprise. Voilà! Famous examples are Hopewell Holdings's two 350-megawatt coal-fired power plants for the Shenzhen Special Economic Zone in China's Guangdong Province. And its billion-dollar highway from Hong Kong to Guangzhou.

Gordon Wu got into the BOT business in a strange and interesting way. In the 1980s, Hopewell Holdings built a 1,200-room hotel, but the project was going nowhere without enough power. So the company offered to develop the Shajiao B Plant on a BOT basis. It designed, constructed, financed and will operate the power station for ten years. Then it belongs to the province.

Wu's BOT superhighway connects Hong Kong with Shenzhen, Guangzhou and Zhuhai. Conceived of when the region was basically a rice paddy, the project is now in the heart of China's fastest-growing area. And the highway project has led to similar deals to build power plants. Wu has a number of power projects under way, including a $40-million plant in Navotas, outside Manila. Wu's firm is also involved in Indonesia, India, Taiwan and Vietnam. Yet infrastructure projects represent less than 10 percent of company earnings. Some projects are under discussion in power-hungry Pakistan and India. Wu wants to standardize power plant design through buying materials in bulk to cut costs, an age-old strategy. His economies of scale can offer electricity to power-hungry countries for less than state-owned companies.

BOTs are not risk-free or for short-term investors. There are profits to be had, but pitfalls abound, too. The biggest problem is the same force that makes BOT schemes possible and profitable—political pressure.

In February 1994, twenty-three international banks that had loaned the Thai government $250 million for a highway in Bangkok declared they wanted out and demanded full repayment. The problem was that people resisted the toll hike that was supposed to make the project profitable.

Undaunted, the Thai government is seeking private contractors for a BOT project to build an elevated railway in Bangkok. There are plenty of takers. The appeal for many is a steady flow of earnings. Lance Gokongwei, a senior vice president at JG Summit Holdings Inc., says the Philippine conglomerate's investments in power-generation projects are "almost like an annuity." Of course, quips the *Asian Wall Street Journal*, that is, "if governments never change, consumers never demand rate reductions, monopolies are never broken up, fuel prices never fluctuate and demand forecasts always come true."

Pakistan's $1.6-billion Hub power project, considered "a landmark in private sector financing in the third world," will add 13 percent to the country's generating capacity by 1997. Britain's National Power invested $100 million for a 25 percent equity stake. The project was negotiated through eight changes of government. Legal documentation, says the *Financial Times,* weighed more than sixty pounds a set. Pitfalls aside, BOTs remain an attractive means to develop infrastructure projects on time and within budget, and regional and international players can reap handsome profits.

The Dam Project

Anyone who doubts the efficacy of Wu's BOT model should look at Bangkok, where more than sixteen agencies have tried to unsnarl traffic. Or at China's long winding path to the Three Gorges Dam project.

First suggested by Sun Yat-sen in the 1920s, the Chinese have long wanted to dam the Yangtze River in order to manage and control flooding, and at the same time generate power. In the 1940s, U.S. engineers from the Bureau of Reclamation worked with the Chinese to design a dam. In the 1950s the Russians took over. The very idea of altering the path of the river the Chinese call "the Great" evokes strong emotions, and has even sparked almost unheard-of public dissension among Communist Party members. Environmentalists oppose it, and no one knows how the government will relocate the 1.2 million people who live in twenty cities and counties that will be flooded by the giant reservoir. No other dam in history has faced such a huge relocation problem.

But Premier Li Peng is determined to pull it off. Some 18,000 workers toil twenty-four hours a day, clearing the path for the diversion channel, dynamiting canyon-size grooves in hillsides and building the massive locks that will carry ships over the mountains toward Central China. But it may be economics not politics or the environment that determines the fate of the dam project. The World Bank is not coming forward with the cash, and so far neither are foreign investors. The government increased electric rates—as much as 25 percent for some residents—to generate revenues. That only renewed opposition. Still the workers keep digging.

Multinationals on the Scene

Many multinational megafirms are betting their bottom lines on Asia's infrastructure. General Electric and Westinghouse are competing for power projects with other giants like Siemens, ABB Asea Brown Boveri, Hitachi, Mitsubishi Heavy and Toshiba. Still others are vying for the opportunity to manage plants that are up and running. For example, Mission Energy of California will run a $2.5-billion coal-fired plant in Java. CMS Energy, a subsidiary of Michigan's Consumers Power, operates power plants in the Philippines. AT&T, Motorola, GTE, IBM and the Baby Bells are scrambling for market share in telecommunications. So are Alcatel Alsthom of France, Canada's Northern Telecom, Germany's Siemens and Japan's NEC and Toshiba.

But it is not just the global companies that are gaining a foothold in Asia; many small ones are getting in on the action. And some prove quite successful because they are so much more flexible. Plus, many small firms secure a local partner who knows the terrain and understands the subtleties of Asian business cultures. Notes Robert Fernstrom, a vice president at Salomon Brothers in Hong Kong, "The projects that are really moving ahead are the ones with good local sponsorship."

Among the established and emerging regional players staking their future on the infrastructure boom are:

- South Korea's **Anam Group**, a $1-billion electronics concern, is designing truncated radio systems, already successfully used by Motorola in Japan, for transportation companies in Southeast Asia and China.
- **China Power & Light** of Hong Kong will plan and design power projects in China, and will manage those in which it holds an equity stake.
- Malaysia's **IJM Corporation** is known for completing projects on time and within budget. Major contracts include a $22-million industrial estate in Kedah State and two power-plant expansions for state-owned Tenaga Nasional Bhd. IJM is also vying for a piece of the $30-million water-supply project for Ho Chi Minh City.

- **IPCO International, Ltd.** not only came up with the idea, but also funded the project to develop Singapore's water supply in Labuan, Malaysia, at a cost of $47 million, and now owns and manages it. IPCO seeks projects in Indonesia, Malaysia, Thailand and China for the near future and Indochina and Burma over the longer run.

- **Triveni Engineering Works Ltd.**, one of India's largest steam turbine and sugar mill machinery manufacturers, earns 40 percent of its revenues from infrastructure development. Triveni recently completed the first part of a sewage treatment plant for New Delhi and is presently working on an effluent-treatment facility for a steel plant in the state of Andhra Pradesh.

So there are deals to be made and many contenders. That the need is great is not in question. And many are willing to risk much for a great return. What many analysts and observers do question is whether Asia can *afford* to build all the infrastructure it needs. A more pointed question may be: Can it afford not to? Enter the global investment community.

Funding the Future

Asia's stock, bond and futures markets are undergoing phenomenal growth. In 1987, Asia's stock markets (excluding Japan) were capitalized at $195 billion. Today they are more than $1 trillion. Institutional investors, companies and individuals are plunging headlong into the world's fastest-growing financial markets. The next ten years will revolutionize Asia's capital markets, says *Asian Business*. Portfolio managers and investment bankers in the West, it argues, will see Asia "as an integral part of the global market place for capital." The goal, of course, is to create the financial institutions and instruments to handle the investments Asia needs for its infrastructure.

In country after country Asia is modernizing stock markets, creating futures markets and pushing banks into global competition. In the last several years, China, Thailand, India and Malaysia have set up securities and exchange commissions to bring a semblance of order to their burgeoning stock markets.

Morgan Stanley, in 1994, became the first U.S. investment house to set up a joint-venture investment bank in China. The American insurance giant American International Group (AIG) started a $1.2-billion fund that will buy direct equity shares in infrastructure projects. The projects will then be listed on local stock markets.

Asia's Stock Markets Come of Age

Indonesia's stock market is fairly typical of the region. Established in 1977, the Jakarta Stock Exchange listed only twenty-four companies one decade later. Despite the country's steady economic growth, capitalization was just $68 million. So the government took action. It simplified listing requirements, removed restrictions on daily price fluctuations, taxed bank interest payments and permitted foreigners to buy up to 49 percent of listed companies and to set up joint-venture securities firms. By 1994, capitalization hit $45 billion.

From 1987 to 1994 a balanced portfolio of shares listed on the nine largest Asian stock markets outside Japan returned about 22 percent a year, calculated *The Economist*, compared with 15 percent from U.S. shares. But as might be expected, the path to relative stability is not a smooth one for Asia's stock markets. In China, a 40 percent plummet in a two-day period in October 1994 prompted a flurry of companies to list on the Hong Kong or New York exchanges rather than in their home market.

India has a long history in stock markets—its first was in the nineteenth century. The market currently lists more than 7,000 companies, but suffers a lack of "screen-based trading." Every transaction requires thirty-five different manual checks—enough to send many traders elsewhere.

Going Public

Because of pressure from all sides, including the need for funds to expand regionally, acquire new technology and open new markets, business families intending to cash out and governmental efforts to redistribute wealth, Asian companies are gearing up to go public. Some of the most tightly held private companies in Asia are expected to list within the next few years. For example, Philippine companies are looking to the stock exchange for sources of funding and market capitalization grew from $5.9 billion in 1990 to $55 billion in November 1994.

Elsewhere in the region, merchant bankers are enjoying a boom in their business of helping clients list their stocks on exchanges. The market is responding; besides the institutional investors, the increasingly affluent middle class is looking to the stock market to have a stake in the economy. The spectacular oversubscription rates, such as that achieved by Denway Investment Limited, may not be repeated, but public offers are still being oversubscribed. Denway Investment Limited from China, when listed on the Hong Kong Stock Exchange in 1993, recorded 647 times oversubscription and attracted $31 billion to its offer of $52 million in a, to say the least, bullish market when China fever was over the top.

Intensifying Regional Competition

Asian governments are intent on developing and promoting stock markets at home. Discontented that Hong Kong and Singapore dominate the financial and capital markets for the region, governments in Taiwan, Malaysia and Thailand are working on reforms and liberalization of their own exchanges. For example, Malaysia recently announced a package of wide-ranging reforms in order to promote Kuala Lumpur as a regional fund management center. Officials believe that the quality of life in Kuala Lumpur and the affordable cost should make the city more attractive relative to the rising costs of operation in Singapore and Hong Kong. Besides, Kuala Lumpur's market capitalization of $218 billion is more than double that of Singapore's, which makes Malaysia's bourse the largest in Southeast Asia and the fifth largest in Asia.

Stock markets are only one vehicle of entry into global financial markets. Private capital, bond issues, securities, pension funds and insurance pools are also part of the mix.

Money Finds Its Greatest Return

Money is information and confidence in motion. Right now, and for the foreseeable future, the world is betting on Asia. Five years ago only a tiny proportion of America's $5-billion net equity flow went into Asia. By 1993, U.S. equity investments in Asia hit $12.9 billion, one third of the $40 billion total. Similar volumes of capital are flowing in from Japan, the United Kingdom and Europe.

But Asia's capital pool is swelling, too. Taiwan's foreign exchange reserves are nearly $100 billion; Singapore's exceed $70 billion. "Economic growth has spawned mutual funds, pension funds and insurance funds that need solid but stable management," says *Asiamoney*. Hong Kong has $87 billion currently being managed, and Singapore will open up $28 billion for foreign fund managers in its effort to attract more fund management companies to relocate in Singapore. "The fund management business in Asia is expected to double in the next five years," reports *Asiamoney*.

Asia also has extraordinary reserves of private wealth. According to the head of one international bank, the biggest foreign exchange positions—$250 million—are held by individuals, not by corporations. These individuals are increasingly taking positions in mainstream capital market deals.

Mobilizing Savings

A sign of Asia's coming of age is when the corporate bond markets that cater to Asian companies issue long-term debt in local currencies to meet their local currency obligations. The recently initiated dragon bond market is a first step. Dragon bonds have been described as "ordinary debt issues, denominated in a major international currency, aimed at raising capital from the growing pool of Asian wealth in the so-called dragon economies of South Korea, Hong Kong, Singapore and Taiwan."

Thus far, these issues have been restricted to solid corporations, governments and a few outside the region. But they demonstrate the level of sophistication toward which Asian financial markets are heading. Over $4 billion worth of dragon bonds have been sold; however, most of the issuers have been West European institutions, and most of the buyers Europeans as well.

Although dragon bonds are listed in Asia, they go through Europe's Euroclear and Cedel systems. But in time Asian corporations and institutions will be as comfortable issuing bonds in domestic currencies as they are in the international bond markets. The potential of Asia's bond market prompted Moody, the U.S.-based credit-rating agency, to open a Hong Kong office. Financial analysts around the globe acknowledge that the combination of pressing long-term financial need and increasing deregulation in the financial industry will ensure a future for corporate bonds.

In the coming years Asia will see a flurry of bank mergers, buyouts and takeovers similar to the anxiety-provoking U.S. bank brawls of the late 1970s and the 1980s. Banks owned by family conglomerates that operate on *guanxi* (personal connections) will continue to play a vital role, but so will foreign banks. Joint ventures between foreign and Asian banks will become commonplace. These efforts will be government sanctioned as the last barrier between maintaining a semblance of control over domestic capital markets and the uncontrolled international markets that move hundreds of millions of dollars through cyberspace in a matter of seconds.

This trend is clearly evidenced in Vietnam, whose "rush to catch up with the rest of the region's economies has made the development of an efficient banking sector a priority," according to the *Far Eastern Economic Review.* "Reflecting this, Vietnam's banking sector has grown exponentially. Not only have over a dozen foreign banks been granted licenses to date, but domestic banks are now allowed to acquire the capital and skills they so badly need through foreign partnerships."

In its capital markets, the market solution is the way forward in funding Asia's future.

What About the Future of Our Children?

Asia must build an infrastructure to support its aspirations and empower itself to compete in the global information age, achieving in a matter of years what took the United States and Europe decades to accomplish. Everywhere the pace of change is frantic and the impact on both people and the environment is not always positive. The distribution of wealth is often inequitable and the pace of development uneven within individual countries and the region at large. The first tentative efforts to redistribute wealth are under way, but lopsided growth will probably continue to trouble the region. Furthermore, corruption is alive and well. In many places political connections will guarantee profits in the emerging private sector.

Asian capitalism is not American capitalism—that is, trusting market forces over state intervention (except, of course, for baseball strikes). Look at Japan's MITI (Ministry of International Trade and Industry), which, to the chagrin of some free marketers, is one big reason behind Asia's success—and a great example of Asia following its own path. Borrowing liberally from various economic models, Asian leaders are fusing ideology and economic reality.

No one can turn back the clock, but many wish to slow the rate of development long enough to examine its impact on people and on the environment. In three years China's economy expanded 40 percent. Steel production has helped China maintain that incredible growth rate. However, sulfur dioxide emissions from the coal-fired furnaces have made Beijing one of the world's most polluted cities.

Pollution is also evident in Hong Kong, Bangkok, Manila and India's largest cities. In Indonesia, logging for paper and pulp has stripped the nation of its trees, with no organized plan in place for reforestation. Major infrastructure projects like China's Three Gorges Dam will uproot 1.2 million people, many of whom will drift to urban areas where there is little work for the unskilled and nowhere to live.

Drug use and commercial sex are on the rise throughout Asia, with a resulting increase in the incidence of AIDS. HIV is still rare in Japan, where condoms are widely available and used, and intravenous drug use is almost unheard of. But these problems are expected to become epidemic in India, Thailand, Indonesia, Burma, Cambodia, Vietnam and Malaysia. In Chiang Rai, in northern Thailand, one in five young males is HIV-positive. In India's northeastern Manipur State, 55 percent of IV drug users have the virus.

Some fear economic development will take precedence over cultural preservation. Cultural sites such as temples and ancient cities hold enormous economic potential. Consequently, capital-hungry countries are turning them into tourist attractions, compromising the integrity of the fragile sites.

In many countries corruption is a way of life. "Over the years, corruption has been allowed to continue, until now it has become a monster," said Param Curaraswamy, a human rights activist in Kuala Lumpur. "Corruption in China has now reached epidemic proportions and few escape the squeeze." In the countryside, local officials divert grain payments to real estate schemes. City folk must pay kickbacks for everything from telephone lines to treatment at public hospitals. As the economy booms, people can, and do, pay—which only encourages the corrupt officials. As one Western diplomat in Beijing put it: "Where there's meat, you're bound to have flies."

The story is the same in India, where of all the barriers to entry the greatest is "debilitating corruption." The amounts of money that changed hands prior to the selection of a cellular phone company in four cities were legendary. In the end, the Department of Telecommunications chose a different vendor for each city. Motorola, with the best service record in the world, wasn't selected. But four unknown companies, with no history but lots of political clout, were.

Keeping the Best in Government

In Singapore, with a population of fewer than 3 million, the prime minister earns $797,000 a year and top cabinet ministers make $535,000, while the country's per capita income rings in at just over $16,000 a year. In the United States, with a population of more than 260 million, the president earns $200,000 and cabinet members make $148,000. Singapore pays government officials on a scale based on private industry. And Prime Minister Goh Chok Tong says that the high salaries are justified "against the cost to you of having an incompetent and corrupt government." In 1993 all Singaporean civil servants were given year-end bonuses equal to three-and-a-half months' salary.

Does paying well keep the best in government and eliminate the evils of corruption? Singapore hopes so. But increasingly, talent is flowing to the private sector, where the rewards can be even greater.

The Power of the Market

Despite its imperfections the world has come to accept the free-market system as the way to organize economic life. How the free market evolves in each Asian country will depend on the ingenuity of its government and the vigor of its business leadership. The excitement so far is in the free market. Consider the Philippines. When the telephone service was run by a state monopoly, 98 percent of Filipinos were waiting for a telephone, while 2 percent were waiting for a dial tone. Today, private companies are competing for the loyalties of telephone users as they create a state-of-the-art telecommunications system.

A Free-Market Asia Holds the Key for the West

The Asia boom will provide the West, especially the United States, one quarter or more of its total economic growth for the years just ahead, according to an analysis by *The Economist*. Asia and the United States are the two places in the world that allow entrepreneurs free range to revitalize and build up their economies, and they are the two places that will truly prosper as we move toward the next century.

Nevertheless, many issues and problems persist—at least in the Western mindset—as barriers against the full potential of this economic bonanza. For example, many in the West blame Asia for the accelerated loss of jobs at home. The response, they argue, should be more protectionist policies. But the main factor behind disappearing low-skilled jobs in Western societies is the mobility of capital and technology, not Asia's new market competitiveness.

In reality, Asia's infrastructure boom and the need for capital goods herald great opportunities for Western companies and their workers. Furthermore, low-skilled workers are at peril *anywhere* in the world. Asia's matured economies lose labor-intensive, low-tech manufacturing to cheaper Asian locations. Hong Kong and Singapore are already putting programs in place to prepare themselves for the dominance of service and information in their economies.

Some Western companies have backed away from doing business in Asia because they think there is a lack of concern about the environment. My dialogue group in Singapore, one of Asia's richest countries —with a per capita GNP of more than $20,000—was dominated by discussions of environmental deterioration. Strong voices on the subject are also raised elsewhere in Asia. If anything, I hear more people in Asia talking about environmental concerns than I do in the West.

As Asia grows richer, the environment will become a great preoccupation and Asians will be more uncompromising about the trade-offs between the environment and economic development. Polls show that in South Korea, Taiwan, Malaysia and the Philippines a significant number of people are prepared to have their earnings reduced in exchange for a less polluted environment. Many middle-aged, well-off urban people in Taiwan are moving out of the cities to build settlements in the quiet countryside. With the convenience and access provided by Asia's increasingly sophisticated telecommunications facilities, a small reverse flow from cities to the countryside has begun. The opportunity for the West lies in helping with its technological know-how and experience to make existing Asian industries more environmentally friendly.

Western companies need an Asian strategy that will demonstrate an understanding of, respect for and commitment to the region. Asian talents are increasingly motivated to work with Western companies that see their own future aligned with Asia's. To begin with, a Western company should decide on a strategic city to anchor its operations. It does not need to be a capital city. Many Western companies, for example, operate out of Penang, Malaysia, rather than the capital city of Kuala Lumpur. In China, the capital city of Beijing is the place *not* to be. Most of the action is in Guangzhou, Shenzhen, Fuzhou and Shanghai. It depends on the industry and nature of the business. Also, discard the national border mindset. Select a location that allows maximum and easy access to the most efficient combination of land, talent, ideas, technology and markets, a judgment best made with the help of an Asian partner.

There is an acute shortage of management talent in Asia, and the situation will become more critical as the boom accelerates. But although professional managers are important, entrepreneurial talent will pay greater long-term dividends. Remember that Asia is a long-term project and talent will be needed for many years to start, build and sustain a business. With increasing demand for business talent, loyalty is waning, and job hopping is fast becoming a favorite pastime in some Asian capitals. Those companies that innovate and are more creative will keep the best talent. Commit resources to train and develop a talent pool.

The key is to be flexible and cultivate relationships to learn to operate in Asian cultures. As economies modernize, greater political openness will follow. But Westerners should not insist on Western legal arrangements. Quality partnerships and trust (with which the Chinese Overseas have operated for centuries) will prove far more successful. A Western legal system does not necessarily help. The Indian High Court has more than a million backlogged cases, which at the present rate of disposition will take more than three hundred years to clear.

Because Asian multinational companies are eager to bring in management experts to develop management controls and more efficient structures, opportunities for Western citizens with technical skills will grow dramatically—good news for those affected by all the downsizing in the West. Much in demand will be system and process engineers, architects and designers, financial analysts, telecommunications specialists, international fund managers and environmental specialists. But for their part, Asian companies would be wise to avoid overcontrol and excessive professionalization so they do not lose the communitarian touch, the soul of their enterprises.

The twentieth century began with a utopian view that communism could bring the best quality of life to everyone. It is ending with the realistic understanding that a market-driven society brings the greatest prosperity to the greatest number. By shifting to market-driven economies, Asia between 1970 and 1990 reduced the number of desperately poor Asians from 400 million to 180 million, even while the populations of these countries grew by two thirds. Never before in the history of humanity have so many people been raised from poverty in such a short time. A record 123 Asians made *Forbes* magazine's 1996 listing of the world's wealthiest people. Of the 123, 82 were non-Japanese, up from 27 in 1991.

Free-market mechanisms and the technological revolution have expanded the coverage of the market economies of the world from 1 billion to more than 4 billion people. Three quarters of them are in Asia. The free market, a Western idea and what it can do, is a triumph for everybody.

CHAPTER FIVE

From Farms to Supercities

"*A*T *six minutes past midnight on December 5, 2006, the human being will become primarily an urban animal.*"

In ordinary times, people move from country to city, city to country, and back again. Sometimes the shift is noteworthy, sometimes it is just a little hatch mark on a census taker's tally. Old towns die and new ones are born as industry or agriculture move from place to place. But in Asia these are not ordinary times. The usual rules don't apply.

People are migrating from farms to cities in such extraordinary numbers in Asia that planners and policymakers must devise dramatic ways to cope. That is not easy. Jakarta came up with a plan; it declared itself a closed city (unsuccessfully, I might add). Beijing's city officials decided to charge new residents as much as $11,600 to move into the capital.

UN predictions paint a stunning picture of urban life in Asia in 2010. Thirty cities will have populations greater than 5 million (compared with only two U.S. cities and six European cities). Shanghai and Bombay will each have 20 million people. Beijing, Dhaka, Jakarta, Manila, Tianjin, Calcutta and Delhi will have more than 15 million. If current patterns persist—and there is little reason to doubt they will not—the ultimate shift from rural to urban will change the character and context of Asian society.

Seven of the thirteen cities whose populations exceed 10 million are in Asia. Some Asian cities double in population every ten to fifteen years. By the year 2010, half of China's population will live in urban areas—up from 28 percent in 1994. The urban migration of rural poor is so great that ethnic ghettos—Chinatowns in China—are springing up. Between 1984 and 1994 more than 400,000 moved from Zhejiang Province to Beijing, so many that there is now an area of Beijing known as Zhejiang village, which has its own clinics and nurseries. Only the Zhejiang dialect is spoken. Zhejiang migrants are known for their clothing production.

Country to country the statistics are mind-boggling:

- Tokyo, with 30 million people, is larger than 162 countries.
- Vietnam's population has grown more than 60 percent since 1975. Ho Chi Minh City's population surged from 2.5 to 5.6 million.
- Since 1960, Bangkok's population has tripled in size to 7.1 million.
- Bombay's population has increased 400 percent since the 1950s, and almost three hundred rural Indian families move to Bombay each day in search of work or a better quality of life.
- Asia's urban population will increase by 600 million during the next 25 years.

The social and environmental costs are incalculable. Already traffic, garbage and smog choke many Asian cities. Unemployment and underemployment are epidemic, and there are chronic shortages of all kinds, including housing, water, power and transportation. Yet for many, a modern, global community is an urban community. Despite the mind-numbing problems, urban life offers opportunity and hope, both in short supply in tiny rural villages.

"We have only two things in the countryside," says a rice miller in the farming community of Yongchon, South Korea. "A growing number of graves, and a growing number of aging people waiting to get there." For that simple reason—and because urban migration furthers the economic goals of some governments—it will continue.

The Hong Kong Model

Two places to find solutions to the problems of urban migration are Hong Kong and Singapore, both of which successfully evolved out of poverty and decay to become models of urban planning and control.

In the 1950s, Hong Kong was a huge shantytown populated by Chinese seeking refuge from the communists. In 1953 fire consumed the homes of 50,000 people and urban planners had to figure out how to house these people as well as the hundreds of thousands of Chinese who kept pouring into the city.

How did they do it? "We had to rehouse these people, and we realized we'd also have to keep building to house the other refugees as they poured in, or we'll always be just a huge squatter's camp," explains Ted Pryor, Hong Kong's main urban planner. "The lesson we learned is that you begin rehousing as soon as you can, but you do it very conservatively and with modern standards."

Forty years later urban planners flock to Hong Kong to study how the colony works. Hong Kong residents have housing—more than half the population lives in modern public housing developments—and business has ample office space (albeit pricey). And while the city has one of the highest population densities in the world, 50 percent of its land is reserved for parks, nature preserves and farms.

Hong Kong apparently learned its lesson well. In 1994, *Fortune* magazine named it the world's "best city for business."

The Singapore Model

Arguably, Singapore is the world's most modern city, if measured by its telecommunications infrastructure, and definitely one of the most conservative, if measured by its paternalistic social policies. But they work for Singapore and urban planners flock to the tiny nation-state to see what makes it tick.

So keen is the world's interest in Singapore that its Foreign Ministry created eighty positions to deal with inquiries and tours. In 1990, forty-eight foreign dignitaries came to study the Singapore model; by 1993, there were 231. What they found was a city built on a "malarial swamp" that had evolved into a model of efficiency with electronically controlled roads, fast-moving traffic and few signs of pollution.

While Bangkok builds more roads to cope with its traffic congestion, Singapore levies a hefty tax to make cars less attractive to residents. And while many Asian cities struggle to apply, however loosely, basic democratic principles, Singapore's government officials rule with an iron fist. It wouldn't fly in most Western cities, and it is growing increasingly difficult to rule by municipal fiat in most Asian cities, but in Singapore the population seems willing to give up some basic civil rights in exchange for a clean, virtually crime-free urban community.

Here are the policies that Singapore officials see as the key elements of the "Singapore Model," as summarized by *Asiaweek* (July 13, 1994):

1. **Strong Government**
   Decisive leadership is seen as providing all-important stability. The People's Action Party has dominated politics for nearly 40 years, aided by a weak opposition and supportive local media.

2. **Long-Term Planning**
   Government guidance keeps the economy on track. Socialist in style, it supports the free market. Pragmatism rules.

3. **Foreign Investment**
   Instead of protecting its markets, Singapore puts out the welcome mat for overseas investors and multinationals.

4. **Clean Administration**
   Politicians and civil servants have a reputation for honesty; corruption is dealt with harshly. The government works to recruit the best and the brightest.

5. **Education for All**
   Singapore's emphasis on educating everyone, including women, raised the level of skills and gave the country the ability to handle high technology.

6. **No Welfarism**
   Rejecting Western-style welfare policies, Singapore stresses working through the family and the individual, such as with the Central Provident Fund. It has also encouraged home ownership.

7. **Family Values**

The family is the basic unit of society, the ultimate safety net. Fostering respect for authority has enabled the government to implement policies with little open dissent.

8. **Law & Order**

To keep the crime rate low, leaders swear by harsh punishments such as caning and hanging. Internal security laws allow authorities to clear the streets of gangs and secret societies.

9. **Communal Harmony**

Sensitivity to other cultures is stressed in a multiracial society. Everyone must know two of the four national languages.

10. **Nationhood**

Singapore promotes national identity over ethnic allegiances. Regular campaigns promote national "goals," from being more courteous to stopping smoking.

"We're somewhat embarrassed by the quite sudden interest in the Singapore experience in the last few years, not just by nations in the region, but also by big countries like China and India, and by distant ones like South Africa, Kazakhstan and the new Palestinian state," comments Brigadier General George Yeo Yong Boon, a key cabinet minister in Singapore. "Singapore has become a ready-made model for them to study, not only for our successes, but also our mistakes."

Building a Mini-Singapore in China

Deng Xiaoping was so impressed by the city that he encouraged China to tap into the Singapore experience. From this evolved the township of Suzhou, a sort of "mini-Singapore" under construction in a coastal area fifty miles west of Shanghai. The planned community will encompass twenty-eight square miles of residential, commercial, light industrial and recreational areas, and it is expected to be finished in 2009, when Singapore-Suzhou Township will be home to 600,000 residents and employ 360,000 people.

This extraordinary project is one ninth the size of Singapore, and is located in China's fourth-fastest-growing major coastal city. The township is being developed as a multicompany, multinational joint venture. Some 19 Singaporean- and Indonesian-based companies together own 65 percent of the project; 11 Chinese companies own the remaining 35 percent; $20 billion is being invested.

Modeled after Jurong Town, a self-contained suburb of Singapore, Suzhou is considered a showcase of what Singaporean leaders call a "transfer of software," or management and organizational skills, to China. Suzhou Mayor Zhang Xinsheng, a Harvard-educated former minister of tourism in China, is convinced that with Singapore's help the township will be able to merge Western civilization with Oriental style.

If successful, and there is no reason to believe that they won't be, Singapore officials plan to proffer the model elsewhere. "In five years, we'll see the beginning of Jurong Town Corporation taking shape in Suzhou, and in ten years we should be able to repeat the project anywhere else in China or Vietnam," explains Senior Minister Lee Kuan Yew. A similar development zone near the city of Wuxi, China will have an estimated $6 billion in foreign investment by the end of 1996.

If You Build Them, Will They Come?

China is breaking ground—by creating new cities out of whole cloth. Currently, an estimated 87 percent of the Chinese population live in rural areas. The government would like to reduce that to 50 percent. But the country's already overburdened urban centers cannot accommodate significant population increases. Hence, the "new city" concept. China created fifty new cities in 1994, increasing the number of its urban centers to 620.

The Chinese government intends to move 440 million people—the equivalent of the combined populations of America and Russia—into new cities. To do so, China will increase the number of its townships, with three thousand targeted for renewal by the year 2000. More than five hundred townships have been chosen for a pilot urbanization project. In the Beijing-Tianjin-Tanggu area, towns will be built to serve the larger cities. In Heilongjiang, Jilin and Liaoning provinces, new towns will be built to serve as trading centers. And Nanyang in Henan and Xiangfan in Hubei will be transformed from grain producers to industrialized communities.

If planners are successful, by 2000, 45 percent of the population of Guangdong Province will live in urban areas—up from 39 percent today. Since 1978 the number of Guangdong cities with populations exceeding 500,000 increased from one to eight. The province's small towns grew from 132 to 1,321.

In China, urbanization and modernization go hand in hand. Both are sweeping the nation. In just three years the rural farming area of Pudong, across the river from Shanghai, was transformed into "a modern development zone," with conveniences like flush toilets and gas stoves. Residents of Pudong, which was created to ease Shanghai's congestion, can now commute to the urban center via a long suspension bridge, one of the most dramatic I have ever seen.

Haikou, the capital of Hainan Island in China's largest economic zone, is in the midst of a $9-billion facelift that will replace farms and fishing villages with an international center of light and heavy industry, trade and tourism. It will be home to 1.5 million people.

Indonesia's Kampung Improvement Program (KIP), begun in Jakarta and Surabaya in 1969, is a critical component of Indonesia's city housing system. More than five hundred *kampungs* (urban centers) have been rehabilitated. Integral to KIP's success is involvement with community residents by, during and after the process.

While policymakers focus on immediate urban needs, others look to the future. In Japan, Taisei Corporation's Alice City project would "move everything that need not be on the surface, underground." The hub of its 250-acre dream city, Alice Terminal, is envisioned as a four-hundred-foot-wide complex going six hundred feet down into the ground and covered with a clear dome. The surface of this subterranean complex would be landscaped with parks and gardens, and served by underground transportation that would link it with similar complexes.

Although the Alice project is a long way from completion, Tokyu Construction's Geotrapolis, another underground project, is already under way and should be finished by 2020. It will consist of three large commercial areas below Tokyo connected by an underground transportation system.

China's Floating Population

Urban migration is perhaps the most dramatic in China, where more than 100 million people—equal to 40 percent of the U.S. population—have left rural communities in search of a better quality of life. Lured by the potential for wages that are three times higher than in rural communities, migrants flood into Beijing's main railway station at the rate of one thousand people an hour. Officials estimate that 70 percent of the people riding Beijing's subways on any given morning are "rural job seekers."

The experience is the same in virtually every city in China.

- Approximately 11 million migrants work in Guangdong—one million of whom sleep on city streets.
- More than 10 million migrants have flocked to the "golden triangle" of Shanghai, Nanjing and Hangzhou. Shanghai alone is home to 3.5 million.
- Six million people have migrated out of Sichuan; another 4 million are "on the move" within the province.
- Between 1990 and 1995 more than 300,000 people left Duyun, a rural community in the mountains of Guizhou Province—ten times the number of people who worked in the province's industrial sector.
- In 1991, 200,000 farmers left Jiangxi Province in search of higher wages. In 1993 that number jumped to 3 million.

Though the numbers are staggering and the strain on urban infrastructure enormous, China's government views the relentless urban migration not as a problem but an opportunity. Called *mang liu* (blind flow), refugees from rural poverty are considered "the engine of China, an inexhaustible supply of cheap labor, a floating population helping to rebuild the country," reports the *New York Times*.

The *People's Daily* calls migration the "inevitable choice" for peasants "looking for higher objectives." It is considered a *stabilizing* force, supplying needed labor in the cities while minimizing the economic strain on the countryside. "Migration has negative effects on transportation, infrastructure, birth control and social order," concedes the *People's Daily*, "but these problems can be solved, so we should not consider it something bad and stop it."

Fan Gang, an economist at the Chinese Academy of Social Sciences, thinks the tide of migrants is quite a positive development so far. "It has helped transfer wealth from rich to poor areas of the country," Professor Fan argues. "If you don't have the problem in the city, you'll have it in the country."

A *New York Times* article says migrants are "one reason that 5,000 factories can be simultaneously under construction in China's coastal province," and Richard Blum, a political science professor at the University of California at Los Angeles, comments that migrants "cushion the transformation of the Chinese economy." They are a giant "shock absorber" flowing from one area of the economy to another.

Rather than discourage this massive rural outflow, China wants to control, organize and apparently encourage it. In the next few years it will set up 15,000 rural employment agencies and their urban counterparts. "Our goal is to coordinate employment between cities and the countryside," explains Cai Haishan, a project manager with the Ministry of Labor. "Our system will make peasants part of city life."

Of course, this assumes economic growth will continue unchecked for the foreseeable future. If not, if there is an economic downturn or a recession, results could be disastrous. **As it is, by the year 2000, there are expected to be 268 million people unemployed in China—more than the entire population of the United States.**

"It is a double-edged sword to be sure," says Richard Blum. "They may be an efficient buffer helping to transform the economy, but they are also a large pool of marginal people subject to the vagaries and insecurity of having no rice bowl they can count on. They are dying in grotesque industrial accidents, they are locked in the dormitories at night, and they create a pocket of potential human misery wherever they cluster."

Liu Binyan, a Chinese intellectual living in exile in the United States, believes migration to the cities "always" marks the end of a dynasty. "This is not to say the current government is about to fall," he adds, "but if it reaches the point where this large floating population does not find work and does not have enough to eat, then there will be big problems."

Vietnam: Cities Booming, Farms Busting

In Vietnam, the story is much the same. "Drive along Giang Vo Street in Hanoi early in the morning and you will find lines of young men, squatting on their haunches on the pavements," says *The Economist*. "They are casual laborers who have drifted into Hanoi from the countryside in search of work on the city's building sites."

No wonder. Both Hanoi and Ho Chi Minh City are sizzling along with a 20 percent annual economic growth rate.

Economic reforms, including private enterprise farming, are planned for the rural areas, home to 80 percent of Vietnam's population. The government tries to locate industry in the countryside—in the words of *The Economist*, "to persuade reluctant oil companies to site a big new refinery deep in the country, rather than on the coast where they want to put it." But apparently this is not enough, as 51 percent of Vietnam's population is still below the poverty line. By contrast, the percentage of the population in poverty in China is 9 percent, in Indonesia 15 percent and in the Philippines 21 percent.

"Vietnam needs to tackle rural poverty if it is to engage the bulk of its population in its development and secure sustainable economic growth for the longer term," the World Bank concludes. "Broadly based economic growth—with policies that absorb and make productive use of the rural labour force—will expand employment and income-earning opportunities for the poor in Vietnam. Policies that fail to benefit farmers will bypass most of the poor." *The Economist* warns: "The growing gap between the cities and the countryside also has uncomfortable social implications."

How Ya Gonna Keep 'Em Down on the Farm?

Other governments and private leaders are trying to stem the urban tide—and the problems that accompany it—by building a better life in the countryside. The South Korean government, for example, is investing $53 billion on rural improvement projects, including housing, education and health care facilities.

In Thailand, one million people moved from rural homes to Bangkok and other cities during the dry season between November 1992 and May 1993. This alarming rate of migration prompted the development of the Thai Business Initiative in Rural Development—T-Bird. "We wanted people in rural areas to have jobs in their home villages instead of coming to Bangkok, where they have problems," says Suchart Suksom, production manager of the Canadian-based Bata Shoe Company. "The quality of their production is very high." Bata is in good company. Others involved in the project include Mobil Oil, Bristol-Myers Squibb, American Express and 3M. It is a goal of the project developers to have five hundred companies involved in T-Bird by 1996.

In Indonesia, urban poverty is more common than rural poverty because the government made rural development a top priority with policies like guaranteed rice prices, investment in irrigation, and subsidized fertilizers and pesticides. From 1960 to 1980 agricultural output increased 4 percent a year. "A small scale farmer on the Indonesian island of Sulawesi, Mr. Asikin [Mohamad] has transformed his family's life from subsistence struggle to rural affluence," says the *Washington Times*. "His 1.25 hectare [three-acre] rice paddy in Lompengang Village, outside Barru, produces two to three times what it did for his father. The family's sturdy hut on stilts now has electricity, running water, and a television. With money and motivation, his two children will most certainly finish secondary school, if not college."

Extending rural credit early on was a critical part of Indonesia's rural success story and proved a wise move politically and economically. In the early 1970s, notes the *Times*, Indonesia launched a "rural credit program for most of the country's 60,000 villages, and a commercial bank, Bank Rakyat Indonesia (BRI), that now reaches 2 million rural residents—one quarter of them women."

Indonesian rural policy radically cut numbers below the poverty line. In 1971, 68 million were counted as poor; in 1990, even with a 50 percent increase in population, the number of poor decreased to 18 million. But Indonesia's recent surge in economic development may threaten those gains. The government seems to understand the need to keep productive, irrigated rice fields from conversion to commercial, residential or other use. Nevertheless, the temptation to use the land and labor more profitably is always there.

In fact, in the not-too-distant future, Indonesia could well become an importer of rice as its agricultural industry develops alternative crops for the hot and dry climate of its eastern islands, an area that so far has been bypassed by industrial development. These crops would be grown for export in an effort to give this rural area a share in the country's wealth. "If so, Indonesia will be able to congratulate itself further," observes Singapore's *Business Times*. "For if a policy of such importance as rice self-sufficiency were to outlive its usefulness in less than a generation in such a large country, that would be a startling achievement indeed."

Asia faces enormous challenges over the next decade or so as it shifts from a society that is rural and agrarian to an urban, industrial society. Country to country, the shape and scope of the challenge varies. But many may find that they must import the grains they once exported to the world.

The Changing Face of Agriculture

"Considered one of the eight wonders of the world, the Ifugao rice terraces in northern Luzon are one of the Philippines' main tourist attractions," reports the *Bangkok Post*. The Ifugao tribes have sculpted a fantastic landscape out of Banaue's mountains. "But now Ifugao traditions are fading and the terraces that have ruled the people's lives for 2,000 years could go the same way."

Neither animal nor machine can work the "skyways" of Banaue's mountains in the Philippines, which are carved out of steep slopes that tower hundreds of feet above the valleys. Thousands of tourists come each year to see the splendor of the terraces. But that popularity, coupled with continued industrial development, is compromising the integrity of the slopes. Furthermore, young people are leaving the tedious way of life, which requires that the rice be tilled by hand and that the mud and stone retaining walls be maintained the same way. They prefer to make and sell handicrafts to the tourists or work the tourist trade in some other capacity.

Some believe the rice terraces will disappear in fifteen years. For the people living in the remote villages of the Philippines where "life retains the rhythms of the past, dictated by the seasons and instructions of tribal priests," the demise of the terraces would be more than the loss of livelihood. It would be the end of a way of life.

What is happening on the terraces of the Philippines is occurring elsewhere in Asia on a far greater scale. Industrial development is devouring agricultural land at a phenomenal rate. In China, in 1994, more than 1.76 million acres of farmland were put to other uses. China has diverted 990,000 to 1.15 million acres of farmland annually for nonagricultural uses. In Shandong Province, the "breadbasket of China," peasants have learned how they, too, can prosper when they give up farming. On the fertile acres in the Yellow River's alluvial plain, grain crops have been replaced by a slaughterhouse, a drug-making plant and a furniture factory. In Xishan, a farmer turned blue-collar worker boasts that "Not even a single villager grows grain now. We're not country bumpkins here."

China is still one of the world's biggest grain producers. "But the rice capital of the world is facing an agricultural upheaval," says the *Asian Wall Street Journal,* which also concludes that the trend spells opportunity for the "American Midwest, Argentina's campos and Australia's wheat belt: China is finding itself more and more dependent on the world to meet its food needs."

China's government claims to be working toward food self-sufficiency, but will not stop destruction of farmland for industrialization. If the pace of economic development is to continue, then so must the relentless plowing under of land. People's tastes have changed. Chinese eat greater quantities of meat and much of the grain they grow goes to feed livestock. Lastly, China's young people have embraced Deng's mantra, "To be rich is glorious," and farming is not their avenue to riches.

"Other East Asian miracle economies went down this road," reports the *Asian Wall Street Journal.* "In Japan, Taiwan and South Korea, once equally obsessed with food self-sufficiency, villages became towns,

towns became cities, and industry crowded out agriculture." These countries are now among the top markets for farmers in the United States, Australia and Argentina, which have a lot more farmland per person.

China is already a top wheat importer. But some estimates say that early on in the next century China will consume 30 million to 50 million tons of imported grains annually. By 2030, China will import 90 million tons of wheat—about half the total of world grain exports today. As one might imagine, this is welcome news to countries—including the United States—that have gaping trade deficits with China. China purchased $1.1 billion worth of U.S. farm products in 1994. "Would I tell Americans to put every fallow acre of land into production? Not yet," says a China-based grain expert who advises U.S. industry. "Would I tell them to start gearing up? You bet."

There's No Place Like Home

Perhaps the greatest challenge facing the countries of Asia is how to renew a sense of belonging and purpose. As rural inhabitants stream into new urban centers and industrial development forces farmers from their land, the integrity and security of community are threatened. It is a natural, albeit painful, part of the evolutionary cycle.

A story in the *Bangkok Post* describes this need for community: "A mega-city of nearly 10 million people, Bangkok is the heart of the country's business sector, has the country's top educational facilities, and is the center of the country's service industries. It has attracted people from diverse cultural backgrounds and social classes from all over Thailand, and, indeed, the world. Yet when academics and Bangkok Metropolitan Administration officials got together recently to assess the capital's cultural strengths . . . they found themselves unable to come up with anything at all."

"People feel powerless and alienated because they cannot effect change in their environs," says Dr. Ubonrat Siriyuvasak, a professor at Chulalongkorn University. "The sense of belonging will return if people have a chance to help right the wrongs that exist in their communities. . . . A sense of community, which is crucial in bringing the Bangkokians together to solve their problems."

That sense of community is weakening everywhere. In Guangdong, Shanghai, Beijing, wherever there is a plot of land with potential as a commercial development project, residents are relocated. And forced migrations from city centers to suburbs are occurring wherever escalating land prices tempt local authorities.

"One of the many certainties in China under communism has been a roof over the head, and it is likely to be one of the last to go," reports *The Economist.* "Governments do not want to see people thrown onto the streets where they could make trouble. But what the state gives, the state can reallocate, and much of the urban population is moving house, whether it wants to or not."

In Beijing, center-city office space sold for $4,000 a square yard in 1994, and urban "villas" for $3,500 a square yard. Beijing's urban real estate is the fourth most expensive in Asia, after Hong Kong, Tokyo and Shanghai. What's more, developers are earning 50 to 85 percent on their investments. Small wonder local authorities think nothing of relocating thousands of people who pay as little as $1 a month to rent apartment space in the urban core.

In Shanghai's center, most of the old housing has been torn down. What was once the city's museum is now an office building. The local municipal building has been turned back into a foreign bank. But what of the residents? Many have lived in Shanghai for generations. What happens to them?

In Thailand, during the past decade the government attracted both Thai and foreign investors to its eastern coast. Once a beach and some rice fields, it is now "prime commercial real estate." In 1969 the government invoked the Land Reclamation Act in Tambon Tungsukla in Chon Buri Province, compelling villagers to give up their land. Says the *Bangkok Post,* "The much-touted slogan 'sacrifice for development' means simple villagers have no choice but to go when the government says so."

But the residents of Laem Chabang, a fishing village and one of the oldest communities in the area, are resisting government plans to make it the center of a new industrial zone. Nearby farmers have been forced off their land, denied compensation and relocated to areas where they cannot grow rice. The fishermen fear the same fate, but they also fear losing their homeland. As one mother said, "We were born here and have lived here all our life. We would rather die here than move out."

The love of land is a factor in the equation that government bureaucracy seldom allows for. Kastorius Sinaga, a lecturer in the Social Sciences Postgraduate Program at the University of Indonesia, Jakarta, writes about the struggle of poor farmers from the Parbuluhan Village in Dairi Regency, North Sumatra, who refuse to give up their rights to over three thousand acres of communal land. "Viewed from a development perspective, the farmers' resistance seems to be counterproductive. The existence of an agro-industrial plantation in this remote and underdeveloped village will afford a long and glowing list of benefits."

But what the government fails to take into consideration, argues Sinaga, is the depth of attachment to the land. "For rural communities, resistance movements to land release plans are deeply rooted in existing local cultures and social beliefs about the meaning of land. With this in mind, one of the well-known reasons for resistance to development in rural areas is the love-of-land and love-of-birthplace phenomenon."

It is more than a love of land and it is not unique to rural communities. It is a love of community, a need for the familiar, the reassurance that comes from a sense of belonging, of shared heritage, of standing on common ground. And as Asia continues its relentless drive toward modernization, this "clan identity" must be factored into the equation.

The Economist, not known for mushy liberal sentiment, describes a pitiful, moving scene: "In the northern city of Tianjin, a man sits in a one-room flat that he took over from his grandfather. On the other side of the street is a vast building site. It will gobble up his home within the next few months. He complains that although the authorities have promised him a flat in the high-rise block that is to be built on the site of his present home, the rent there will be very much higher. But is he not looking forward to having running water and an inside toilet? He looks at the walls of his flat, which have not seen a new coat of paint in decades, and at the metal bowl which serves as his bathroom, and says 'no.' His flat may not be much but, to him, it is home."

Symbol of Success

Meanwhile, the tide of urban migration rolls on and development continues. Shanghai, Singapore, Kuala Lumpur, Taipei and Bangkok are Asia's emerging "supercities," each determined to supplant Hong Kong as the great commercial crossroads, or to in some way replicate Hong Kong's unparalleled success. But Asia is now too large and too wealthy for just one more Hong Kong. "There will be more than enough for competitive Asian capitals to grow and prosper," predicts Hong Kong Director General of Industry Denise Yue.

Asian cities are also racing to put up symbols of success—by building the tallest building in the world. **Of the world's top ten tallest buildings scheduled to be completed in the 1990s, nine are in Asia.**

In the near future, Shanghai, Jakarta, Chongqing (China), Taiwan, Hong Kong and Kuala Lumpur will each have a tall building symbol, heralding their economic arrival. Malaysia arrived first with its Petronas Twin Towers standing at 1,476 feet and eighty-eight stories each in 1996. The towers will be the tallest in the world, topping the Sears Tower in Chicago by twenty-two feet.

In a sense this symbolizes Asia's competitiveness with the West. The world's tallest buildings *will be in* Asia.

While in the West tall buildings have been symbolic of wealth and power, why must the East mimic such gross lack of taste and efficiency? Asia has a great opportunity to demonstrate an Asian model of success. Eco-friendly work and human-scale living environment would make a powerful statement. Asian city planners have a great opportunity to devise an Asian way of creating work and living spaces best suited for their inhabitants, and the harmony of wind and water *(feng shui)*. At a time when Asians are racing toward greater heights, one of the world's most successful companies is putting things back into perspective. The tallest building in the suburban corporate headquarters of Bill Gates's Microsoft near Seattle is only three stories high, not as tall as the neighboring Douglas firs.

The West Can Be Key to the Infrastructure

The considerations in the face of Asia's rapid urbanization are wide-ranging for Western companies wishing to do business in the region, among them decisions about where to locate production, marketing and operating bases and the search for opportunities to provide new products and services. Those new products, in turn, range from childcare and eldercare (for nuclear families who now live away from grandparents) to mobile phones, motorcycles, highways and bridges.

The Thai Farmers Bank reported that traffic jams in Bangkok had caused demand for mobile phones and pagers to soar. (Last year in Bangkok, I got a call at 7:45 a.m. from the sponsor of a speech I was giving that evening. He didn't really have anything to say, and after a few minutes I realized he was caught in a traffic jam and was making calls to entertain himself. Mobile phones as entertainment: the growth of mobile phones in Bangkok has been in direct proportion to time spent in traffic jams.) In fact, the net profits of telecommunications firms in Bangkok increased by 140 percent in 1994 compared to 1993; net profits for the mobile phone business jumped 150 percent in 1994.

The demographic landscape and cost structures (rent, labor and amenities) in Asian cities are changing rapidly. Apart from Tokyo, Hong Kong and Singapore, other Asian cities are quickly climbing up the cost ladder. For example, in Bombay, one of the world's most densely populated cities, rents for prime office space are the highest in the world—slightly more than in Tokyo and four times more than in Manhattan. Foreign companies rushing to gain a foothold in Asia must examine very closely the fast-changing demographics and cost structures in order not to incur very high learning costs. In Bombay, because of scarcity, tenants have to pay several years of rent in advance—sometimes as much as five years—before occupying the premises. Such mistakes can be avoided if Western companies look at Asia, or India, as a whole and not be captive to a capital city or a particular country.

Because of the urbanization of Asia, the greatest opportunities for Western companies lie in the introduction of technology and design to build environmentally friendly dwellings for Asian cities and to help build Asia's urban-suburban transportation systems.

CHAPTER SIX

From Labor-Intensive to High Technology

MANY Westerners still associate Asia with low-wage, labor-intensive industries. Workers in Japan are well paid, most recognize, but in Taiwan, Korea—and certainly China—people earn considerably less than their U.S. or European counterparts, don't they? To a large extent, yes. That's one reason Asia is so competitive.

But as the global economy continues to shift from its industrial past to the full potential of the information-based future, the key to productivity will not be inexpensive labor but the best use of high technology.

Good news for the West, right? Good news for the leaders in high technology, for the United States, Japan and Germany? Not exactly.

In reality, the countries of Asia have envisioned the future more clearly than most. Asian entrepreneurs and their governments, by and large, realize that the fulfillment of high technology will weaken their primary strategic advantage—cheap labor. Furthermore, they saw the handwriting on the wall a decade ago. Larger global forces are converging to make all of us rethink what we are doing. And while the United States and Europe sank into the political quagmire of protectionism, Asia forged ahead.

Today, Asia's sophisticated urban centers, its savvy, technology-seeking, incentive-supplying governments and global high-tech companies, as well as a new breed of U.S.-educated and now repatriated business leaders, have consciously leapfrogged over the industrial age and are pioneering the information age.

That, of course, does not apply everywhere. Hong Kong is said to have the world's most sophisticated phone system (Singapore might disagree). In Sri Lanka, however, it has been said it is "faster and easier to travel by car to any destination in the country than to try to make contact by telephone." If you can find a phone, that is. In India, there is less than one telephone per hundred people, one of the lowest penetrations in the world. But the state telephone company employs more than 500,000 people; the ratio of employees to telephones is 1 employee for every 17 telephones. As I exclaimed in Bombay recently, "That's not a telephone company! That's an employment program!"

Yet, the point remains: the shift in Asia from labor-intensive to high technology is well under way. It is happening even in Asia's developing countries. The question is, what are the implications of Asia's headlong rush into high technology for the rest of the world, and in particular for Asia's competitors in the United States and Europe? That question cannot be addressed without a detailed look at the advanced and very impressive state of technology in Asia today.

The Opportunities Ahead

Virtually every country in Asia is creating policies and removing bureaucratic barriers that might impede progress toward a high-tech, fully wired future. Yet no matter how they have traveled on the information highway, all Asian countries must address the same three basic challenges:

1. To make current manufacturing operations more efficient through technologically advanced production techniques.
2. To develop and support "homegrown" high-tech industries.
3. To create a telecommunications infrastructure capable of support-

ing an information economy and integrating into the global information network.

Tigers and Dragons and Geese

What makes this drama so fascinating is Asia's unique approach to development, the so-called flying geese formation which jump-starts regional growth. The "Four Tigers" are already prosperous. But success brings rising costs. Where's a new millionaire to invest? In Asia, the answer is often right next door. Malaysia, the Philippines, Indonesia and Thailand, where costs are still low, attract their neighbors' wealth.

The result is the creation of interregional growth hubs, each component of which offers a critical element in support of industry. One such hub ties Singapore to southern Malaysia and the Indonesian archipelago in support of a burgeoning electronics industry. Singapore brings the technological know-how, and the telecommunications and transportation infrastructure, while Malaysia and Indonesia offer labor, water and electric power. It's a dynamic triad, win-win-win situation. A similar effort links Malaysia and Indonesia to Thailand.

The powerful economic links between China's southern Guangdong Province and Hong Kong are legendary, even though there are no official trade links because of unresolved political issues. Throughout Asia politics is giving way to pragmatism.

Taiwan: A Microcosm of the Region

If you want to understand what is happening in Asia, look at Taiwan, which has been transformed from an agricultural backwater country to an economic colossus—in just forty years. The GNP rate averaged more than 9 percent in the 1960s, 10.2 percent in the 1970s and 8.2 percent in the 1980s. It is expected to increase between 6 and 9 percent in the late 1990s.

Much of Taiwan's prosperity was built on exports, which continue to soar. In 1995 total exports amounted to $111.7 billion, while imports totaled $103.6 billion. Taiwan held the world's second largest foreign-exchange reserves in 1995. In decades past Taiwan exported labor-intensive manufactured products such as textiles and footwear. No more. Now the island nation is a leader in high technology.

Success Drives Up Costs

Economic prosperity improved Taiwan's standard of living but also drove up the costs of labor and land, and put a strain on the country's infrastructure. The very attributes that attracted manufacturers there in the first place were being compromised. Taiwan's government and people faced the choice of giving up on manufacturing or creating a strategic plan to make existing industries more competitive, while at the same time increasing the country's attractiveness to high-tech companies. Taiwan chose the latter. Then, in 1991, it embarked on a whopping $300-billion, six-year, national infrastructure development plan (since scaled down).

Taiwan realized its comparative advantage in traditional labor-intensive manufacturing had begun to decline, says Fred C. H. Feng, deputy director of the International Cooperation Department of the Ministry of Economic Affairs for Taiwan. "We now have to increase our productivity and upgrade our industries away from labor-intensive products to more high-tech products with greater value added."

That was a smart, sophisticated vision. But how was a country like Taiwan supposed to implement it? Basically through strategic alliances with leading global companies. Taiwan needed their state-of-the-art technology and determined to create an environment so hospitable that the world's information leaders could not resist.

Taiwan's goal—to become a regional center for international corporations—was realistic, considering that it lies between northern and southern Asia, is near China, and has a skilled labor force, immense capital and a long tradition of supporting the manufacturing needs of multinationals. Taiwan's incentives to companies with expertise in its newly selected "strategic industries" include the loosening of banking and financial regulations (foreign banks can now open branch offices in Taiwan) and the relaxation of rules forbidding foreign institutional investors to buy and sell securities.

As a sign of Taiwan's new political pragmatism, the Mainland Affairs Council considers all matters dealing with cross-straits relations and aims to work toward a smooth reunification. Meanwhile, although China and Taiwan technically remain in a state of war, economic bonds between the two countries grow stronger.

A Principal Source of Foreign Investment Capital

As a holder of large foreign-exchange reserves Taiwan rapidly became a main source of investment capital. Taiwan's Ministry of Economic Affairs says that the country is the world's seventh largest overseas investor. The vast majority of this investment is in Asia, mostly mainland China, where Taiwan has invested more than $25 billion. And much of these investments have been in labor-intensive manufacturing, partly because land and labor costs have increased so much at home.

The Taiwanese have also invested in Vietnam (where they are the largest foreign investor), Malaysia and Thailand (where they are the third-largest foreign investor) and Indonesia. Taiwan's investment is happily received by its Asian neighbors, but some say it drains money away from the country's own industries. Taiwan's domestic economy is undergoing restructuring, moving up the value chain.

If Taiwan is to navigate the straits of the global information society, not to mention convince top information companies to invest millions, it must invest significant resources at home. Thus, the six-year infrastructure development plan. A critical first step is its commitment to a fully digitized telecommunications network following on the heels of Singapore's digitized network, which was completed in 1995. The race is on in Asia to go fully digital.

Industries of the Future: Taiwan's Top Ten

Though observers who espouse the "let the market decide" model might wince (and I am among them), Taiwan's choice is clear. It will follow the Japanese approach and "pick favorites." Taiwan offers significant financial incentives to companies in these ten "strategic" industries: telecommunications, information, consumer electronics, semiconductors, precision machinery and automation, aerospace, advanced materials, fine chemicals and pharmaceuticals, health care and pollution control.

Companies in these categories stand to reap an impressive set of benefits including administrative and financial assistance. The Industrial Development Board "may subsidize up to 50 percent of the financial management, quality control, production management, material management, marketing, in-service training and design costs of a company that meets the strategic-industry criteria," reports the *International Herald Tribune*. Such companies also enjoy "a five-year tax holiday and may be exempt from import tax on equipment imported for R&D work."

Taiwan serves as an economic development model for the region as the government explores all avenues to prosperity in the twenty-first century. Taiwan also targets expatriates who left the country for academic reasons and stayed away for political reasons. Now they are encouraged to return home to build the country's future.

Strategic Asset: Reversing Asia's Brain Drain

Hsinchu Science-Based Industrial Park, south of Taipei, is a sort of haven for repatriated engineers. Of the park's 155 companies, more than half were founded by Taiwanese engineers who returned to Taiwan from the United States. "The original thought was that since there were so many Taiwanese scientists and engineers in Silicon Valley, that if we could get some of them to come back and start businesses, they could help us start a high-tech industry here," says H. Steve Hsieh, the park's director general, who has a Ph.D. from the University of Wisconsin. "Many people went to the United States . . . because Taiwan was under martial law. Some of these people got into a middle-age crisis. So we've tried to recruit them to come here and start high-tech companies."

Middle-age crisis, as well as long stints with certain U.S. firms, can certainly create an entrepreneur.

Nobel laureate Dr. Lee Yuen Tseh returned in 1994 to Taiwan to head the Academia Sinica, Taiwan's most prestigious research institution, at the invitation of President Lee Teng Hui. "In the 1960s, most young people didn't feel that there were good opportunities in Taiwan. The best and brightest went to America," he says. Dr. Lee sacrificed a comfortable life and gave up his U.S. citizenship to return. In his new position he is now crusading for the return of the diaspora of Taiwanese intelligentsia worldwide, including such prominent figures as Harvard paleontologist Chang Kwang-chih, physicist Frank Fang and botanist Yang Shang-fa. He set up the Foundation for the Development of Outstanding Fellows, which raised almost $30 million from business circles to help scholars and scientists relocate to Taiwan to teach and conduct research.

"I'd been at IBM long enough," says Wu Tao-yuan, a Stanford University Ph.D. in electrical engineering and former head of R&D for IBM in Silicon Valley. "I saw that my future was limited there because of the nature of the beast. Taiwan presented a much greater opportunity for me."

"I was at Stanford in applied physics," says Yau You-wen, who returned to Taiwan from the United States in 1993. "[I] went on to Honeywell, and later IBM. What brought me back were the opportunities." Yau is now the director of quality at the Taiwan Semiconductor Manufacturing Company, the country's largest fabricator of integrated circuits.

The 155 companies in the Hsinchu Industrial Park are privately owned but have received money from the government's National Science Council for land, buildings and research. Total 1995 sales were expected to total $9 billion. By 2003, Hsieh expects sales to hit $50 billion. U.S.-educated Taiwanese engineers are largely responsible for the park's success. Around 1,500 returned expatriates now work in the park. Several of the park's tenants are among the country's largest high-tech firms. Microtech, for example, founded in 1980, captured 15 percent of the world market for desktop scanners.

In the past five years an estimated six thousand experienced managers and engineers have returned to Taiwan, many with doctorates. Says Hsieh, "I want to see a whole series of little Singapores created here in Taiwan." A second park will be built near the southern city of Kaohsiung (the world's third-largest container port after Hong Kong and Singapore). Hsieh envisions a third in central Taiwan and two more by the year 2020. Hsinchu is also expanding.

In the wake of generous government incentives, Taiwan, Hong Kong, Singapore, South Korea and others may offer upcoming generations even greater opportunities for professional growth than U.S. high-tech firms. Asia does a lot of things right when it comes to technology. But this new move to reverse the brain drain, more than any other single action, should give U.S. information giants pause.

Shifting the Balance of Power in Technology Development

The commitment to bring thousands of U.S.-educated Asians home introduces the very real possibility of a dramatic shift in the balance of technology power. Nearly half of the 1993 engineering Ph.D. recipients at American universities were foreign nationals, many of whom stay in the United States to work in Silicon Valley or top research-and-development centers such as AT&T Bell Laboratories. These talented foreigners are vital to the success of U.S. technology-based companies.

"As more of these high-tech journeymen head homeward with their skills and network of contacts, they are closing the technology gap," says *BusinessWeek.* "Take the case of South Korea. Thanks partly to U.S.-trained researchers who have returned over the past decade, Samsung Inc. is in a dead heat with Japanese chip makers to dominate next generation memory chips."

More than one hundred AT&T Bell Laboratories' "alumni" have returned to Taiwan, making the island "an export power in semiconductors and multimedia gear." *BusinessWeek* calls Hong Kong "a hotbed of telecom and audio gadgets, with hundreds of entrepreneurs," and cites Allan C. Y. Wong, a U.S.-educated former NCR Corporation electrical engineer who built VTech Holdings Ltd., a $500-million-plus maker of educational toys and cellular phones, into a global company. The new repatriated technology masters "tilt the balance of technological power toward the emerging markets in the next century," concludes *BusinessWeek.*

At the very least, they will accelerate the pace at which Asia plays catch-up with the West. In the past three to five years the technology playing field has been leveled. In many areas the United States, Europe and Asia are on equal footing. Asia's farsighted governments are doing everything in their power to pave the way for the transfer, from creating special high-tech parks and economic zones to investing in research and development initiatives to secure a future for homegrown innovations.

R&D Payoff

Few have been as successful as Singapore in setting goals for technology development and achieving them. Its sophisticated telecommunications infrastructure grew out of the 1986 National Information Technology Plan, which aimed to create the first fully networked society—where all homes, schools, businesses and government agencies are connected through an electronic grid. That will probably happen by 1999.

Singapore has a superb track record in shifting from imported to indigenous technologies. "Just 10 years ago, the island's economy was still heavily geared to basic manufacturing," reports *Asian Business.* "But since then, the city-state has turned itself into a hotbed of R&D activity, with local labs busy working in areas such as computers, medical technology and basic engineering."

The Institute of Molecular and Cell Biology (IMCB), which receives funding from both the government and the private sector, has a multinational group of two hundred scientists, including more than one hundred with Ph.D.s, and a support staff of sixty technicians. The Singapore government is making a long-term investment in R&D, and the island's Ministry of Education has a special $35.7-million budget for basic research at the island's two universities. The R&D focus covers biotechnology and pharmaceutical, microelectronics, computer software and computer imaging. South Korean companies increased their R&D spending by 25 percent in 1995, to $3.9 billion.

"South Korea's R&D efforts to move into high-tech have secured a prominent position for its semiconductor industry," notes *Asian Business*. "Now the country is the third-largest exporter of memory chips, after the United States and Japan. South Korean producers hold about 30 percent of the market for the 4-megabyte dynamic random access memory (D-RAM) chips that have become standard equipment for the latest generation of personal computers."

Asia's Answer to Silicon Valley: India, Inc.

India first offered incentives to high-tech companies in 1986. Today, Bangalore, with seven software development parks and 5 million people, is one of the world's largest exporters of computer software. Bangalore's population has doubled in recent years, attracting many returning émigrés.

Pradeep Singh spent ten years in the United States at Texas Instruments and Microsoft. After returning to Bangalore, he launched NetQuest (India) Private, which sells electronic services and software products. G. Jagannath Raju earned a Ph.D. from the Massachusetts Institute of Technology and started Systematics Inc., a Lexington, Massachusetts–based robotics company. Government incentives lured him back home after twenty years. He plans to build robots for India's nuclear power plants, mining industry and aircraft manufacturers.

India's software development firms are connected to U.S. and European customers through a telecommunications network that was the brainchild of some Indian software writers. Infosys now has sales of $28 million. "Passengers traveling by many international airlines, including American Airlines, Swissair, or Singapore Airlines . . . have software companies in India to thank for the fact that these aircraft run anything like on time," writes Dewang Mehta, executive director of the National Association of Software and Service Companies (NASSCOM). The London underground runs on an Indian program, too, he says. So do bank accounts at Citibank, American Express, Deutsche Bank and Hong Kong & Shanghai Bank.

"There was a time when the world used to speak about Japan, Inc.," comments N. Vittal, secretary to India's Department of Electronics. "What is now emerging is India, Inc., particularly in the area of software. The government of India has provided all the requisite inputs— training for manpower, high-speed data communications, red-tape-free systems—in fact, a veritable red carpet for the industry."

That government strategy is paying handsome dividends. Since 1989, India's software exports have averaged a stunning 40 percent increase a year, hitting $1.2 billion in 1995. What's more, India's software industry is no longer selling programming skills, but what Ed Yourdon, author of *Decline and Fall of the American Programmer,* calls "expertise in managing entire projects." The engineers' identity is almost irrelevant, he says. Customers care about cost, quality and on-time delivery. "Indian software firms offer considerable project management expertise, high quality testing and quality assurance capabilities, and an overall 'infrastructure' to assure that the project will run smoothly," says Yourdon.

China's urban centers will also compete in the high-tech bonanza. In 1985, China established special economic zones for technology. By 1994, there were twenty-seven state-level zones along the coast, sixteen inland and nine in remote districts. Another twenty-five regional zones have been upgraded to state-level zones. "Electronics Street," in Zhongguan, a district of Beijing, is the site of numerous universities and research institutes.

In 1993, Shanghai's computer industry rang up $80 million in annual sales. It aims for $2 billion by 2000. A high-tech software development park will be home to 30,000 engineers. They can only hope to be as successful as Bangalore.

Aiding and abetting the transfer of technology power are the global companies that came to Asia in search of cheap labor and discovered a wealth of talent, energy and an extraordinary work ethic.

The Global Workforce—Asia Benefits

Singapore's R&D effort aimed to attract global information giants. The result: A who's who in electronics—Motorola, AT&T, Digital Equipment, Hewlett-Packard, IBM and Matsushita—arrived to take advantage of government incentives.

- U.S.-based Motorola Electronics opened an R&D facility in Singapore to develop consumer electronic products aimed at Asian markets. It was Motorola's fourth R&D unit, and only its second outside the United States.
- National Semiconductor chose Singapore for its high-tech R&D center, which will be the only facility outside the United States making semiconductors to U.S. military standards.
- The $35-million Motorola Innovation Center develops pagers in Singapore. It was here the Scriptor pager was developed almost entirely by Singaporean industrial designers using software developed in Singapore. The plant employs seventy-five local engineers.
- Hewlett-Packard opened a plant in Singapore in 1970 to put together computer keyboards. It is now the worldwide R&D and production center for H-P's portable ink-jet printers.

Major U.S. information firms are making a home in India, which claims the second-largest pool of English-speaking scientific talent after the United States. India boasts more than 100,000 software engineers and technicians. Hundreds of companies, many locally owned, supply software to Western customers, says *BusinessWeek*, which predicts the number of engineers could double by the year 2000. An Indian engineer with five years' experience earns $800 a month and a slot in the upper middle class.

The Training Edge and Skills Crisis

Penang, Malaysia, is home to Hewlett-Packard's worldwide base for microwave components and is taking over from a Palo Alto site responsibility for hard-disk drives. Such global shifts in production responsibility, R&D and assembly would not be possible but for the intensive emphasis on training in the cutting-edge companies cited.

Penang's Skills Development Center, a 360-student polytechnic institute for high school and university graduates, was funded by fifty-seven foreign firms and the Malaysian government. Intel contributed a $140,000 microprocessor lab. Seagate Technology, Inc., operator of a hard-disk plant, donated a 20,000-square-foot "team building park" for leadership training. Motorola gave $320,000 for PC software training and a bachelor of science program. "Originally, they set up plants in Asia chiefly for cheap labor," writes *BusinessWeek.* "But many of these assembly shops have gathered so much know-how that they now do critical design-and-engineering tasks."

Multinationals still get what they came for—inexpensive labor. A circuit board designer in California earns between $60,000 and $100,000 a year. Comparable talent in Taiwan makes about $25,000. In India or China, you can employ the cream of the crop for less than $10,000. And today Asia's labor is as well trained as the West's. Plus, many employers find the work ethic and attitude superior.

There are even greater savings on the "back end," the painstaking work that produces software, reports *BusinessWeek.* Nursing a concept from blueprint to computer code to prototype or test model takes hours and hours of work. In China, where a keypunch operator earns $75 a month and a graphics designer $400 a month, a company like Bilingual Education Computer Inc., which designs interactive CD-ROM programs, can produce a product for one quarter to one tenth the cost of U.S. production.

Advances in telecommunications mean knowledge-based operations can be located anywhere. Software shops in Taipei, Singapore or Penang can serve end-users in New York or Frankfurt. "Conventional notions of comparative advantage are getting blurred in the process." Similarly, "Citibank taps local skills in India, Hong Kong, Australia, and Singapore to . . . develop products for its global financial services. . . . And everyone from law firms to U.S. nonprofit groups cut costs in managing and analyzing documents by hiring 'outsourcers' such as

International Data Solutions Inc. in Herndon, Virginia, which employs thousands of workers in the Philippines."

According to the research firm Dataquest Inc., there are an estimated 350,000 information-technology engineers in Chinese research institutes and state companies, with average salaries of about $105 a month. Since China's list of priority industries includes electronics and telecommunications, undoubtedly its academic institutions will soon begin cranking out engineers at a rapid clip.

Improving Product Quality

"As recently as five years ago, a China-products fair could still bring a wry smile to the faces of browsing foreign traders," says a story in *Nikkei Weekly.* "The clunky toaster; the cheesy-looking welder; a tank-sized refrigerator looking as if it belonged at the head of a May Day parade. At best functional, always 20 years out of date, Chinese products were destined almost exclusively for Third World markets." But now international market analysts believe that within three to five years, China will export consumer and industrial products equal in quality or better than Japanese ones.

How is such a turnaround possible? The answer, of course, is technology transfer. Since the late 1970s the heart of China's industrial policy has been acquiring foreign technology. To date, Chinese companies have signed over 5,600 technology-transfer agreements with developed nations worth more than $40 billion.

No other developing country has purchased as much foreign technology as China.

No wonder China's domestic steel industry is rapidly overtaking Japanese imports, helped by joint ventures with the Japanese themselves, mostly in Dalian. The high yen is part of it, but the main reason can be traced to vast improvements in the quality of Chinese steel. China is also moving into the high-tech steel market, once Japan's domain. Still, consumer electronics remains the greatest concern to

Japan's manufacturers. Already, China's acquired expertise in color-television production technology allows it to crank out TVs on a par with anything Japan exports.

Japanese consumer electronics exporters worry about Taiwan's new reputation for high-quality, affordably priced goods. "Leading the 'Made-for-Taiwan' charge," says a Taiwan ad in *BusinessWeek*, "are two corporate visionaries—Frankie Hong, chairman of Proton, whose TV and other electronics products are penetrating global markets, and Stan Shih, chairman of Acer, a hot computer maker. Acer, in fact, is by far the largest brand-name exporter in Taiwan."

One high-end, top-quality product to emerge from Taiwan's newly revamped manufacturing sector is Philips's Taiwan Brilliance 1720 monitor, a favorite of software programmers and graphic designers the world over. Philips undertook exhaustive research to learn what end-users really needed.

Proton's state-of-the-art TV, a wide-screen, fully digital DT-3660, is setting the standard for interactive capabilities. It is programmed to handle every known signal from a laser disc to a camcorder or TV game. It is an all-purpose, interactive entertainment center equipped to replace PC monitors, telephones, fax machines and videocassette recorders.

South Korea's Lucky-Goldstar, Hyundai and Samsung are making their mark on global high-tech markets. Samsung is number one world-wide in the production of D-RAMs, memory chips that store computer data. The company just broke the record with its 256-megabyte D-RAM, the world's most powerful chip.

Goldstar is creating alliances with GE Appliances, Zenith Electronics, Texas Instruments, Hitachi, Siemens and others to secure a global position similar to its leading one at home in consumer electronics. It is a leading player in the memory-chip market, and is out to capture the market for thin-film transistor liquid-crystal displays presently held by Sony and other Japanese producers.

"No longer the so-called Hermit Kingdom that treasured its privacy after countless invasions over the centuries, South Korea today is opening its windows to technology and trade as it has never done before," says *BusinessWeek*. "And nowhere is this happening more visibly than in the offices of the country's highly diversified conglomerates, now facing free-market competition at home and in foreign markets and, as a result, pouring $35 billion into new plants and products to improve their competitive advantage."

These are exhilarating times for Asia. As the region takes its place in the global community, it is emerging as an economic powerhouse, a sophisticated producer of high-tech products. Only two factors could slow down the region's headlong rush toward prosperity: education and telecommunications capabilities. If either were insufficient to meet the challenges of the information age, growth could come to a screeching halt.

Where Will the Engineers Come From?

"In our view, the biggest challenge of all facing Asia is education," reports Hong Kong–based Political & Economic Risk Consultancy Ltd. "China can pump all the billions of dollars it wants into its phone and rail systems. It will be money wasted, however, unless those responsible for operating these systems are educated in efficient management techniques."

Well said. But they are not the only ones who think so. The World Bank estimates that "one quarter of all investment in rail systems, power plants and other infrastructure is wasted through technical inefficiencies largely due to poorly trained operators."

Asians have made extraordinary gains both in academic and hands-on training. There are thousands of repatriated engineers and hundreds of thousands of homegrown technical graduates. Are they enough to keep pace with the region's development? Not even close. "The shortage of skilled workers is so serious [in Asia] that in some places it threatens to derail growth," claims an article in the *Far Eastern Economic Review:*

Malaysia, Thailand and others in the region face serious labor shortages.

- In Thailand, some 6,000 engineering students graduated in 1993; the demand was for thousands more;

- Malaysian universities graduate fewer than 6,000 engineers each year; annual demand is for 10,000;
- In 1994, Hong Kong allowed 1,000 Chinese professionals to emigrate, hoping to meet the need for more computer experts; and
- South Korea expects to increase the number of engineering students from 280,000 to 340,000 by 1999. Already, South Korean engineers with graduate degrees number more than 60,000 annually, but that is not enough.

"It's a very serious problem," says Somsak Tambunlertchai, an economist at the Asian and Pacific Development Center in Kuala Lumpur. "These countries need to move up the comparative-advantage ladder. And the lack of skilled manpower is a serious constraint." Don Carkeek, managing director of Digital Equipment Corporation (Thailand) Ltd., who supervises three hundred sales and service people in Thailand, comments, "The demand for skilled, talented, well-educated people far exceeds the supply. Look at the daily newspapers—the classified ads go on and on and on about requests for people with skills background."

Demand for India's 20,000 computer science students who graduate each year is so high that industry wages are increasing 20 percent a year.

Business Fills the Gaps

As a matter of survival, business attempts to fill the educational gaps. In South Korea, Samsung, Hyundai, Kia Motors and Pohang Iron & Steel built their own high schools, guaranteeing that the skills of graduates match the needs of the business. Daewoo supports a university, and Pohang's Institute of Science and Technology took top honors as South Korea's best institute of higher learning—winning out over the prestigious Seoul University.

Elsewhere in the region, Toyota's Shenyang plant trains employees on site. Microsoft gave twenty-five personal computers to a training facility in Shanghai. Honeywell provided CAD/CAM systems, and

Matsushita Electric Works Ltd. gave the machinery to develop robots. Labs and high-tech sites will be opened.

At Motorola's training center in Beijing, workers learn to brainstorm, define goals and understand the concept of corporate vision. Difficult as it is to find skilled workers, people with management expertise are even harder to find. That is one reason repatriated Asians are in such high demand. Motorola sent employees from its Singapore office to Copper Mountain in Colorado for an Outward Bound type of team-building experience, to strengthen collaboration and employee bonds.

What's more important, one might ask: education or infrastructure? For Asia to prosper, the infrastructure must be developed even as educational needs are identified and filled. It isn't either/or. It's both.

The Information Age Is Here

AT&T sold China a high-speed digital transmission system between Hong Kong and Guangdong Province that can carry "more than 30,000 voice and data calls over a single optical fiber line." It is said to be as good as, if not better than, the lines linking New York and Washington, D.C. "This technology is as advanced as anything we have commercially available," says Christopher Padilla, AT&T's director of government affairs. "In effect, we're helping China lay down its first information superhighway."

Since the end of Cold War–era export controls, high-tech manufacturers in the West have sold enormous amounts of technology to China. During the last six months of 1994, AT&T sold China more than $70 million in previously restricted equipment. "Only a few years ago," writes the *Asian Wall Street Journal*, "such a voluntary transfer of Western brainpower to a Communist country would have been unthinkable."

• France's Alcatel SA received $1.2 billion in orders for telecom equipment in China in 1994—more than double the 1993 orders.

• Motorola will invest another $1.2 billion in its China operations. Of that, $720 million will go into a silicon wafer plant in Tianjin. Motorola is intent on creating a wireless system for China.

• IBM is helping China build an information infrastructure, and Digital Equipment also sees a bright future in China.

• During 1996 China expects to spend $11 billion on fiber-optic lines, switches and phone connectors, plus an additional $49 billion by 2000.

Asia Gets Wired

Forget fax machines, fiber optics, satellites and cable. In much of Asia, the issues are telephones and transmission lines. Asia without Japan has more than half the world's population, but just one tenth of its telephones. In the next decade China will install 98 million telephone lines. But that will only be one for every ten people. The number of telephone lines in China is expected to increase from 48 million in 1994 to 110 million by 2000. But to accomplish that goal, 10 million to 11 million new lines will have to be installed every year until 2000, the equivalent of installing Britain's telephone network every three years —at a cost of more than $100 billion.

Asia's developing countries must spend $90 billion to $120 billion by the year 2000 just to meet basic phone service, reports the World Bank.

• Bangladesh wants 150,000 phone lines installed as soon as possible.

• India has 9 million phone lines—one line per hundred people— and would like to increase that to 20 million phone lines by 2000. The price tag: $13 billion. There are 4 million people on the waiting list for telephones in India, some of whom have been waiting for five years.

• Indonesia will spend $10 billion on telecommunications by the year 2000, much of it on phone lines. There are now 1.65 lines per hundred people, most of those in Java.

• Malaysia will spend $20 billion to bring its telecommunications system closer to world standards.

Singapore has one of the highest phone densities in the world, one of the most sophisticated telecommunications infrastructures and among the most ambitious plans for growth. What officials in Singapore realized early on was that it isn't land-based phone lines, or cellular, or fiber optics, or microwaves, or satellites. It's the mix of all of those technologies.

Converging Technologies

"In places like China and India, the information superhighway will have to be wireless, because it is cheaper and faster to install," notes Paul Kan, chairman of Champion Technology of Hong Kong, a company that plans to have around fifty ventures in China in 1997. Wireless is one route, but it is not the only way to go. China already has more than 22,000 miles of fiber-optic lines and plans to install seventeen fiber-optic trunk lines by 2000. Fiber-optic submarine systems connect Hong Kong with Japan, Malaysia, Singapore, Taiwan, Thailand and Vietnam. Hong Kong, Singapore and Japan all plan to connect every home via fiber optics. South Korea will spend $60 billion on its information superhighway through 2015. One of the first projects will connect eighty major cities by fiber-optic cables by 1997.

Meanwhile, mobile phones are a hot item throughout Asia, most notably in Hong Kong, where more than 737,000 people carried a cellular phone in January of 1996—167 times the estimated number of users in 1985. Between 1990 and 1994 the number of mobile phones in Beijing increased from 20,000 to 1.57 million. By 1997, there will be more mobile phones in Thailand than land-based ones. In 1996 the number of people in China with pagers will surpass the number of people in the U.S. with pagers.

Between 1984 and 1994, the number of outgoing calls in China and Vietnam increased close to 30 times. Eight of the ten countries with the fastest increase in outgoing overseas calls are in Asia. Keeping all these people talking could require at least twenty to thirty new telecommunications satellites for the Chinese market alone (including Hong Kong) in the next decade, reports *The Economist*. Inmarsat, a London-based consortium of telephone companies in seventy-five countries, plans to have twelve high-orbit satellites, from which people can call anywhere in the world from a hand-held phone.

The latest trend is in "low earth orbiting" satellites that offer greater clarity through smaller and lighter-weight phones. Already eleven different satellite services are planning "low earth orbiting" systems. Among them are Motorola's Iridium project, which will connect sixty-six satellites; and TRW's Odyssey, connecting twelve satellites.

Virtually every country in Asia has an aggressive plan to link up to the global economic village. Asians are already aficionados of the Internet, and it is only a matter of time before all of them will be able to reach out and touch someone anywhere in the world anytime via computer, telephone, fax, cellular phone or satellite.

It is increasingly clear that the West can no longer count on maintaining leadership in technology development.

The Chinese Network's Talent Pool

One of the more surprising and interesting sights in Hong Kong is at the tiny park in front of the huge Hong Kong & Shanghai Bank: on weekend afternoons as many as two thousand Filipinos, mostly maids, gather to pass the time during their days off. They are only the most visible of the foreign workers needed in Asia, now a land of labor shortages. Finding, training and retraining employees is one of the few restraints on growth in the region.

Only a trickle now, in time we are likely to see a major migration of workers from West to East. This shift is now being led from the high end, highly educated professionals, many of them part of the returning brain drain. According to Lai Mao-Nan, director of the National Youth Commission in Taiwan, up to 50 percent of the 220,000 Taiwanese who went abroad for masters and doctorates since 1970 have returned to their homeland. According to the Hong Kong government, about 12 percent of the 462,000 people who emigrated during the last ten years have returned. The Hong Kong Institute of Human Resource Management estimates that for every hundred professionals who emigrated two years ago, twenty others returned from overseas. Among the returnees:

Woo Chia Wei, the founding president of Hong Kong University of

Science & Technology. Woo, a physicist, became the first Chinese-American to head a major U.S. university when he was appointed president of San Francisco State in 1983. Since heading the University of Science & Technology, he has recruited more than 450 mainly U.S.-trained scientists, engineers and management specialists. About 75 percent of his faculty are ethnic Chinese educated in the West.

Dr. Chris Tan, a noted biotechnologist in Canada and the United States, returned to Singapore to head the National University of Singapore's Institute of Molecular and Cell Biology. Since his return in 1987, Dr. Tan has helped the institute recruit more than three hundred research fellows, most of them Asian returnees who have earned doctorates and lived and worked in North America.

Millions of Asia's best and brightest went to the West during the past thirty years, primarily to the United States, Canada and Australia. *Asia Inc.* estimates that there were about 8 million who did so. The current reverse brain flow could develop into a tidal wave of returnees as Asia seeks to lure them back to help drive the growth into the next century. Ronald Skeldon of Hong Kong University describes the attraction to the reverse flow: "In Hong Kong and Singapore, you have high-salary, low-tax economies; in North America, you have low-salary, high-tax economies."

There is also an increase in the number of Western expatriates flocking to Asia. In Hong Kong, for example, the number of Americans, Australians and Canadian expatriates—including ethnic Asians who hold foreign passports—has more than doubled from 45,300 in 1985 to 97,000 in 1994.

For productivity to increase, the quality of human resources matters more than the quantity. Asia has been smart in pouring its resources into primary and secondary education rather than higher education. Now as the Western world passes into the information age, and some parts of Asia leapfrog into the new age, Asia is in urgent need of higher educational development and reform. Education services in science and technology and research and development could become a major Western export to the East.

But Asia is in a relatively stronger position to enter the information age than most people think. The region has several advantages.

• Asia has a young population that makes it more technology comfortable. Asian youth are so fascinated with technology that they are willing to try anything. An expatriate executive at Microsoft in Singapore was amazed at how much interest teenagers have in computers compared with their peers in the United States. He said, when he returns home, the common talk among teenage girls is about becoming beautiful, going out on a big date and other stuff about having fun. In Asia, the girls are talking about Pentium, how many megabytes you need to run a certain software and Windows 95. They are ready for cyberspace.

• As a latecomer to development, Asia has a golden opportunity to install the latest state-of-the-art infrastructure. A new airport in Asia can install the latest air traffic controller computer system. Almost all the airports in the United States have computer systems dating from the 1970s. Moreover, the young population does not have to be retrained; they don't have to unlearn the systems of the industrial period.

• Although there is a shortage of engineering talent in Asia, concerned governments are making efforts to remedy the situation. There is endless talk about education reforms and some are already going forward. Increasingly, Western engineers are being hired and efforts are being made to recruit from Western countries. Many of the high-tech and telecommunications projects around the region are managed by expatriate engineers and experts. Many more will be needed.

A promising opportunity lies in collaboration with the Asians. Technology-hungry Asian companies and governments are eager to make joint ventures and form strategic alliances with Western companies that possess the technology, know-how and personnel. The synergy of capital, market and talent in East-West collaborations will do wonders for the world in the spread of scientific and technological innovation.

With the reversal of the Asian brain drain will come the emergence of strong global enterprises with large capacities to buy talent from the West. If Asia can find a way to achieve economic growth and better integrate quality of life values into its societies, it will become an attractive alternative workplace for many people, especially young people in the West. Westerners may need some time to get used to the Asian work ethic, but if the quality of personal and professional fulfillment is significant, it may be a price that many will find worth paying.

Technological leadership, the West's domain for many years, will probably continue in some areas. There are no guarantees. But technological application, proving the power of technology to millions of new participants in the global economy, will depend on many highly educated and skilled people with an understanding of ways to use science and technology to improve people's quality of life. From this standpoint, India and China will dominate the twenty-first century by the sheer number of skilled technicians who will be able to deliver new products and services to the world. In the process, the future of professional services may shift from West to East and the prosperity associated with these services will follow.

CHAPTER SEVEN

From Male Dominance to the Emergence of Women

A tiny Buddhist nun living on the eastern shore of Taiwan has created a massive medical enterprise and transformed a mining town of 350,000 into a cradle of compassion. Starting with nothing, she built and now runs an 800-bed hospital employing 140 full-time doctors, 500 nurses and 900 staff members, as well as a nursing college and a medical school. Her followers, 4 million strong, some 90 percent of whom are women, raise more than $100 million a year to support the work of these remarkable entrepreneurial women.

It is a measure of the high regard in which she is held by her disciples that one of them told me that Master Cheng Yen is six feet two inches tall. In fact, she is five feet four and weighs no more than ninety pounds. This fifty-nine-year-old dynamo with deep-set eyes and a powerful gaze is testimony to the revolutionary change ahead as the women of Asia extend their extraordinary energies into economic, political and community life.

It is, in fact, a revolution that has already begun—a quiet, yet powerful revolution.

Though most still live by centuries-old traditions, millions of affluent, professional Asian women will enter the twenty-first century as a force the entire world—not to mention Asian men—must reckon with. Educated and business-minded, they are pioneering new roles in politics, demanding full partnership with men and playing leading parts in the entrepreneurial explosion of the Pacific Rim. A new generation of women, including daughters of well-to-do Chinese Overseas, is taking the reins of the family business or launching family-financed businesses.

Granted, Asia's women leaders are an elite on a continent where wealthy states sit alongside countries still racked with poverty. And there is great disparity in achievement and opportunity between urban and rural women. Still, the patterns that will change the lives of hundreds of millions of Asian women are already in place. First, women are well educated. In Taiwan, for example, women ages twenty to twenty-four match the college graduation rates of their male counterparts diploma for diploma. As any Asian will tell you, education is the first step.

Second, Asian women have made substantial, mostly unrecognized inroads in the workplace. Country by country, all across Asia, the labor force participation rates for women compare favorably with those of Europe. Against the backdrop of widespread structural change, this first generation of Asian women professionals, politicians, company presidents and corporate managers has achieved financial independence comparable with other women worldwide and with their male colleagues. A sample of statistics from across Asia tells the story:

- In Japan, nearly all currency traders are women.
- The number of female managers in Singapore has nearly tripled in the last decade.
- One in five management jobs in Hong Kong is held by a woman.

And yet Asia's quiet, women-led revolution is not simply the story of women managers. It is the story of women farmers and laborers, too. In retrospect, Asia's economic miracle would not have been possible without their participation.

- Korea's industrial base was built by a legion of women working at the repetitive, dead-end and poorly paid jobs in electronics, textile and toy factories.

• Thousands of rural women, predominantly indigenous Malays, migrated to the cities to work in the electronic factories of Malaysia. Over the last decade they have successfully helped the nation make the transition from a largely agricultural-based economy to one that is rapidly industrializing.

• Singapore's early industrial expansion in the manufacturing of electronics was made possible by the thousands of pairs of nimble hands of women in the assembly plants.

Education and financial independence will deliver what Asian women may value most—options. In a part of the world where women's lives have been role-bound for centuries, new options are already emerging. But as ever, new opportunity does not come without challenge. Assuming new roles can be a confusing, exciting and painful process. Yet, for millions of Asian women there is no turning back.

"This is a revolution without marches or manifestos," writes Sally Solo about Japanese women in *Fortune* magazine. "There is little confrontation, because of the nature of the change and the nature of those who are changing. For one thing, it is a revolution based on economic necessity, not ideology."

A Confluence of Circumstances

A confluence of trends and circumstances has accelerated women's entry into Asia's economic life and heightened the enthusiasm with which they embrace these new opportunities. The three critical factors are:

1. *Opportunity.* Asia's exploding economy and the small populations of some Asian powerhouses (Singapore has fewer than 3 million people, Hong Kong 5.5 million, Malaysia 20 million) mean labor shortages and full employment. Business must tap all human resources. Furthermore, many international companies with facilities in Asia are accustomed to hiring women.

2. *Education and Demographics.* Women in Asia possess the educa-

tional qualifications to exploit these new opportunities. They are more educated than their mothers (in some cases more than their male colleagues), entering the workforce, marrying later (if at all) and having fewer children. Many Chinese couples choose to remain childless. In Shanghai, 85 percent of couples prefer a one-child family. In large cities, more than 10 percent of couples are childless, and in 70 percent of these families, women are making the decision.

3. *Technology.* Instant access to global events via international broadcast systems gives Asian women a window on a world that earlier generations could not even fathom. And, in the workplace, the new technology is gender-blind.

"Women in Asia have made far greater inroads into business, partly because the shortage of educated talent has overcome prejudice more rapidly, partly because business families have recognized the value of commercial talent," reports Singapore's *Business Times.* "Thus, in only one generation some Asian countries have created a corps of career women who are upwardly mobile, globally minded, affluent and ambitious. That is no mean feat."

Indeed, one could argue the time frame is more like one decade. Furthermore, it has happened with no coordinated effort, no affirmative action in business or government and no well-organized women's movement. In some countries, women are creating organizations to help other women, but that effort is quite recent and not widespread. In Asia, the feminist movement, for all intents and purposes, is nonexistent.

Still, the trend from male domination to a partnership society in which women take their place beside men in business, academia and politics is evident throughout Asia—and gaining momentum.

Voices of Asian Women

The combined influence of education, technology and rapid economic growth has set the stage for Asian women to become more assertive about their rights and more aggressive in pursuing their ambitions. They are seeking to establish a new order, a fairer, more open and equal social system.

But in Asia, women who speak out risk being accused of "aping the West blindly," as one local newspaper put it. Comments Dr. Kanwaljit Soin, a Nominated MP in Singapore: "When women's groups call for steps to be taken to change attitudes which are lagging behind social and economic realities, policy makers tend to respond by suggesting that these are the shrill cries of a minority of women who are selfishly demanding doctrinaire equality and symmetry for their own ends."

Soin is calling on the government of Goh Chok Tong to create a task force to consider policies that might help balance the dual demands of family and work. Soin laments the strains on Singaporean families, who, she argues, confront "ever higher standards" at school, the office and on the shop floor. "[The issue is not a tussle] between so-called liberated women and men and families," she says, "but it is essential that society reexamine how best adjustments can be made on attitudes and in work conditions that will allow for a better balance between the demands of family life and economic activity."

From property ownership to inheritance rights, from employment to abuse and domestic violence, women are demanding prompt social change. In Malaysia, for example, Minister Datuk Napsiah Omar, a woman, got the country's parliament to pass a domestic violence bill at the eleventh hour, and the Sisters of Islam, a study group of Muslim professionals, called for the creation of a comprehensive gender policy within Muslim culture that takes into account contemporary realities.

Women in Thailand, Taiwan and Hong Kong are beginning to speak out on gender issues. "I always say if females are kept down, you lose half the country," says Charatsri Teepirach, governor of the Thai province of Nakhon Nayok and Thailand's first and only woman provincial governor. "I don't fight for women's liberation, but if we utilize this portion of human resources, we can do things. . . . As a lady, I feel I have to work harder, because I am being watched. If I fail, there will be a good excuse for them [the ministry] not to appoint any more women as governors. So, I have to work hard."

Others argue that women must first look within to find the road to success. "If we want to see advances in the careers of women or their success in business, the woman has to remove these limitations, her self-imposed limitations," says Gloria Tan Climaco, chairman and managing director of SGV & Company, Asia's largest management and accounting firm, and an affiliate of the U.S. accounting firm Arthur Andersen. Such limitations, she argues, may exist because of the tradition: ". . . years of subtle messages that this is what you should do as a good woman, as a good mother, as a good wife. It takes someone to sit down and think through what she wants to do with her life, to figure out whether she wants to remove the limitations."

Women in the Workforce

If the percentage of women in the workforce is any indication, many Asian women have followed her advice. Women are represented in the Asian workforce in percentages that look remarkably like Europe:

Vietnam	47	Taiwan	38
Thailand	46	Hong Kong	37
Indonesia	45	The Philippines	36
China	44	Malaysia	35
Japan	41	Sri Lanka	27
Korea	40	India	24
Singapore	50		

Labor Shortages Spell Opportunity

According to a World Bank study, Indonesia alone will need an estimated 26,000 people to fill midmanagement positions each year. A University of Indonesia Management Institute study concluded that the number of new management jobs created each year in that country was closer to 100,000.

Elsewhere in Asia, the same "problem"—full employment, a result of expansive economic growth—is creating monumental opportunities for women. Companies that might have discriminated against women are in such dire need of talent that they promote without regard for gender—unless, of course, a position is deemed unsuitable for women.

Changing Economic Structure

Asia's rapidly expanding service sector will create greater employment opportunities for women. Taiwan, Singapore and Hong Kong's service sectors already constitute 61, 68 and 77 percent, respectively, of those countries' GNPs. In some countries, women are already dominating in these sectors. For example, in Korea, women hold 60.6 percent of service sector jobs. Japanese women hold 54.9 percent. As one male executive commented to a reporter who was conducting a survey for the magazine *Asian Business:* "You can't afford to ignore 50 percent of your talent."

In Thailand, between 1974 and 1990 the number of female managers grew almost fivefold, compared to a twofold growth in the number of male managers. In Singapore, the majority of women managers, 51 percent, are in commerce. The percentage of women managers in finance, insurance and real estate is around 18 percent, in manufacturing 14 percent, and in community, social and personal services 9 percent.

Indeed, the growth of women managers in Singapore is a dramatic story. Over the past ten years their numbers have increased from 8,644 to 22,580. Some 62 percent of female managers are between twenty and thirty-nine years of age; the percentage of male managers in that age group is 47 percent.

In Malaysia, women have been successful in human resources and personnel management, public relations, job training and education. Few hold positions in engineering and law. Similarly, in Taiwan, women hold managerial positions predominantly in personnel, advertising, mass media or research and development.

While professional women in Singapore, Taiwan and Hong Kong participate in Asia's financial and trading sectors, thousands of well-educated Filipino women took over the management of their households and care for their young and old. Hundreds of thousands of Filipino women work as maids in the affluent urban centers of Asia.

High Achievers/High Finance

Against all cultural norms, Asian men are slowly accepting the presence of women at work. At least women are honest, they rationalize. But it also appears that women's traditional role as family money managers has opened doors to them in the global world of high finance. In any event, that is an area where Asian women have achieved marked success.

Elizabeth Sam, senior executive vice president with Overseas Chinese Banking Corporation Ltd. (OCBC), directs the bank's investment banking and treasury division, managing the investments of the bank, its subsidiaries and customers, as well as directing investment banking, the stock market, and the provision of nominee and trustee services and treasury operations. A former chief manager of the Monetary Authority of Singapore and a main board director of Mercantile House Holdings PLC, a UK-listed company, Sam joined OCBC in 1988. She is chairman of the Singapore International Monetary Exchange Ltd.

Rosario N. Lopez held the position of chairman of the Philippines Securities and Exchange Commission, for which she had previously served as chief legal counsel.

Chin Ean Wah, a Chinese-Malaysian educated in Singapore, runs the Morgan Stanley Institutional Fund, Inc.–Asian Equity Portfolio, which realized a stunning 106 percent return in 1993. Chin is successful, she says, because she and her four associates visit three hundred to four hundred companies a year. "In Asia, far more than elsewhere, the company is synonymous with the man behind it, usually an entrepreneurial founder. We need to know his motives, connections, and how he treats shareholders."

Two other Asian women at the pinnacle of success in high finance are Naoko Takemura, associate director of asset management at Nomura Trust, who is responsible for Nomura's Japan Fund, Asia Fund and Asian Emerging Market Funds; and Chok Kwee Bee, the senior general manager at Arab Malaysian Merchant Bank. Chok oversees the bank's activities regarding listing of Malaysian companies and mergers and acquisitions.

Throughout Asia women dominate the world of fund management

and currency trading. In fact, in Japan, almost all currency traders are women. One explanation for this phenomenon is that women are better at foreign languages than men—a key skill when dealing with international monetary markets. Or maybe women are just better at managing money.

An article published in the *Far Eastern Economic Review* entitled "Where to Put Your Money," featured a "How the Experts See It" column. Three of the five experts quoted were women: Diahann Brown, senior fund manager at Thornton Management (Asia); Winnie Lee, director at Aetna Investment Management; and Elizabeth Tran, chief investment officer for Asia at IDS Fund Management.

Asia's Dual Income and High Savings Rate

In Asia's rapidly growing young families, women's income is needed to supplement the household income in order to cope with the rising cost of living, both in the acquisition of consumer and luxury goods and the high cost of education and retirement.

Although discrimination between sexes in payment of wages is banned in most Asian countries, in Japan the average wages of women account for only about 60 percent of those of men—even among full-time employees. So the wage gap is not just a women's issue but a family issue, and demands for pay equity can be expected to rise.

Furthermore, Asia's high savings rates were in part due to women having control of the family's purse strings. Most Japanese men turned over a big proportion, if not all their salaries, to their wives. This is also widely practiced among Chinese and Muslim families.

Up Against the Glass Ceiling?

Dr. Irene H.S. Chow, a senior lecturer in the Department of Organization and Management at the Chinese University of Hong Kong, reports that in Hong Kong one in five managerial positions is held by a woman. Yet her research also showed that while men and women say they respect the skills of female managers, they would still prefer to be managed by a male. Presenting a research paper at the Conference of Women in Management held at the university, Chow concluded that women in Japan and South Korea lag far behind women in Hong Kong, Singapore and the West, but that all women face barriers when attempting to reach the boardroom.

In 1994, China honored seven women who overcame enormous obstacles, not the least of which was prejudice, to achieve positions as chief executive officers. Yet, when the session of the local Shenyang People's Congress nominated Zhang Furong as a candidate for the thirty-seven-seat standing committee, the protests were loud and vigorous.

"Some people questioned my qualifications, asking why the congress should need a female entrepreneur as a member of the standing committee when there are so many male CEOs in industry and business," says Zhang. But she didn't flinch. She stood her ground and won the seat, noting in an interview: "There are still very few women who have reached the top of the business, industrial as well as political echelon. I have only one or two women colleagues whenever there is a gathering of business and industrial CEOs in the city."

For many women, the struggle for respect and responsibility isn't worth the energy. They would rather stake their own claim in the business world. Entrepreneurship is flourishing among women in Asia.

The Long March to Equality

To appreciate how far Asian women have moved toward equality—and how far they have to go—one must understand the Confucian-like ethos present throughout Asia, even in non-Confucian societies. Developed from ancient religious practices, the Confucian rule of life relied on rites, family, social attitudes and hierarchy to impose and maintain order. Controlling one's feelings, for example, is considered necessary and desirable to achieve moral serenity.

Within the Confucian social order, men and women have defined places and roles for the purpose of achieving harmony—yin and yang. Males are strong and aggressive (yang); women, passive and nurturing (yin). And from the Asian perspective, being subservient is not necessarily undesirable. In the Confucian system, women are to be revered. Children are taught to be filial to their mothers. Daughters-in-law are told to respect their mothers-in-law (who, in many cases, are the most powerful person in the household), and in traditional polygamous Confucian families the first wife enjoys prestige and enormous power over subsequent wives. In exchange for total submission, women are promised lifelong care. First they are looked after by their fathers, later, by their husbands or brothers.

These norms, stitched into the very fabric of Asian society, will not change easily. Asian society believes that while there should be mutual respect between husband and wife, nonetheless, the husband sings and the wife accompanies. Though revered, women remain subordinate to men and are expected to live according to the three rules of obedience and the four virtues *(sān cóng sì dé)* for women's right living. While at home, daughters submit to their fathers *(zài jiā cóng fù)*, once married they submit to their husbands *(chū jià cóng fú)* and in old age to their sons *(lǎo lái cóng zǐ)*. The virtues include the codes on good morals *(fù dé)*, right speech *(fù yèn)*, appropriate work *(fù gōng)* and proper looks and attire *(fù róng)*. Confucius also opined that "a woman without talent is a virtuous woman."

In their excellent book, *China Wakes,* Nicholas Kristof and Sheryl WuDunn note that for thousands of years, girls had to bind their feet, remain illiterate and try to survive with no identity or dignity of their own. When Mao Zedong declared that "Women hold up half the sky" the Communist Party decreed a number of changes to improve their status. "The party outlawed prostitution, child marriages, the use of concubines and the sale of brides." Women's organizations were formed, and an official policy of respect and equal treatment of women was instituted. "The party encouraged women to join its ranks, to become officials, to run factories and to do things they had never done before." China witnessed a dramatic increase in the number of women participating in the industrial force, from 600,000 in 1949 to more than 50 million today.

After Deng Xiaoping's economic reforms, women were given greater economic opportunities, but not without discrimination and abuse. Millions of women now work, churning out electronics, shoes, apparel, toys and all kinds of labor-intensive consumer products in congested, dirty factories.

As women grow more independent, more active in society, more influential in their communities, a new ethos will take the place of ancient traditions. Meanwhile, certainty reigns. Still, women are in the workforce. They are more and more visible and vocal in local and national politics. And in the future their numbers will increase.

A Women-Led Entrepreneurial Explosion

"The greatest concentration of entrepreneurial talent the world has ever seen is dispersing throughout the Pacific Basin, and establishing the most extraordinary commercial network in history," said Paul Meo, chief of the World Bank's international trade division, at the beginning of the decade. Today, the world is feeling the impact of that entrepreneurial explosion in Asia and discovering that women are a critical part of its driving force.

Five out of six new businesses in Japan are created by women. They own some 2.5 million businesses, most of them with fewer than five employees. And while women managers are still rare in big companies, women are starting and managing small and midsize firms in increasing numbers:

- In Singapore, 38 percent of women managers own their own firms, and about 20 percent of business owners are women.
- In China, women make up one-third of the self-employed. A new program has now been designed to integrate women business owners into the modernization process.
- In Indonesia, women, in particular those in the powerful Javanese ethnic group, have traditionally been active in the labor force and made family decisions. In Jakarta, a growing number of women are opting for entrepreneurism.
- In the Malaysian state of Kelantan, women are generally the breadwinners. They own most small and midsize businesses in the community.

• In Thailand, women-owned businesses are concentrated in agriculture, services, retail and manufacturing.

• In Singapore, most, but not all, women-owned businesses are in fashion, food, travel or employment. Throughout the region women own highly successful businesses in many economic sectors.

The Trend Setters

Thailand-based Dusit Thani Group, the country's leading hotel chain, ranked in the top hundred best-managed businesses by *Asiamoney* magazine, was founded and is managed by Chanut Piyaoui, who serves as chairperson. Chanut launched the business in 1970 with no family resources to draw on. She mortgaged her home and sold her jewelry. Today, her international corporation has 63 hotels in 17 countries. She was honored with the title Khunying, awarded to women of outstanding achievement by the King of Thailand. Chanut simply says of her success, "I wanted a hotel like the ones I stayed at in America."

Another successful entrepreneur in a nontraditional business is Mutiara Djokosoetono. After graduating from law school, she pursued a successful career in academics for twelve years. Left with three children after the death of her husband, she turned two rented cars into a taxi company at a time when such vehicles were scarce in Jakarta. Today, she is president director of the Blue Bird Group, the largest taxi company in Indonesia with a fleet of over three thousand vehicles operating in Java, Bali and Sumatra.

Western China is home to Rabiya Kadir, an ethnic Uighur Muslim who lives in Urumqi, the capital of Xinjiang Province. When Deng Xiaoping began his economic reforms in 1978, Kadir was a housewife with an unquenchable entrepreneurial spirit. Beginning with the equivalent of $10, she bought and sold textiles, clothes and food to local residents. In 1982 she invested her profits in a small shop that, in the next decade, she parlayed into Arkida Industry & Trade, a huge complex of trading and manufacturing interests. Its profits quadrupled between 1992 and 1993. Kadir's personal net worth is an estimated $15 million. "I am just an entrepreneur," she says modestly. "I concentrate on making money and how I can contribute to the economy of Xinjiang Province."

Independence Through Entrepreneurism

Throughout Asia thousands of women, full of ambition and energy, are starting new businesses in record numbers. Explains Singapore's Claire Chiang, human resource director of the Wah Chang Group and former president of the Association of Women for Action and Research, "There is nothing like being on your own. I think women will increasingly feel the need to control their life situations, finances and their time. We want it all, work and family. We can have it especially through entrepreneurship." Chiang sees the entrepreneurial explosion among women as a reaction to on-the-job discrimination and the glass ceiling. She is an entrepreneur herself and one of the first two women to be elected to the Council of the Singapore Chinese Chamber of Commerce.

Kuala Lumpur's Khatijah Ahmad realized she had hit the glass ceiling at age thirty while managing a department of 2,500 at a semi-governmental enterprise. "I could see I would always be No. 2." So, she negotiated a sixty-forty venture with international money broker Atley & Pearce. Khatijah offered better deposit and loan rates than local banks and turned a profit after just three months. Now her KAF Group, a multi-services finance house, which is listed on the Kuala Lumpur Stock Exchange, turns in $2.3 billion a year and has five hundred employees. Market capitalization is $243 million.

Of her extraordinary success Khatijah says, "You agonize for a short period of time, then you take the plunge. After that first decision, I just took one step at a time." Her timing was also flawless, as the Malaysian government was deregulating the financial markets and creating unprecedented opportunities.

Women in Fashion

Joyce Ma is credited with single-handedly creating an international fashion market for Hong Kong. Born in China, Ma moved with her family to Hong Kong in the early 1950s. In 1969, recognizing a dearth of designer outlets for the increasingly fashion-conscious Asian women, she launched Joyce Boutique Holdings. Today, the company has twenty-seven Hong Kong outlets, several stores in Taiwan, two in Manila and plans to expand throughout Southeast Asia. Ma recently spent $7 million to refurbish and expand the Joyce Boutique in the Kowloon Regent Hotel. There are more than 27,000 Joyce credit-card holders, and company revenues doubled in the last two years. Says Ma of her success: "What I've tried to do is create a space in which human beings, not shoppers, are free to dream."

Hanae Mori is described as "the first Japanese designer to break into the international fashion scene . . . the doyenne of the industry." She opened her first shop in central Tokyo in 1951 and had her first show in New York in 1965. By 1977, she had become the first Asian given membership in the exclusive Chambre Syndicale de la Couture Parisienne, whose members include Yves St. Laurent and Christian Dior. She also was awarded the Order of Merit, considered "Japan's highest cultural honor." And she enjoyed the honor of designing the bridal dress for Crown Princess Masako Owada. Mori now presides over an empire worth more than $450 million, with more than seventy stores worldwide. She is considered one of Japan's most successful businesswomen.

Martha Tilaar has spent twenty years developing a line of cosmetics that blends traditional Indonesian mixtures and treatments with products discovered in her travels around the world. Comments Tilaar, "I had always thought that everything from the West was the best, so it was a great shock to me . . . [when people] told me to go back to my own country, study my own culture and develop my own beauty products. It changed my behavior and my way of thinking. It told me that I had to be myself, that I had to be an Indonesian." Her cosmetics business is now a multimillion-dollar operation.

Media

"The power of women can especially be seen in the media," says Diane Ying, who along with two colleagues started the economic monthly *Commonwealth* in the early 1980s. Today, the Chinese-language periodical is Taiwan's number-one financial and economic magazine, and is regarded as the "beacon" for the business community. The magazine attracts more advertising dollars than any other monthly magazine in the country. Ying is the only woman to sit on the National Unification Commission, which advises the president on policies toward the Chinese mainland. Taiwan's two largest newspaper groups, the United Daily News Group and China Times Group, are also managed by women.

Hong Kong's Sally Aw Sian runs a flourishing newspaper empire. Her group controls Hong Kong's third most popular Chinese paper, *Tin Tin Daily News,* and the English-language *Hong Kong Standard,* along with the flagship Chinese-language dailies: the morning *Sing Tao Jih Pao* and the evening *Sing Tao Wan Pao.* She is also a world leader in newspaper publishing for Chinese communities in North America and Europe.

Women Excel in Science and Technology

It is not just in "women-friendly" enterprises that Asian women excel. Dr. Choo Yuen May, for example, is the senior research officer for the Palm Oil Research Institute of Malaysia and is a recipient of the World Intellectual Properties Gold Medal for best woman inventor. Dr. May graduated from Waikato University, New Zealand, with bachelor of science and master of science degrees, and received her Ph.D. from the Malaysia Institute of Chemistry. A winner of numerous awards, she has 143 publications to her name and holds twelve patents.

Pearleen Chan is the managing director of Singapore Network Service Pte Ltd., which she founded in 1988 to implement the first nationwide trading network, Tradenet, through which she introduced Electronic Data Interchange Technology to Singapore. Throughout Chan's twenty-year career in information technology she has been an integral player in the development of the country's state-of-the-art telecommunications infrastructure, widely reported to be the most sophisticated network anywhere in the world.

Chan also played an active role directing the computerization of the civil service at the Ministry of Finance and National Computer Board (NCB). She is chairperson of both the Asia EDIFACT Board and the national IT Standards Committee, and is a board member of the Information Technology Institute/Institute of Systems Science Common Management Board.

Spearheading the development of high-tech industries in China is Dr. Yu Ching Yu, president of Asia Simulation & Control System Engineering Ltd. Sent to the United States by China to learn simulation and control technology, Yu now heads a team of two hundred engineers and scientists in a design and simulation engineering company based in the southeast city of Zhuhai. Her factory is a "showcase" for the progress China has made in technology development and is a frequent tour destination for visiting dignitaries, including Deng Xiaoping, Li Peng and Senior Minister Lee Kuan Yew.

Women Transforming Politics

In Asia's future, many of those visiting dignitaries may be women. "If we want to bring about major change, we have no choice but to get into politics," says D. Rounnag Jahn, a Bangladeshi political scientist at Columbia University. "And while it is in our interest to join politics, it is also true that women are better equipped to transform politics."

Some would disagree, but no one can deny that women are moving rapidly into the political arena.

- In China women make up 21 percent of the parliament.
- In Taiwan the government reserves about 10 percent of its locally elected seats for women.
- In Bangladesh, Hong Kong, India and the Philippines women make up 10 percent or more of the legislatures.

Three legislative councillors in Hong Kong, Anna Wu, Christine Loh and Emily Lau—called ACE by the media (for their initials)—represent a new phenomenon: women as "professional politicians." They are "leading challenges to the sacred cows of Chinese and colonial tradition . . . giving gender issues a broader airing and helping dispel the still-strong notion that politics is an art best left to males."

Hong Kong is a bellwether for political change in Asia, and these three women are leading the charge. Christine Loh pressed for changes in rural inheritance laws, and in 1994 the government repealed the law barring women from inheriting rural property. Anna Wu came to office in 1991. Early on her agenda was pressing Hong Kong to sign the United Nations Convention to Eliminate All Forms of Discrimination Against Women. Now she is challenging the government to set up a commission on human rights. Meanwhile, former journalist Emily Lau is the only directly elected female in Legco. (The rest are appointed.) She called for a ruling to open all of Legco's sixty seats to popular election. That initiative lost by only one vote.

All of Asia is being "politicized" and throughout the region women are making inroads. Even in staid, conservative Japan, women are taking their place beside men in the political arena. Takako Doi, former chairperson of the Social Democratic Party of Japan, is the first woman speaker of the lower house of Japan's Diet. "There was the general perception that female candidates could be used like equipment to gather votes," says Doi about women previously appointed to office. But now, the number of women elected to the lower house is increasing steadily.

"The most politically active and passionate among Asian women are perhaps to be found in the Philippines," notes *Asiaweek.* A woman became president in 1986. Though she reluctantly came to power after the assassination of her husband, President Corazon Aquino gave women more prominence in her administration than in previous ones. In the May election of 1995, women had a strong showing. Gloria Macapagal Arroyo topped the elections to the powerful Senate, the first woman to do so. She is considered a serious contender for president or vice president in the next election. Three other women were also elected to the senate in 1995, as were 19 to the 215-seat House of Representatives.

Miriam Defensor Santiago came close to winning the presidency of the Philippines in 1992. A former judge and head of immigration with a reputation as a corruption-buster, she is tooling up to compete again in the next presidential contest.

There is a growing awareness of the value of having women in positions of political power. Some key leaders are actively encouraging women to get involved in Thailand, for example. Khunying Supatra Masdit, who at the age of twenty-nine was the youngest person ever elected to the Parliament, after four terms decided not to run again, but to turn her attention instead to encouraging and helping women win political office. To achieve her goals, she founded the nonprofit Center for Asia-Pacific Women in Politics. Based in Manila, its purpose is to "give information and training to women on how to get elected, how to govern, how to make policies, build constituencies, and maintain a political base. We also support women who are already in office." Masdit was the convener of the Women's Forum at the United Nations Conference on Women held in Beijing in September 1995.

Focus on "Soft Issues"

"My government and I will continue our quest for peace," says Chandrika Bandaranaike Kumaratunga, Sri Lanka's first female president. She has vowed to end the civil war with the Tamil separatist rebels. Chandrika follows in the footsteps of her mother, Sirimavo Bandaranaike, who became the world's first female prime minister after the assassination of her husband, Solomon Bandaranaike.

Bangladesh's former prime minister, Khaleda Zia, widow of President Ziaur Rahman, who was assassinated in 1981, worked on increasing education and vocational training, particularly for girls. She also set up no-collateral loans to enable women to pursue business opportunities. Sheikh Hasina Wajed won the 1996 election.

Women in Government and Civil Service

In China, women faced tremendous difficulties in getting to the center of power. They are now in the top leadership, though in very small numbers. According to a government white paper published in 1994, there are sixteen deputy and full ministers in government. Eighteen women are serving as provincial governors and deputy governors. In China's 517 cities, there are 317 female mayors and vice mayors. Twenty-one percent of the representatives in the People's Congress are women. Women now hold jobs in more than half of China's township administrations, achieving the goal set by participants at a 1990 conference on the empowerment of women. Beijing now has eighty-six women in the executive and People's Congress—up 56.4 percent since the previous session. Women hold positions of influence in 88 percent of Beijing's districts.

Clearly, women in China are more actively involved in government than at any time in history. A few, like Wu Yi, minister of foreign trade and economic development, often called the "part Dragon Lady," have risen to national prominence. Wu is the only woman cabinet minister in the male-dominated People's Republic of China. She played a key role sorting out tariffs, trade barriers, copyright laws and the complex process China must complete in order to rejoin the world's international trade organizations. Her stately manner and dignified air attracts notice wherever she goes. She is frequently mobbed by fans requesting her autograph. A legend in her own time, she is said to have spurned the advances of Yang Shankun, then China's president, by stating that she was "far too humble to accept such an exalted position."

Wu made a sensational debut in her first confrontation with U.S. trade delegates. When a peeved American counterpart supposedly exclaimed, "We are negotiating with thieves!" she calmly replied, "And we are negotiating with robbers. Look at your museums. Do you have any idea how many of the items were looted from China?" In charge of $200 billion in Chinese foreign trade, she has wooed and won negotiators from around the globe.

Women are becoming more visible elsewhere in the region.

• Charatsri Teepirach, a provincial governor in Thailand, mentioned earlier, is an architect by trade. She comes from a position as director general of the Interior Ministry's Town and Country Planning Department.

• Anson Chan, who serves as the chief secretary of the Hong Kong government, is the territory's highest-ranking civil servant. She is considered to be in the running to head Hong Kong after the 1997 takeover.

• Malaysia's minister for international trade and industry, Rafidah Aziz, has been enormously successful in promoting foreign investment.

• In Singapore, Dr. Chan Heng Chee, a former ambassador to the United Nations, went on to head Singapore's Institute of Southeast Asian Studies, a think tank that specializes in research on political and economic affairs. She is now Singapore's ambassador to the United States.

Opportunity for advancement will increase as legions of women assume responsibility for government programs at every level. In Pakistan, for example, Prime Minister Benazir Bhutto, now in her second administration, is implementing "women-friendly" policies. She appointed Khalida Rashid Peshawar High Court Judge. Sindh's Majida Rizvi, also appointed by Bhutto, was the first woman provincial judge. That should change soon, however; henceforth 10 percent of government jobs are supposed to be held by women.

Karma, Gender Imbalance and Techno Time Bombs

Asia's historic preference for male offspring and the horrific practice of female infanticide, still practiced in rural Asia, especially China and India, are extracting a sort of karmic retribution in the form of gender imbalance, which has the potential of creating endless social problems. With the arrival of the ultrasound scanner and the strict enforcement of the one-child policy, many Chinese couples abort a female fetus so that they can later try for a son. Because of this widespread practice, it is estimated that by the end of the century China will have some 70 million bachelors destined not to marry.

South Korea's demographic profile is even more unsettling. Kim Min Kyong, head of the National Statistical Office's population statistics section, says that "By 2010, for every 100 girls, 130 boys will reach the marrying age. Some 30 percent more unmarried men than women."

In India, there are already just 929 women for every thousand men. Realizing the seriousness of this gender imbalance, governments are banning "technical means" of determining a child's sex and advising people to let nature take its course. The gender imbalance is sure to shake up age-old assumptions about women, marriage and family. Already India's social activists have been pushing the government to work toward uplifting the status of women. In rural India, where three quarters of the country's 940 million people live, government studies have documented parents' neglect of their daughters.

Elsewhere in the region, as communities become more modernized, cultural and economic imperatives to bear sons seem to have subsided with increased prosperity and any gender imbalance is what nature intended. "That may soon happen in China, India and Korea. But if it doesn't, these societies will learn the hard way that it doesn't pay to fool with Mother Nature," opines *Asiaweek*.

An Ounce of Prevention

Thailand's Charatsri Teepirach, governor of Nakhon Nayok Province, hopes education will help wipe out child prostitution in the province. "If they have higher education there will not be many prostitutes out here," she argues. She visits known haunts of child prostitutes to encourage them to go to school and sends doctors to educate girls about the dangers of AIDS and other sexually transmitted diseases.

In Asia, where the sex trade is big business, young girls are often kidnapped, even sold into prostitution by their families. But education *is* a way out. "Girls who go on to secondary school have a 99 percent chance of staying away from prostitution," says Mechai Viravaidya, chairman of the Population and Community Development Association.

Some 90 percent of Asian prostitutes have a sixth-grade education or less; more than half never completed fifth grade, reports Chakrapand Wongburanavart, dean of social sciences at Chiang Mai University and director of Thai Women of Tomorrow. If girls stay in school beyond the sixth grade, he argues, "they will likely continue their education and . . . reject the idea of becoming prostitutes. Then they can be trained for other jobs."

Thai Women of Tomorrow has already given a thousand scholarships of $120 each to high-risk sixth-grade girls in Pha Yao and Chiang Rai provinces. Half the money comes from U.S. foreign aid, half from private donations. The girls study to be secretaries, dressmakers and health-care assistants.

According to Amihan Abueva, head of the Manila-based Salinlahi Foundation, a child-welfare organization, "In Thailand, the Philippines, Sri Lanka and Taiwan there are around 200,000 [child prostitutes]." And that's considered a conservative number. "If you include India, Bangladesh, [and] Pakistan, the number can easily reach more than 1 million in Asia. Recently, child prostitution has spread to Cambodia, Vietnam and Korea." The foundation is part of the nineteen-country network End Child Prostitution in Asian Tourism organization (ECPAT). It is ECPAT's goal to make people aware of child prostitution and to force governments to take action against it, including making available educational opportunities.

Harnessing the Energy

Increasingly, entrepreneurship is seen as one way to lift women and children out of poverty. A new breed of financial institution is harnessing and directing that entrepreneurial energy to address the pressing issues created by poverty. A main goal of the Friends of Women's World Banking Association of Thailand is to encourage and support women in business. It offers information on starting and managing small businesses and guarantees the loans women take out to finance their self-employment activities.

Similarly, the Dhaka-based Grameen Bank in Bangladesh lends money to individuals to help them help themselves. Started in 1976, the bank has loaned around $1 billion to 2 million families. The repayment rate is an incredible 98 percent. Most borrowers are women. The bank now has 1,042 branches and 11,000 employees serving half of Bangladesh's 68,000 villages.

State-owned companies in Indonesia donate 1 to 5 percent of profits to a fund the Young Indonesian Pribumi Business Association helps manage. The fund provides money and training to small-business owners. Additionally, Indonesian banks are required to set aside a fifth of their funds for small businesses.

Lastly, India's Self-Employed Women's Association (SEWA) offers credit to poor, self-employed women working as weavers, garment workers, embroiderers and domestics. The SEWA bank has about $1 million in working capital, which comes from its 46,000 members. Repayment rates from women borrowers are 96 percent. Other banks wish they could claim such stellar repayment rates. Throughout Asia women have demonstrated that given the opportunity, they can accomplish whatever they set out to do.

Education as Equalizer

If knowledge is power, then education is the great equalizer. In Asia where literacy rates are high, women increasingly pursue higher levels of academic achievement. "The real hope for women lies in education," says Chua Jui Meng, minister of health in Malaysia. When women and men both continue their education, she argues, "We have achieved parity."

In Asia, women's education levels have improved dramatically in the past decade. In some countries, they achieve higher levels of education than men. And, as a result, they are increasingly well prepared to assume positions of authority in politics, business and society.

Singapore government statistics demonstrate that women's participation in the labor force increases with education and is substantially higher for women with secondary education. In 1991 more than 80 percent of women with university educations were active in the labor force. What's more, these women are usually "better educated than their male counterparts." About 60 percent of working women have at least a secondary education; the comparable statistic for men is 48 percent.

In Thailand, as in most countries, education is the single most important route for women's advancement into managerial positions. As early as 1990, the number of female students at the college level exceeded that of men.

In Hong Kong, more and more women are studying management. In

1991, for example, women made up half the graduates in the full-time undergraduate business program at the City Polytechnic of Hong Kong —and 75 percent of the graduates in international business. Furthermore, in 1990 women made up 38 percent of the students earning business degrees from Hong Kong Baptist College. The number of women studying business administration at the Chinese University of Hong Kong jumped from 5 percent in 1979 to 11 percent in 1989.

In Taiwan, 10.4 percent of women and 10.5 percent of men between the ages of twenty and twenty-four years were either "in or had completed four-year universities and colleges" in 1992. Taiwanese parents place tremendous importance on education. In some ways, women college graduates have an edge over their male peers. Men must serve two years of military duty after school, whereas women can go right into a job. And by the time their cohorts return to the labor force, they are already more advanced in their careers.

Women Breaking New Ground in Asia

In Malaysia, the percentage of women in technical studies jumped from 4 to 36 percent between 1970 and 1990. Female undergrads make up 50 percent of physical science students at the Universiti Malaya (UM), Universiti Sains Malaysia (USM) and the Universiti Pertanian Malaysia (UPM). On the postgraduate level women make up 60 percent of the students at UM and UPM. A training program in the Philippines teaches women nontraditional skills like carpentry, welding and masonry.

In Tujia autonomous county of Shizhu in southwest China, in the area of the Three Gorges Dam, Li Shuqing is raising rabbits using modern farming techniques. In 1994 she earned 20,000 yuan ($2,366) selling rabbit fur—a handsome sum anywhere in China, but particularly in rural areas. Some 100,000 women in the country have already learned similar techniques. Many women now contribute to family finances and win leadership positions in their communities.

In Indonesia, a largely female Environmental Bamboo Foundation (EBF) led by designer Linda Garland is pioneering a global movement to create an industry using bamboo as a wood substitute for products ranging from spectacular "hardwood" floors to water filters, construction materials, musical instruments, pharmaceuticals and food. Bamboo's use as an environmental resource for eco-tourism and sustainable business is now being integrated into the policies of several Indonesian ministries, an example of a bottom-up, grassroots movement eventually taking hold at the highest levels of government.

Education is the "alternative to being bound, ignorant, and kept in a 'golden cage' through early arranged marriages," said the Javanese noblewoman Raden Adjeng Kartini, who spent her life expanding women's chances for education. She is remembered throughout Indonesia every year on "Kartini Day," which "celebrates the progress women have made over the past century."

A Tale of Two Worlds

In the wake of rapid social change, the emergence of women is a trend many Asians (both men and some women) may view as undesirable. Asians value family, and in the past, by having women stay at home, the twin tasks of bringing up children and caring for the old were taken care of. With women's emergence, child-rearing is viewed as a shared responsibility. Motherhood gives way to parenthood. This is new, and is making many men uncomfortable, undermining traditions and changing the roles of the sexes. But whatever people think, women will continue to question cultural traditions as they search for new roles that work for them.

At Asia's first regional conference for women managers and entrepreneurs held in December 1994 in Kuala Lumpur, a woman in the audience, in her late twenties, who was dressed in the traditional Muslim veil and long-sleeved, ankle-length clothing, congratulated the speakers for their success and said that she was encouraged and inspired by them. But she also shared her predicament with the group: Her husband, she insisted, "would be uncomfortable" if she were to raise her profile. She asked if women have to be high-profile in order to succeed. And, she commented to the audience, "I find that it's better for me to work behind the scenes to avoid scenes at home."

In such simple words are spoken volumes about the varying degrees of progress women have made, and the pressing, but difficult challenge to change social norms and cultural traditions that still stand in their way. Although Asian women have made greater progress in less time than women in any other area, it has occurred more out of economic necessity than out of any will of the masses to make it so.

One manager, a Malaysian woman, dismissed the need for affirmative action. "Look at the Malaysian women," she said. "They are in that enviable position where they work hand in hand with men in the development of Malaysia. Why? Because there are not that many Malaysians. There are only 18 million Malaysians. So, every person counts."

Demographics helps, no doubt about that, but as one journalist puts it in *Asiaweek*, "Abuses and discrimination against women [still] exist in Muslim communities. These have their own unique laws and regulations to protect females and nurture their lives . . . [but] safeguards don't always work. . . . Many women don't know they have a right to divorce their husbands and think Islam permits their spouses to beat them. And a great number regard a role beyond wife and mother as unthinkable."

Similarly, in rural China and India, where more than 2 billion people live, "The rhythm of birth, life and death has changed little from when Confucius and Buddha walked the earth. Farmers with no income other than what they harvest rely on strong sons to help work the land —and support them after they have hung up their hoes. If a son is born, a daughter is a burden. She is less productive in the fields during her youth—and after her marriage guarantees only her in-laws' comfort. In India's predominantly Hindu society, a daughter is 'outside wealth' that is handed over to a husband, usually with a hefty dowry payment. For some, too many daughters can literally lead to bankruptcy."

This is the tale of two worlds for women in Asia. There is still the very real world of arranged marriages at an early age, of women as chattel, or "outside" wealth and of bride burnings and child prostitution. In the other world live women who are college-educated and as prepared as their male counterparts to take advantage of exploding economic opportunities. These are the women who are marrying later, if at all, and having fewer children, if any.

Women in Transition: Changing Mindset

There is a dramatic shift in mindset, especially among young Asian women. Their assertiveness is expressed in leading a totally new and revolutionary lifestyle that Asia's rapidly changing society is learning to adjust and respond to. Among the changing trends are:

- *Marriage:* from *When?* to *Why?*
- *Choice of Partner:* from *The man chosen by the family* to *My own choice.*
- *Children:* from *How many?* to *Why have children?*
- *Relationships:* from *Husband and family first and always* to *What about me?*
- *Options:* from *No to marriage* to *Yes to motherhood.*

The evidence of these changing lifestyles is to be seen everywhere. In Japan, women are abandoning the old aspirations of getting married as soon as possible and embracing a new indifference. The social stigma attached to being single, especially for those in their twenties, is much weaker now. At the beginning of 1990, more than half of the women in Tokyo between twenty-five and twenty-nine were unmarried. Japan now competes with Sweden for having the oldest median age for first-time marriages, twenty-seven for women and thirty for men.

Women are having children later and some, not at all. Increasingly, childbearing is perceived as a burden. Birthrates in Korea and Japan have dropped to among the lowest in the world: fewer than 1.54 children for women of childbearing age in Japan and 1.7 in Korea.

Women are initiating divorces everywhere in Asia. Between 1979 and 1990 divorce rates doubled in China, and they jumped another 300 percent between 1991 and 1994, mostly among intellectual women. In

Japan, Taiwan, Singapore and even conservative Kuala Lumpur, many women are ending marriages and exploring new options.

In Singapore, so concerned were the authorities about the large number of unmarried professional women that a new department called Social Development was created to play cupid, developing ways to persuade women to marry and creating opportunities to meet potential partners (including love boat cruises and weekend barbecues).

Some women are deciding on motherhood without fathers, risking social displeasure. Unmarried mothers are on the rise in Asia.

Becoming Your Own Role Model

Given the rapid pace of social change, coupled with society's own coming to grips with the new realities, a new social order will finally emerge in Asia. Taiwanese author Liou Fey Ying perhaps put it best: "Women only managed to shake off centuries-old bondage in recent decades. There are now role models for the women of the future. Everyone can become a pioneer. There is a wide spectrum of possibilities: becoming an entrepreneur, a professional manager, a wife and social activist. The time has come for a thousand flowers to bloom."

Women-Driven Economics

The average male reader—Western or Oriental—might greet the emergence of Asian women with a skeptical response: a trend, perhaps, but a megatrend? Surely not. I believe such a reaction rates somewhere between ignorance and pure folly. No businessman can afford to ignore the economic implications of the emergence of Asia's hundreds of millions of women consumers, entrepreneurs, community leaders and voters.

Time is money, as the saying goes, and in years past Asia achieved astronomical savings rates because nonworking housewives "made" money by transforming their time into bankable savings. Nonconsumers to the core, they spent their days comparison shopping, avoiding expensive clothing and luxury items, and banked their husbands' salaries. Their daughters are a different breed. The Japanese secretaries with $1,000 Chanel bags and Hermès scarves are legion now.

But of greater structural importance is the simple fact that working women must shell out for transportation, lunch, the baby-sitter—and a working wardrobe. The banker's nightmare is a marketing man's dream. Such is the "progress" of civilization, the "lifestyle" of a maturing economy. In a couple of years those male economists who were blind to the emergence of Asian women will scratch their graying heads, pondering the steady drop in Asia's savings rates—and the power of Asian women as consumers.

A few numbers. Of the 9.9 million women in Taiwan, 4.35 million have full-time careers. There are 5 million households in Taiwan; the woman in each of them commands a disposable income or spending power of $25,000, for a total of $125 billion. Women have control of the family purse; it is they who wield the real economic power. This pattern is the same elsewhere in urban Asia. Marketers the world over will put themselves at risk if they do not start taking a real interest in Asian women. Asian governments know full well that women voters can tilt the balance of power at the ballot box and completely alter the course of their political fortunes, and women are increasingly becoming the target of their campaigns. Asian women will alter the balance of political power and dominate the marketplace as well.

Many American businesswomen have been hesitant to bring their talents to a male-dominated Asia (not to mention the shortsighted companies that ban women from jobs in Asia). But Asia in the twenty-first century will find leadership in its own women and they, in turn, will find partnerships with women in the West, moving toward a global critical mass. Fast-changing societies cannot afford to leave half their talent behind.

The emergence of women will not have to be at the expense of men. Labor shortages—especially for educated labor—will abound in Asia for the foreseeable future. As women gain greater access to educational opportunities, their talents will contribute to the development of new legal systems, new economic systems and a new social infrastructure. But Asian women will find their own way, blending religious commitments and cultural traditions and family obligations with new work styles and economic and political leadership. They will redefine feminism the "Asian way," providing an additional dimension to the richness of ways to improve our common humanity.

CHAPTER EIGHT

From West to East

Most Asian businesspeople in international commerce adopted an English name to accommodate Westerners—Stan Shih, Ronnie Chan, Jimmy Lai, and on and on. My advice to Westerners for the future: get used to Asian names as soon as possible, because more and more Asian businesspeople are dropping their English names.

Through its dominance in markets, technology and capital since the Second World War, the West had an overpowering influence on the world, especially on Asia. The world used to mean the Western world, but a confluence of circumstances is converging to forever alter the global balance of power. Today, global forces are forcing us to confront a new reality: the rise of the East. It is becoming apparent to the East and to some in the West that we are moving toward the Easternization of the world. In the global context, the West is still important, but no longer dominant. The global axis of influence has shifted from West to East.

Global political, economic and cultural forces are reshaping the world. It is no longer just what America and Europe can do. It is what America, Europe and Asia can do together to reshape the world. When Latin America and Africa are integrated at a later stage, there will be total and complete integration of a world system, the single-market global economy.

Only thirty-five years ago East Asian economies, including Japan's, contributed 4 percent of the world's output. Now they contribute 24 percent, the same amount as the United States, Canada and Mexico. By the century's end, if current trends are played out, these economies will be responsible for one third of world output. The World Bank estimates that Asia will account for half the expansion in global trade. The rise of the East began with economic power. Political clout and cultural influence will follow.

The Western World in Transition

The twin forces of global change—the decline of Western dominance and the rise of the East; and the shift from industrial to information societies—are producing the need for painful adjustments. The shock waves are enormous in speed and magnitude. Sitting governments that cannot make a timely paradigm shift will become helpless; economies that cannot restructure will create many unemployed, unhappy voters. Yet this time of change also holds unlimited opportunities for the West if, that is, the West is willing to join in a new world where collaboration replaces domination, and where diversity and convergence are far more attractive alternatives to homogeneity.

The time has come to fully recognize and accept the East. This acceptance is as profound as was accepting that the world is round. And the East is not just Japan and China. The countries of the ASEAN group—Thailand, Malaysia, Singapore, Indonesia, the Philippines, Brunei and Vietnam—have a population of 450 million; the Indian subcontinent has 940 million people. All are powerful forces and players in the reshaping of the world economy.

The Return of Hong Kong

The year 1997 is symbolic for the Chinese as well as for the West. In Hong Kong, colonial rule officially ends June 30, 1997. When Macau returns to China in December 1999, the final chapter of Western domination in Asia will be closed.

For the first time in four hundred years, every inch of Asian soil will be controlled and governed by Asians.

When in 1995 the high-profile Royal Hong Kong Jockey Club jettisoned the tarnished appellation "Royal" and became the Hong Kong Jockey Club, reality started to sink in. The West must now look at Hong Kong with a new pair of lenses, seeing it as a part of China, not as some Western outpost taken back by China. These new lenses must examine all of Asia, beginning now.

For Hong Kong, China is a new master. People feel it already. Hong Kong, like a prodigal son, will now return home. Hong Kong's new official symbol, the five-petaled bauhinia, which has already replaced the likeness of Queen Elizabeth II on coins, is a symbol of its new identity. The international community is well aware of the integration of the mainland and Hong Kong. Any mishandling of Hong Kong will not be in China's interest.

Enter the Dragon

Distrust and suspicion of the mainland Chinese leadership will remain for some time. Martin Lee, the leader of the Democratic Party in Hong Kong's legislature and an eminent lawyer, is dismayed and skeptical. "China wants Hong Kong to be the most prosperous Chinese city. They will tolerate Hong Kong as a Chinese city. They will have control of the executive, the legislature and the judiciary. They will control the universities and the press."

But isn't Hong Kong already a Chinese city?

Tsang Yok Sing, an official Hong Kong advisor to Beijing, finds Lee's fears ludicrous. "We believe China understands very well that to keep the social and economic system in Hong Kong, a democratic system has to develop here. Most people in Hong Kong know they are Chinese. If you ask me, I say it is my country. You can't get away from it." Hong Kong's Chief Secretary Anson Chan reiterated the sentiment; "I am Chinese through and through. I never regarded myself as British. I want to see China succeed."

From West ⟶ East

Fortune magazine ran a cover story in June 1995 proclaiming "The Death of Hong Kong." Not death, but birth. I say a new Hong Kong is being born—**a Chinese Hong Kong**—which may not fit Western standards, and which the West may not be comfortable with. In fact, China itself may not be entirely comfortable with the return of Hong Kong. It is not an acquisition—it is the return of a province. "Ultimately what is required of China is a different mind set," writes Karen Elliott House in the *Asian Wall Street Journal*. "A society that counts its 1.2 billion people as interchangeable commodities is being asked to understand the value of six million people as unique individual assets." House suggests that the United States offer visas to Hong Kong citizens who wish to emigrate.

Years ago that would have been an attractive proposition, but with the explosive growth in Asia in general, and China in particular, how many in Hong Kong would want U.S. passports? Some might, but ever pragmatic, they would eventually return to Hong Kong to make money. When movie producer and actor Michael Hui was asked about his Canadian passport, he said that it was just a travel document. The Canadian High Commissioner in Hong Kong offered to help him get rid of it.

China has made it clear: Those who stay in Hong Kong or return there before 1997 will retain permanent resident status. Those returning after 1997 must stay for seven years to requalify as permanent residents. The moment of truth has arrived: West or East, the people of Hong Kong must choose.

Hong Kong 1997 is symbolic of a world reshaping itself.

The East is taking over Hong Kong, superseding the West's influence. K. C. Chen, former editor of the Chinese-language Hong Kong–based *Huanan Economic Journal*, says, "For years, people complained that it is difficult to adjust and to fathom the Japanese, theirs is a very different world. It is even more difficult to understand and try to work with the Chinese. But Japan is only 126 million people, China has 1.2 billion." The question is obvious: Who can afford to ignore China?

Hong Kong's future governance is a domestic issue of international concern. How the governance of Hong Kong is decided will be representative of the way China intends to reclaim its former glory.

China: The New Superpresence

That China will become the new world superpresence is not a question of "if" but "when." China's economic resurgence, followed by the rise of its political clout and its potentially huge military presence, is a certainty the world must deal with in the next century. The China challenge will preoccupy the sphere of international relations, especially those between China and its immediate neighbors in Asia. Eventually, the world will accept China's return to dominance as a political, economic and military power. China will be a global power, if not *the* global power. The question is, how can the world influence what kind of global power China will become? Among other things, it will be inseparable from the Chinese Overseas network.

China's economic fortunes depend on the open markets of the United States, and investment and technology from the newly industrialized Asian economies. The world is driven by the allure of the Chinese market. The rise of China will be on a scale the world has never seen before, and a policy of containment, for whatever reason, just won't work. The short-term concerns about conflicts and flashpoints are testing grounds for the development of a longer-term strategy for engagement with China. And Asian- and China-driven strategies will be required.

Unlike Japan of the 1930s, China's interest is not in conquests. The complexities of domestic conditions, the need for capital to fund growth, the widening rural/urban gap and impending social instability, the weakening of Beijing's control and authority on the provinces and a whole range of political and economic concerns will undermine China's potential hegemonistic intentions or ambitions. However, the same reasons could force China to reach out to secure valuable resources, such as control over oil and gas reserves in the South China Seas, to address domestic needs.

The negative fears and concerns about the return to glory of the world's former giant are understandable. It will forever change the balance of power between West and East. What the world must now think about is the positive and predictable Asian way of dealing with China: that is to accept and let China reestablish its leadership role in a hierarchical pattern of international relations. By identifying common economic and political interests with China, and acknowledging its supremacy, countries in Asia could accommodate the rise of China and Chinese hegemony. This could thus be the alternative to conflict and instability in the region.

Toward Equal Partnership

In the context of this changing balance, Australia has accepted reality and come to terms with becoming Asian. Paul Keating, prime minister of Australia, writes in *Asiaweek*, "Engagement with Asia has been a major part of Australian policy for over a decade now. . . . For as never before Australia's economic, strategic and political interests now co-alesce in the region around us . . . and importantly, finding a place for ourselves in Asia is also about finding our own identity. Asia is no longer the 'Far East.' It is the 'near north.' "

Australia is experiencing Easternization on a major scale. Half of Australia's immigrants now come from Asia. One third of Australia's exports went to Asia in the early 1980s. By 1994 that had increased to 60 percent, or $38.3 billion. Japan and Korea are the largest export markets, followed by the ASEAN countries (counted together). In 1994 more than 60,000 students from Asia studied in Australia. The West is learning to adjust to Easternization, beginning with Australia.

A Relocation from East to West

Once U.S. and European megamanufacturers outsourced labor-intensive operations to low-wage, low-skill Asian nations. Today that tide is turning. For some time now, companies in Hong Kong, Singapore, Taiwan and South Korea have moved manufacturing operations to less-developed Asian nations. Now wages and incomes are rising in those countries as well, and it is more cost-effective to manufacture and distribute in the countries to which goods are destined to be delivered.

There are ten big South Korean manufacturers in the United States and nine from Taiwan; half opened their doors in the last several years. South Korea has thirty-six companies operating in Britain, Taiwan has sixty-seven. Hong Kong has sixteen manufacturers in Britain, mostly in textiles and electronics. As the former British colony prepares to become part of China in 1997, some Hong Kong companies are moving elsewhere.

The Birth of an Asian Commonwealth

Will Asian nations eventually unite like the European Union? The answer is no. Alliances to date are motivated almost solely by economic self-interest. While Asian countries such as those in ASEAN and the growth triangles sort out their political priorities, they will create economic groups, benefiting from one another's market, labor, resources, capital and technology. Because these marriages are based on economics, they work. And collectively, the countries of Asia are very powerful. Asian governments provide the leadership, create the necessary conditions; private businesses carry out the integration. Western multinationals have played their role, but it is the Asian companies that are raring to go regionally and globally. For now, Asians are eager to engage the West in reshaping the world.

If the United States takes a myopic view of Asia, the results could be devastating. *Wall Street Journal* columnist Albert Hunt argues that "in the final analysis, the simple fact is that Asia is so big and bustling that the U.S. ability to affect change is limited. But at the margin it's critical that the U.S.'s influence be constructive rather than destructive. Otherwise, America will be a mere observer in the Pacific century."

The World's Future Is in Asia

The East will not take away jobs from the West. The predator is technology, not cheap labor. Asia itself loses jobs with new technologies. But with the great reduction of the labor content in manufacturing, it does not make much sense for companies to relocate except for those in textiles and clothing where labor costs can make the difference. According to a study by Charles Oman of the Organization for Economic Cooperation and Development, the share of low-skilled labor in production costs has been falling rapidly—from around 25 percent in 1970 to 5 to 10 percent today.

The markets are in the East, both for consumer and capital goods. The U.S. Department of Commerce has designated ten priority markets as vital for the growth of all American exports. All these markets are developing countries.

The United States already exports far more to Asia than to the mature markets of Europe, while Europe ships twice as much to the developing world as to the United States.

The Asian Way Restated

The typical Western view of modernization, which encompasses ideas on civil liberty, freedom of speech and democracy, is strongly challenged by Asia. Asians place a high priority on family first and seek to devise a more communal and equitable form of development. Centuries of political chaos have so scared the Asian psyche that they will do anything to preserve social and political stability. "Harmony is the goal in our pursuit of modernization," said Korean Professor Dr. Sang-Woo Rhee of Sogang University, in Seoul, Korea.

The West prefers diverse lifestyles. Asia emphasizes discipline and conformity. The West delights in open debate while Asians abhor confrontation, preferring to persuade. East Asia's success may become a new model for the world. But building that model raises many questions. What in the West is good that we want to make our own? What does the West have or do that we want to avoid at all costs? Do we need to reinvent cities? Do we need to create big corporations? In Asia's diverse environment, small and flexible operating units with a common belief system have been the standard. Asia was built on that. Will success and ambition blur our vision? Will we fall into the trap of equating size with success? How do we build on past successes? In family and social welfare considerations, how much do we want governments to intervene? Is Asia at a competitive advantage because it does not have a social welfare system that bogs it down?

The Welfare Debate

Many Asian governments and citizens are discussing welfare and other social safety nets, and not just in the developed countries. China's media are debating welfare because of the risk of social instability resulting from massive unemployment when loss-making state-owned enterprises are scrapped.

State enterprises—which are really massive employment programs —will face the greatest challenge for China and India. Welfare programs are sure to follow closings. Asia's affluent Newly Industrialized Economies (NIEs) will also increasingly have to deal with the welfare question. The challenge is to design systems that do not kill personal responsibility and self-reliance, the cornerstones of individual and national competitiveness.

• Over the past five years South Korea has put in place a national pension scheme and is going forward with a comprehensive health insurance program.

• Malaysia and Singapore have state-regulated savings schemes that encourage home ownership.

• Thailand has recently announced plans to care for the elderly, the disabled and those below the poverty line.

Comprehensive Western-style welfare systems are not on Asia's list of developmental priorities. Most Asians favor preserving self-reliance and individual enterprise as evidenced by the proliferation of small and medium-size businesses in the region, especially in the Chinese-based economies.

It's the System, Stupid

Welfare state disincentives and safety nets can erode personal responsibility. A recent U.S. Census study found that more than 30 percent of Southeast Asian households in the United States depend on welfare. Among Laotians and Cambodians in California, 77 percent of households live on welfare. Southeast Asians represent the highest incidence of welfare dependence for any U.S. ethnic or racial group. An effective and workable welfare system provides opportunity, encourages enterprise, promotes personal responsibility and preserves self-reliance.

Hong Kong's Jimmy Lai, publisher of *Apple Daily*, is a great champion of the free market and individual enterprise. His is a spectacular rags-to-riches story. "In the marketplace," he says, "you vote with your dollars, you vote with your self-interest, your children's interest."

Ow Yang Hsuan, chairman of the board of governors of Singapore's Institute of Policy Studies, maintains that it is the avoidance of Western-style welfare programs and emphasis on family self-reliance that have helped Asia on its road to prosperity. The World Bank noted that "from 1965 to 1990 the 23 economies of East Asia grew faster than all other regions of the world." That growth was due to hard work. There is no miracle. The success of the Chinese Overseas illustrates how self-reliance works as a strategy for upward mobility.

The Asian-American Experience

The pivotal players in the new global configuration of East and West will be Asians living in America and Asians born in America. It is in America where the East and West truly meet. Many Asian-Americans are as comfortable in the Western world as they are in the Eastern. As growing numbers of American-born and/or U.S.-educated Asians return to their native countries to take advantage of the region's explosive growth and dynamism, this Asian-American population will become an important bridge between the two hemispheres.

Bilingual Asians in Growing Demand

"Once upon a time code phrases like 'language barrier' and 'cultural differences' were used to keep Asians out of the choicest jobs in American businesses and professions," says *Transpacific* magazine. "But today, being Asian, especially a bilingual Asian, may be the best qualification for a high-paying career. The former 'language barrier' will soon be called 'language advantage' and 'cultural differences' will soon be considered one of the most necessary attributes for top ranked executives," where the future will be dominated by Asians.

This is not to suggest that discrimination is not an issue for Asians in America; it certainly is. The number of Asians in the top ranks of America's corporations is still quite small. But the tide is changing. According to Koichi "Kris" Fukuda, a partner with Heidrick & Struggles, the world's oldest executive search firm, "There's a tremendous demand for executive managers with a bicultural background." With the right qualifications, in fact, Fukuda feels that Asian executives in any corporation "can write their own ticket."

Heidrick & Struggles surveyed four thousand CEOs in 1993, asking what they looked for in an executive or manager, or what they needed to succeed. "Almost all of them independently, Asian, Caucasian, Black or Latino, gave the same elements," reports *Transpacific* on the survey:

1. a background in the Asian Pacific;
2. more than two languages;
3. at least one advanced degree, preferably an MBA from a top U.S. school; and
4. a degree from two countries.

Clearly, more Asians in America and American-born Asians fit that profile than do representatives of any other population group. And while they gain greater acceptance in the corporate world, many Asian-Americans will be eager to follow in the *entrepreneurial* footsteps of Bill Mow of Bugle Boy, David Chu of Nautica and David Lee of Qume Corporation.

The Big Deal

Transpacific magazine recently profiled six Asian men in America who "live for the action of the big deal." Three of these profiled were investment banker Warren Woo, venture capitalist and self-made millionaire Yosh Uchida, and high-tech deal maker Dennis Paul Kim, who brokers investment deals with technology-hungry Korean companies and small high-tech companies in the United States.

The world of independent filmmaking is full of young, ambitious Asians, including Ang Lee, Tommy Chang and Greg Araki. Until recently Asians were noticeably absent from the executive teams of major entertainment conglomerates. No more. Stephen Chao ran Fox Studios and went on to head QVC's new spin-off channel. Teddy Zee held executive positions in several studios and is now at Columbia Studios. Chris Lee is executive vice president at Tristar. Alex Kitman Ho has won Oscars for producing *JFK* and *Born on the Fourth of July.* Janet Yang is head of development for Oliver Stone's Ixtlan Productions.

America's Fastest-Growing Minority Group

According to the 1990 U.S. Census, Asian-Americans are the country's fastest-growing minority. More than 7 million people (in 1990), a little less than 3 percent of the population, trace their ancestry to Asian nations, up from 1.5 percent in 1980. Most are from China, the Philippines, Japan, India, Korea and Vietnam. Already there are more than one million Asians in Los Angeles. There will be 20 million Asian-Americans by the year 2020.

There are an extraordinary number of successful entrepreneurs among Asian-Americans. Asians excel academically, have entered the professions in large numbers and have the highest household income of all minority groups, and they are beginning to exercise their political clout and realize they have the power of the purse. Asian-Americans are finally being acknowledged for the invaluable contributions they have made to modern American society, but it is an acknowledgment that comes after decades of discrimination.

A Growing Asian-American Middle Class

Says *American Demographics*, "Forget Chinatown: most Asian Americans live in middle-class suburbs." In general, they are educated and have more disposable income than big city Asians. Though assimilated Americans, they tend to preserve their customs. Asian suburbs include Filipino Daly City (south of San Francisco) and Chinese Monterey Park (near Los Angeles). Some twenty-five metropolitan areas in the United States had at least 25,000 Asian-American suburbanites in 1990, or 76 percent of suburban Asian-Americans, reports *American Demographics*. Four of the top ten high-growth areas for suburban Asians are in the western United States. In Atlanta, Riverside–San Bernardino and Dallas, the number of Asian-American suburbanites more than quadrupled during the 1980s. In New Jersey's Middlesex and Somerset counties and in Houston, the number more than tripled, according to *American Demographics.*

Explains Eleanor Yu, president and chief executive officer of Adland and Adland Worldwide, a San Francisco agency specializing in the Asian market, "Historically, inner-city Chinatowns in Los Angeles, San Francisco, and New York were created because of discrimination and because the Chinese were not ready to assimilate. Today, many Asians —even recent immigrants—are ready to assimilate. They speak English, they've been exposed to culture, and they're buying estates in San Marino, Westchester, and Monterey Park." Wealthy Asians have global business interests, and professional careers, and travel frequently.

"Asians in the suburbs assimilate like anyone else," Yu says, but "they do maintain a certain level of Asianness." They watch Chinese TV, among other channels, and you are sure to find stacks of Asian-language newspapers in their homes.

Jeff Yang is counting on that certain level of Asianness. This twenty-seven-year-old Harvard graduate recently launched *A.*, a magazine created for the Asian-American community. He and his thirty-something partner, Phoebe Eng, are modeling the publication after similar lifestyle magazines such as *Ebony* and *Hispanic*. Yang and Eng are not the first to try to tap into the Asian-American population.

Ten-year-old *Transpacific*, believed to be the longest-running Asian-American publication, covers lifestyle and business trends in Asia. *A.* will focus only on Asians in America.

Entrepreneurs Create Their Own Opportunities

Yang and Eng are among a growing group of Asian-American entrepreneurs who are striking out on their own. This trend is dramatically evident in California's Silicon Valley, where Asians have long worked as engineers in America's fast-growing computer companies, yet never made it to the executive suite.

These entrepreneurs are both ambitious and frustrated. Many Asians who came to the United States to study and stayed to work are now ready for more responsibility and greater success. Some say it is not easy for Asians to advance in U.S. firms. "Many Asian engineers are not being looked at as having management talent," says David K. Lam, one of the first Chinese entrepreneurs in Silicon Valley. "They are looked upon as good work horses and not race horses."

Dr. Lam, who grew up in China, Vietnam and Hong Kong, holds a Ph.D. from the Massachusetts Institute of Technology and spent many years at Hewlett-Packard. When passed over in favor of a white American hired right out of college, he quit and founded Lam Research, now a publicly traded company that manufactures equipment used in chip-making. In 1985 he started Expert Edge, a software firm. Like many Asian entrepreneurs in America, Dr. Lam started Expert Edge with financial backing from investors in Asia.

Among the other companies that Asian-Americans have started in Silicon Valley are Everex Systems, which manufactures personal computers; Komag, which produces data storage disks; Wyse Technology, a terminal and computer maker; Qume, a printer company; and Solectron, which assembles products for other companies and was awarded the U.S. Baldrige Award for Quality.

Long aware of the value of networking and the informal information chain, Asian-American entrepreneurs formed their own groups to replace what they lost in stepping outside the establishment. The Asian-American Manufacturers Association, the Chinese Institute of

Engineers and the Chinese Software Professionals Association keep executives in Asian-owned companies in the know. The Mount Jade Association, comprised of high-level executives from both the United States and Taiwan, encourages business relationships between East and West.

The "Model Minority"

At the Vien Dong International Supermarket in the Linda Vista area of San Diego, incense burns and Vietnamese music is piped in over a sound system. Lettuce, tomatoes and onions rest in bins next to Chinese cabbage and gingerroot. Customers can select a two-pound bag of Uncle Ben's Converted Rice or a fifty-pound bag of rice imported from Thailand, New England perch or milkfish flown in from Taiwan.

Vien Dong is one of forty supermarkets in San Diego owned by Chinese, Korean, Japanese or Vietnamese immigrants that give equal shelf space to foods native to their country of origin and to American brands. Opened in 1989, Vien Dong began as a specialty store selling Chinese gifts and firecrackers. It has since grown into a four-store chain. One of its locations is an old Safeway store. What makes it remarkable is that the community it serves is less than 20 percent Asian.

Vien Dong's success is not an isolated phenomenon. Yaohan Plaza, in the prosperous Chicago suburb of Arlington Heights, draws Asian consumers from as far away as Michigan, Ohio and Kentucky. Yaohan Plaza, according to *American Demographics,* "caters not only to the Japanese Americans who account for half of its customers, but also to Chinese and Koreans (30 percent) and non-Asians (20 percent)." Through a direct mail list of 12,000 regular customers, the mini-mall announces sales and promotions that keep its parking lots full.

"Del Monte canned peas are stocked next to Azuki beans," reports *American Demographics;* "Starkist Tuna sits adjacent to broiled eel. Quantities sometimes seem larger than life, with 25-pound bags of rice stacked on pallets and one-gallon cans of soy sauce. On the other hand, the Asian taste for junkfood seems sated by unimpressively small bags of potato chips.

"Chinese come for jasmine rice, very sweet cookies, and special varieties of green tea," continues *American Demographics*. "Koreans buy extra-thin shaved beef and ribs for barbecuing, as well as dried cuttlefish. The store sells more than a dozen types of tofu, and eight varieties of fresh mushrooms, even in the dead of a Midwest winter."

Despite excellent revenue growth and an obviously loyal customer base, including many non-Asians, store manager Shuji Kono hopes to expand his non-Asian customer base. "The Japanese people, they're happy," he says. "But that is not enough. We need American people." His strategy: "We're going to introduce Japanese culture with food."

The Asian Way

Introducing Japanese culture with food. How simple, profound and very Asian. Though each country is unique, there is a certain cadence and rhythm common to Asians, an attitude and way of thinking that is distinctly Asian. It is part Confucianism, part Taoism, part Buddhism and part Hinduism. It is what has made it possible for immigrants and refugees, artists and intellectuals from Asian countries to make a home for themselves in the United States, yet maintain their own style and identity.

To be sure, each successive immigrant group has been discriminated against and oppressed by the groups that came before, but eventually they were absorbed into the vast multiethnic population of America. But that has not been the experience of Asians in America, in part because they cannot appear as "all-American" as an Irish- or German-American could, and in part, because they have chosen to do things the "Asian way."

A Convergence of Cultures

"The East is always interested in the West and the West in the East. We always find that which is different from ourselves to be intriguing and desirable," says Japanese designer Issey Miyake.

It seems that in the world of fashion design Asia is in and Asian designers are hot. Established Western designers such as Ralph Lauren, Jean-Paul Gaultier and Betsey Johnson have all introduced a bit of Asia into their lines. For Lauren it is "Vietnamese pajama pants and long patterned Balinese silk skirts," reported the *Asian Wall Street Journal.* Gaultier called his fall line, "The Long Journey: Mongolia, Tibet, China and Eskimos," while Johnson used Asian models to show off her spandex catsuits in 1994.

Meanwhile, Asia-born designers are striving for international acceptance with a more eclectic influence. Rei Kawaubo, founder of the revolutionary Comme des Garçons line more than twenty years ago, says one of her greatest milestones was to have her work finally accepted as her own and not as a Japanese phenomenon—a feat that took almost ten years.

Indonesian designers Ghea Sukaya, Bijan and Prayudi were recently featured at a gala benefit for the Environmental Bamboo Foundation in Bali. CNN's "style" host Elsa Klensch filmed the event for international broadcast.

When Hangzhou-born Han Feng describes her fashions, the word "Asian" is not on her lips. "I'm trying to get away from being called a Chinese designer making Chinese things. My designs are international," says Feng. And after a quarter of a century of spreading Western fashion styles in Asia, Joyce Ma, called the "First Lady of Hong Kong," is doing the reverse—bringing the East to the West through her $100-million fashion empire.

Guangzhou-born designer Vivienne Tam takes a universal view of fashion. Based in New York, she sells her designs at Barneys and Saks Fifth Avenue as well as at her three boutiques in Hong Kong. "I wondered how well the traditional pieces would sell in Asia. But whatever style is selling the best in New York sells the best in Hong Kong. This somehow exemplifies the way the world is merging together," says Tam.

This convergence of East and West is evidenced also in the art world. In the January 1995 issue of *Art in America,* critic Janet Koplos reviews "Scream Against the Sky," a traveling exhibition of Japanese avantgarde art since World War II. In her critique entitled "How Japanese Is

It?'' she describes the influences on the work of Japanese artists of this period, many of whom have not lived in Japan for decades. And she makes a profound observation, one that is particularly appropriate to a discourse on Asia's influence over the West.

Writes Koplos: ''A complicated question that the show evades is just who or what is a 'Japanese artist.' By the end of the '60s, a number of contemporary artists had left Japan. For Munroe [curator of the show], they remain eternally Japanese, regardless of residence or preference or even citizenship, and regardless of where their influences derive from.''

That, of course, is the question. Because of their uniquely Eastern heritage, do Asians who immigrate to, or seek refuge in, the West remain forever Asian? Are they destined to be strangers in a strange land, or do they, like immigrants before them, assimilate and become Westernized? Or does something quite different happen? Do they take the best of what is Asian and the best of what is Western and carve out a wholly new identity? And by the same token, can the West ever understand the subtleties of Eastern thought, which has so great an influence over their social conduct?

The drama of acculturation is now being played out on the world stage. As the global community becomes irrevocably linked by a seamless information highway, and one's business partner is as likely to be halfway around the globe as on the next block, the experience and influence of Asians on America could well become a model for emergent multicultural communities everywhere. But just as the modernization of Asia is not to be thought of as its Westernization, but as its modernization in the ''Asian way,'' so the integration of Asian immigrants into American society is not to be thought of as the Americanization of Asians. Asian-Americans have the same aspirations and expectations as all other Americans. They expect to be accepted into American society, to work and live where they choose. They want their work to be valued as highly as the work of their peers. At the same time they have not abandoned, nor will they abandon, their cultural heritage. They will be Americans in the Asian way, and both the American and the global community will be enriched as a result.

247

A Bridge Between East and West

In the global village, Asian-Americans, as well as Asians who are educated and have worked in America, will be a bridge between the East and the West. Having lived in both worlds, they will act as mediators and interpreters for business and political communities that are so interrelated that national and regional boundaries are irrelevant. And the Asia Pacific–American community will be mimicked. The best of what is Asia, the best of what is America and the best of what is Europe will converge, and there will emerge an entirely new community model.

This convergence of cultures was described by Kishore Mahbubani, permanent secretary of Singapore's Ministry of Foreign Affairs and dean of the Civil Service College. In an article entitled, "The Pacific Way," published in the journal *Foreign Affairs*, Mahbubani writes:

The Pacific community will be a completely new creation. It will not be an Asian community, nor will it be an American community. If the Pacific has emerged as the most dynamic region of the world, it is because it has drawn on the best practices and values from many rich civilizations, Asian and Western. If this fusion continues to work, there could be explosive creativity on a scale never before seen. . . .

The real success of the Pacific community will come when the learning process in the Pacific becomes a two-way street rather than a one-way street. It took a long time for China and other East Asian societies to accept the common sensical advice of Yukichi Fukuzawa, the Meiji-Era reformer: to progress, learn from the West. Many American intellectuals still believe that all the deep wells of learning are in Europe. Those who travel across the Pacific come to learn about, but not from, East Asia. There is a profound difference between these two approaches. In the past few years, many Americans have been disconcerted by lectures from East Asians, as have many East Asians by American preachings on democracy and human rights. It will take time for both sides to learn to listen to each other.

It may take less time than he thinks. Americans are a pragmatic lot, and Europeans, although still clinging to a belief in their inherent superiority as a rich and venerated bastion of culture and intellectual thought, will ultimately learn to celebrate differences in culture and to accept that diversity is a path to universal prosperity. Furthermore, there is emerging in the global community a new cadre of leaders who are both idealists and pragmatists. They are risk takers who also believe strongly in consensus building. They are open, aware, change-oriented and seek a balance between material success and spirituality.

Leadership for the Future

A new breed of leaders is emerging in Asia. The young Asian leadership in politics, government, business, intellectual and academic areas is reshaping the direction of Asia and the world. Forty-something and ready for their ascendancy to positions of power, representatives of this group can be found in every corner of the globe. Pakistan's Benazir Bhutto, forty-three, Sri Lanka's Chandrika Kumaratunga, fifty, and U.S. President Bill Clinton, fifty, are already in power. Malaysia's Anwar Ibrahim, forty-eight, Singapore's Lee Hsien Loong, forty-three, and the Philippines's Richard Gordon, fifty, plan to be there soon. "Behind them are a legion of well-connected, highly educated technocrats, entrepreneurs, artists and community activists who together will lead into the 21st Century," says *Asiaweek.*

In my travels around Asia, what impresses me most is the knowledge Asian leaders have of the West. A far greater number of people in positions of power and influence in Asia know about the West than do their counterparts in the West know about the East. This knowledge will put them in a more advantageous position in dealing with the West.

After the flap with China over his attendance at his class reunion, we all know that President Lee Teng Hui of Taiwan received his doctorate from Cornell University in the United States. More than 70 percent of his cabinet ministers were trained in the West and 60 percent hold doctorates from Western universities. President Fidel Ramos of the Philippines is a graduate of the U.S. Military Academy at West Point, and Pakistani Prime Minister Benazir Bhutto is a Harvard alumna. Many of Indonesia's top economic planners hold doctorates from the University of California at Berkeley. Throughout Asia government leaders, corporate executives and second-generation business leadership of Asian family companies were trained and educated in the West.

These new Asian leaders are unique among emerging global power brokers. Although politically active, many are not politicians, but rather successful businessmen and -women with a keen interest in maintaining economic stability. Many embrace spiritual ideals but not religious zealotry. While politicians in the West wave the flag of family values when railing against moral decay, Asian leaders are products of Eastern religious thought, which values family over all else. For the most part, members of this group support democracy in principle, but not necessarily the Western application of democracy.

"Under the tutelage of their elders," says *Asiaweek,* "they have been the backbone of East Asia's awesome economic advantages. Now they are about to take charge just as the region is becoming a world-class economic power. . . . They are creatures of their time. In many parts of East Asia they will be the last to know what it is like to grow up in poverty—and to have deprivation as a motivating force in their psychological and ethical makeup."

For the most part, Asia's new leaders embrace the guiding principles articulated by Malaysia's deputy prime minister, Anwar Ibrahim, in an address to the forty-ninth gathering of the UN General Assembly:

Development is the only secure foundation for global peace and security, for the origins of conflicts are often buried deep in socioeconomic deprivation and disparities.

As for civil society, its growth into maturity requires the establishment of institutions for a stable and responsive social order, a democratic participatory arrangement as a means to channel political energy, and a conducive environment for culture to flourish.

In all these, it is the people that matter, their freedom, security and development. All great traditions of mankind, East and West concur in the sanctity of the human person, the family as a fundamental unit of society and the primacy of moral ethical values as the foundation of civilization.

Muslims' Ascendancy to Leadership in Corporate Asia

Tajudin Ramli, the chairman and chief executive officer of Malaysian Airlines, took command of the national carrier after engineering the largest corporate buyout in the country's history. His satellite and telecommunications companies also are well positioned to capitalize on the opportunities presented by rapid economic growth in such a huge region. Tajudin Ramli and a rising crop of corporate leaders who hold to the Islamic faith constitute a new phenomenon in Asia.

For a long time there has been a widespread perception that Islam is incompatible with profit, and that Muslim participation in Asia's corporate sector has been minimal. A question often asked is whether Muslims can participate in the stock market or in banking. Interest is un-Islamic, although fees for services can be charged. There is no straightforward answer to the question of their participation. It all depends on whether or not in the course of a transaction one violates any of the Islamic principles of business. However, a fact unknown to many is that Islam is generally not incompatible with trade and commerce. The Prophet Muhammad has been reported to have said, "A truthful and trustworthy merchant will be gathered [in the day of Resurrection] together with the prophets, martyrs and truthful."

In Asia's corporate world, more and more Muslims are taking the reins, led by many prominent Malaysian businessmen of Islamic faith, together with their counterparts in Indonesia, and an increasing number in Pakistan and India. These leaders, many of them very young, thirty- and forty-something, are ambitious, articulate in English—many of them were educated in the West—and completely at ease with science and technology. Corporate leaders with Islamic faith are fast becoming important players in Asia's economic modernization and will become increasingly visible. In response to this new Muslim visibility, many restaurants in the region are now including *halal* menus, sensitive to the special way the non-pork-eating Muslims prepare their food.

Many people in the world, especially Americans, associate Islam with the Iranian hostage crisis, fighting in the Middle East and terrorism. These incidents have created stereotyped images of Islam, which are a gross distortion of the mainstream religion. Today, the American Muslim community is the U.S.'s fastest-growing religious minority. The United States has 4 million Muslims and 12 percent are Arabs. The groundbreaking endeavors and successes of Muslims in Asia will help change the world's perception of this major religious group.

Dealing with the East

Raymond Wong, a business consultant from Kuala Lumpur, complains about the lack of understanding of Asian cultures by Western businesspeople. "If the West wants to do business with us, they must make it a point to get to know us," he says and recounts at length how warmly he and his colleagues receive their Western counterparts while they are in Asia, and how this warm reception is not reciprocated when they visit the United States at a later date. This cultural divide, especially in styles and expression, is a common source of friction and frustration. Asians are indirect and nonconfrontational. It takes patience and perseverance to navigate their cultural sensitivities.

The Challenge of Asian Languages

Learning the culture begins with mastering the language. And many Asians have implied that Westerners should do so: "When we deal with you, we speak English. Our children speak English, too. It would be best if you could understand and speak our language." But being Asian, they will not say that directly to your face, and you will never know how they feel.

Given the diversity of the region, a wide range of natural languages and local dialects is spoken. Just to acquire a working knowledge of one, let alone several, would call for total devotion. Fortunately, however, the greatest benefit of the Western legacy in Asia is the English language. Because of Asia's colonial past and the U.S. presence in postwar trade and investment, English became the language of commerce and education for some Asian countries. English has been dominant in the business communities, and with the region's rush to join the world economy there has been an upsurge in learning English, especially in Korea, China, Thailand, Indonesia and Vietnam. Even longtime nationalistic Malaysia is reversing its language policy and has begun to reemphasize the importance of English as a means to embrace Western science and technology, so essential for the country's transition from labor-intensive to high-tech manufacturing.

English will remain the language of commerce and international communication in Asia, and its importance will grow as the region continues to liberalize and open up. But in time, a second language will become dominant. Mandarin will move to center stage as the language of Asia.

Mandarin Moves to Center Stage

- In opening a dialogue between Confucianism and Islam, Malaysia's deputy prime minister, Anwar Ibrahim, an ethnic Malay, quoted important verses from Chinese scholars in Mandarin. Southeast Asia's "China driven" orientation has heightened interest in Mandarin.
- Since 1979 Singapore authorities have actively promoted Mandarin as the "mother tongue" of its ethnic Chinese citizens. "School children are already learning Mandarin from a very young age," says Ho Kah Leong, senior parliamentary secretary at the Ministry of Information and the Arts. "Those who want to enter university—and who doesn't in Singapore—have to pass stringent tests of proficiency in Mandarin," reports *Asiaweek*.
- Mandarin is now widely spoken in Hong Kong, which for a long time spoke only Cantonese, and news broadcasts in Mandarin are on most channels in the region's television and radio stations.

Cantonese is a dialect of the people of southern China, and because the Chinese Overseas in Southeast Asia and in the West are mainly from this southern region, there is a distorted perception that Cantonese is the language of the Chinese people. Mandarin is the language of China; Cantonese is only a dialect. Both China and India have many dialects, but all of China has a common written language. Everyone can understand the same written word. In India, the dialects have different written languages.

It is now commonplace to overhear conversations in Mandarin in airline cabins and hotel lounges throughout Asia. It will become a dominant language of commerce in the region. Communication in Mandarin, especially the written language, has long been a challenge, even for Chinese and other Asians. China, Singapore and Malaysia use simplified Chinese characters of Kanji, while Taiwan staunchly retains the complex traditional version. There are so many characters that a typewriter needs several different keyboards. But computers have changed all that. Intelligent software can interpret both simplified and traditional characters, avoiding the need to master the tedious process of remembering the phonetic guide to three thousand essential characters. Technology has enabled Mandarin to be widely used in business tasks, but the challenge lies in its full adoption in contractual and legal realms.

Mandarin's grammatical simplicity has made for a less than exacting contractual language (which Hong Kong lawyers and consultants have experienced in their dealings with Chinese officials). Additionally, a lack of standardization of terms used in translating foreign words complicates the situation. Despite these challenges the economic value of the language will accelerate its elevation to international use. Already, efforts are being made in that direction. One example is the Hong Kong–based, twenty-four-hour Mandarin television channel, the Chinese Television Network, styled to be the CNN for Chinese communities throughout the world and launched in 1994.

Looked upon for a long time as the language of high culture, Mandarin is spreading in Asia, and more will realize its economic value in the coming century. Paradoxically, Mandarin is also fast becoming the language of pop culture. Singers around the region, especially those from Hong Kong, are churning out Mandarin versions of their original Cantonese pop songs, called "canto-pops" by the local English media. It surely makes a lot of sense if the music and lyrics can be understood and appreciated by 1.2 billion people.

When Japan was at its peak, many speculated that the world would have to speak Japanese. That never happened, one reason being that the Japanese never encouraged it. Mandarin is a different story. Because of the large ethnic Chinese population in Southeast Asian countries, the language has been commonplace for a long time. With the increased confidence stemming from affluence, many will embrace Mandarin much more enthusiastically than Japanese. East Asians partially understand the written Kanji used in Japan, Korea and Taiwan. Standardization is urgently called for to accelerate wider application of the language.

A Winning Strategy in Asia

The East-West divide centers on the fundamental differences of their systems. The rule of law, or the lack of it, and human rights issues remain the most explosive minefields in relations between East and West. The West believes that only the rule of law keeps governments from riding roughshod over people in business and in the protection of personal and civil liberties. Without a well-defined legal system and respect for individual rights, businesses cannot be assured of security.

Asia, especially China, has a long history of rule by man *(rénchì)*. Asian cultures are "relationship-driven" rather than "rules-" or "system-driven." Asians dislike formal conflict resolution, preferring to work out differences through negotiation. The Chinese people deal with emotions *(qíng)*, logic *(lǐ)* and law *(fǎ)* in that order in the organization of interpersonal relations. "The Chinese dislike technical and legalistic solutions, because the sophisticated background to implementing them isn't there," says Andy Sun, executive director of the Asia Pacific Legal Institute and adjunct professor of law at George Washington National Law Center in Washington, D.C. Many Asians believe that harmony in long-term relationships is preferred to reliance on the legal system, as once in court, "face" is destroyed. In Chinese minds, everything, including differences, is negotiable as long as "face" is preserved. That is why *guanxi* (personal connections) is so important in dealing with Asians.

But acceptance of the rule of law will evolve as Asia modernizes. The enlightened middle class with their newfound wealth will push for change from the bottom up. In Asia, navigate gently, don't push to gain ground. If you need a buffer, get a Chinese Overseas partner.

East-West Harmony

As the East grows more materialistic and high-tech, spirit-starved Westerners grow more Eastern.

The West is importing Eastern spiritual traditions and practices with an almost unquenchable enthusiasm. Yoga and meditation are mainstream fare among fifty-something housewives. Chinese acupuncture and Japanese acupressure are available in any major U.S. city, and even skeptics swear by their healing powers. Reincarnation and Kundalini energy and Right Livelihood pepper everyday conversations of many Americans and Europeans. Korean ginseng is sold at the local health food store, and Chinese herbs are coming on strong. Millions of women who are interested in Goddess psychology might have a little Kwan Yin statue next to a Virgin Mary icon. The person doing Tai Chi in the park is either an eighty-year-old Oriental or a thirty-year-old Occidental.

Far from a passing fad, the real aficionado has moved on to the next layer of Eastern wisdom and embraces it with great gusto: getting Jin Shin Jyutsu treatments, investigating a psychic surgeon in the Philippines, studying Korean Shaman tradition, Vispassana and Metta meditation, and Taoist meditation, not to mention Qigong, the four-thousand-year-old science of internal energy cultivation.

How rich the world will be when both the cultures and the economies of West and East converge.

The Asian Model?

John Hung, an expatriate Westerner who has lived for a long time in Hong Kong, gave me an excellent illustration of the difference between Eastern and Western societies. He said, "A bus driver looking from his window at a passing Rolls-Royce said to himself, full of hope, 'I may not sit in that car, but my son will.'" In contrast, Hung continued, Westerners have a strong entitlement mentality on a wide range of things. They insist on their rights, "whereas Asians aspire."

During the last 150 years of progress and prosperity enjoyed in the West, much of Asia was in poverty. Now, Asians are on their way to an economic renaissance that will provide an opportunity for them to reassert the grandeur and glory of their past civilizations. With the application of science and technology, Asians could present the world with a new model for modernization that combines it with both Western and Eastern values, one that reconciles freedom and order, individualism and community concerns. The most profound consequence of the rise of the East is the birth of this new model for modernization. Asians are modernizing in the "Asian way" and, in the process, presenting the West with both the challenge and the opportunity to follow their lead into the twenty-first century.

NOTES

Chapter One: From Nation-States to Networks

18 Information on China from various sources, including "Without You I'm Nothing," *Far Eastern Economic Review*, June 23, 1994; "The Chinese takeover of Hong Kong Inc.," *The Economist*, May 7, 1994; and "It's Already 1997 in Hong Kong," *The Economist*, December 18, 1993.

20 Bustanil Ariffin statement from "APEC Ministers Plan Packages to Help SMES," *Business Times* (Singapore), October 24, 1994.

21 Hong Kong banker quote from "The New Power in Asia," *Fortune*, October 31, 1994.

23 Yoji Hamawaki information from an interview by the author.

24– Billionaires' profiles from various sources, including "The Bamboo
25 Network," *Forbes*, July 18, 1994; and "Asia," in the July 15, 1996, issue; Nina Wang quote translated from "Profile of the World's Richest Chinese," *Forbes Zibenjia*, June 1994.

30 Wang Gungwu quotes from "The Chinese Entrepreneur and His Cultural Strategies," a paper given at the Second World Chinese Entrepreneurs Conference, Hong Kong, November 22, 1993.

34 Li quote from an interview by the author.

34 Shih quotes translated from the Taiwan-based *Excellence* magazine and Hong Kong–based *Yauzhou Zhoukan* magazine.

35 Lee quote from the Second World Chinese Entrepreneurs Conference in Hong Kong in November 1993.

38 Yukiko Ohara statement from "Japanese Banks' Bad Loans Constitute Bigger Burden Than U.S. S&L Debacle," *Wall Street Journal*, June 7, 1995.

Notes

38 Terry quote from *World Business*, January 1995.

43 Takeshi Nagano, Morita and Aoshima quotes from "Bring on the Clowns," *Far Eastern Economic Review*, April 20, 1995.

44 Ishihara quotes from *Boston Globe*, April 15, 1995.

45– Retired government official quote from "Focus: Japan," *Far Eastern*

46 *Economic Review*, June 15, 1995.

46 Michio Watanabe quote from "Should Japan Be Sorry for Its Conquests? A New Furor Erupts," *International Herald Tribune*, June 6, 1995.

Chapter Two: From Traditions to Options

52 Lai quote from "The Information Rebellion," *Far Eastern Economic Review*, April 14, 1994.

53 Quote by Chen Li from an interview by Foong Wai Fong in Beijing.

53 All Lee quotes in this chapter, unless noted, from "Culture is Destiny," *Foreign Affairs*, March/April 1994.

54 David I. Hitchcock, *Asian Values and the United States, How Much Conflict?* (Washington, D.C.: Center for Strategic & International Studies, 1994).

56 Anwar Ibrahim quote from his speech at the Islam and Confucianism Civilization Dialogue on March 13, 1995.

57 Noordin Sopiee quote from "The Asian Way," *Asiaweek*, March 2, 1994.

57 Muzaffar and Rhee quotes from interviews by the author.

57 Kishore Mahbubani's call to the West in Hitchcock report. Mahbubani's article "Go East, Young Man" appeared in *Far Eastern Economic Review*, May 19, 1994.

58 Modern vs. Western quote from the Hitchcock report.

60 Muzaffar quotes from an interview by the author.

60 Anwar Ibrahim quotes from "Mahathir Strikes Chord Among Japanese," *Nikkei Weekly*, December 12, 1994; and "Press Freedom Is an Asian Value," *Asian Wall Street Journal*, December 10, 1994.

61 Lee Yuen Tseh quote from an interview by the author.

61 Tu's explanations from "Confucianism Is No Ban to Asian Democracy," *Asian Wall Street Journal*, May 23, 1995; and "China Looks to Confucius and Marxist Theory Fades," *Asian Wall Street Journal*

Weekly, October 10, 1994. Fukuyama's quotes from the *Asian Wall Street Journal,* May 23, 1995.

62– Confucian values in Singapore education from "Confucianism, New
63 Fashion for Old Wisdom," *The Economist,* January 21, 1995.

63 De Bary quotes from "China Looks to Confucius as Marxist Theory Fades," *Asian Wall Street Journal,* October 10, 1994.

63 International Confucian Association quote from "Confucian Works Still Inspire," *China Daily,* October 6, 1994.

64 Koh quote and list from "Reports of America's Sorry Demise May Just Be a Bit Exaggerated," *International Herald Tribune,* October 8–9, 1994.

65 Mahathir quote from "Rediscovering Islam," *Wings of Gold,* March 1995.

66 Family statistics from various sources, including Hitchcock report and "Asian Family Values Are Under Attack," *Window,* September 23, 1994. Lu quote from the *Window* article.

67 PDA in Japan from "Japanese Lovebirds Kiss Off Tradition," *Asian Wall Street Journal Weekly,* November 14, 1994.

67 Nobue Nakamura, Ken Lyle and Misao Kawaii quotes, and Tokyo Dome event from "Dirty Dancing: Japan's 'OLs' Take It Off," *Los Angeles Times,* December 15, 1993.

68 Lu quote from "Asian Family Values Are Under Attack," *Window,* September 23, 1994.

68 Beijing survey from "Modern Family Values Evolving in Beijing," *China Daily,* January 23, 1995.

68 Wahid Supriyadi quote from an interview by the author.

68 Lam Peng Er quote from an interview by the author.

68 Marzuki Darusman quote from an interview by the author.

68– Atiya quote from *Bangkok Post,*
69 February 13, 1995.

69 JJ's quote from "Shanghai Dances to a Different Tune," *Business Times* (Singapore), September 17–18, 1994.

70 Cheng and Yan information from "20 Years of Asian Growth," *Far Eastern Economic Review.* November 24, 1994

70– Qufu and Kong Qingx information, and Luo quotes from "Entrepre-
71 neurial Zeal in Name of Confucius," *Asian Wall Street Journal,* March 15, 1995.

71 Values education list from "Teaching Asia to Stay Asian," *The Econo-*

mist, October 8, 1994; "Confucianism, New Fashion for Old Wisdom," *The Economist,* January 21, 1995; and "The Classics Are Back," *Asiaweek,* June 21, 1996.

72 Almonte quote from the *Manila Times,* April 9, 1995.

72 Liak Teng Kiat quote from "Life of the Party," *Far Eastern Economic Review,* December 29, 1994/January 5, 1995.

72– Kim Dae Jung quotes from "Is Culture Destiny?" *Foreign Affairs,*
73 November/December 1994.

73 Aung San Suu Kyi quotes from "Listen: The Culture of Democracy and Human Rights Is Universal," *International Herald Tribune,* December 7, 1994.

73– Lee quote, studies on the economic benefits of democracy and richest
74 countries quote from "Democracy and Growth, Why Voting Is Good for You," *The Economist,* August 27, 1994. Mahathir quote from "How Free a Choice?" *Asiaweek,* April 21, 1995.

74 Lingle article information and suits from "Singapore, Contemptible," *The Economist,* January 21, 1995; and "Singapore's Philosophers," *Wall Street Journal,* October 19, 1994.

75 Chan Heng Wing quote from "Singapore Makes Clear in Letter Its Tolerance of Criticism Is Limited," *Asian Wall Street Journal Weekly,* January 2, 1995.

75– Louis Cha quote from "Free Press Can Triumph over China's Influ-
76 ence," *South China Morning Post,* April 23, 1994.

76 Cheong Yip Seng quote from "Speaking of Asian Values," *Asiaweek,* December 14, 1994.

76 Quote on voting from "How Free a Choice?" *Asiaweek,* April 21, 1995.

77 Chuan Leekpai quote from "Democracy in Asia," *USA Today,* December 16, 1994.

77 Commission for a New Asia statement from "The Asian Way," *Asiaweek,* March 2, 1994.

77 Koh quote from an interview by the author.

77 Kim Dae Jung quote from "Is Culture Destiny?" *Foreign Affairs,* November/December 1994.

77– Thomas quote from "The Universality of Human Rights," *New Straits*
78 *Times,* January 26, 1995.

78 Li quote from "Inching Forward on Rights," *Far Eastern Economic Review,* April 7, 1994.

78 Religion and rights quotes from Kim Dae Jung's article "On Asian Democracy," *Asiaweek*, April 28, 1995.

78 Human rights code from "Regional Briefing," *Far Eastern Economic Review*, April 6, 1995.

78– Trade unionist and Leipziger quotes from "Business First, Freedom
79 Second," *Time*, November 21, 1994.

79 Statistics and quote on Christianity from various sources, including "The Pope Sees 'Harvest of Faith' from Fields of Asia," *Washington Times*, January 30, 1995; "The Great Awakening," *Asiaweek*, August 17, 1994; and "Blessed Are the Rich," *The Economist*, December 10, 1994.

79– New Age spiritualism in Japan from "Japanese Embrace New Age
80 Lifestyles," *Nikkei Weekly*, October 17, 1994.

80 Crowell visit to China described in "The Great Awakening," *Asiaweek*, August 17, 1994.

81– Quotes on Buddhism, Luang Poh Koon, Yantra Ammaro Bhikku and
82 Phra Dhammakaya information from *Far Eastern Economic Review* May 4, 1995.

82 Quotes on Christianity and Islam from a special report on Islam in *The Economist*, August 4, 1994.

82 Quotes on Islamic movements and by Khalid Ahmed from "March of the Militants," *Far Eastern Economic Review*, March 9, 1995.

83 Mohammed Sadli quote from "In Other Words," *Far Eastern Economic Review*, March 9, 1995.

84 World Bank age statistics, retirement schemes information and quote from "Honor Thy Father," *Far Eastern Economic Review*, March 2, 1995.

84– Lai quote from an interview
85 by the author.

86 Noordin Sopiee quote from an interview by the author.

86 Yung Wei quote from an interview by the author.

86 Francis Fukuyama quote from *The End of History and the Last Man* (New York: Avon, 1992), p. 324.

Chapter Three: From Export-Led to Consumer-Driven

87 Gallup poll data and Burkholder quote from "First Poll of China Finds Materialism Alive," *Washington Post*, February 16, 1995.

89   Gray quote and income list from "Middle Class Top Dollar," *Asian Business*, March 1994. Thailand income list from "Retailing in Asia," *The Economist*, September 25, 1993.

90   Ferrier quote from "The Hard Sell, Advertisers Target Asia's Affluent Consumers," *Far Eastern Economic Review*, November 24, 1994.

91   Description of purchasing power parity from John Naisbitt, *Global Paradox* (New York: Morrow, 1994), pp. 180–181.

93   Kanoui statement from "Economic Liberalization," *Asian Wall Street Journal*, October 10, 1994. Car data from "A New Taste for Quality" *Far Eastern Economic Review*, December 7, 1995.

93   Credit card data from "Will They End Asian Frugality?" *Asiaweek*, March 10, 1995; "Citibank Blitzes Asia," *Forbes*, May 6, 1996; and "The Card That Could Rule Our Lives," *Asiaweek*, November 3, 1995.

94   Malls in Bangkok reported in "The Mall, the Merrier," *The Economist*, August 27, 1994, and "Retailing in the Philippines," in the May 18, 1996, issue.

95   Manager statement from "Born to Shop," *Far Eastern Economic Review*, August 19, 1993.

95–   Decline of auto industry information and Brooker quote from "Asia:
96   Last Hope for Car Makers," *Asian Business*, May 1994.

96   The people's car quotes from "China to Churn Out Personal Cars," *International Herald Tribune*, September 23, 1994.

96   Quote on incentives to buy cars from "Chinese Will Be Encouraged to Buy Cars," *Financial Times*, September 23, 1994.

97   Quote on auto industry response for a Chinese family car from "China's Quest for Inexpensive Family Car," *Asian Wall Street Journal*, November 21, 1994. Meyerand quote from "Boom-at-a-glance," *New York Times Magazine*, February 18, 1996.

97   Smil quote from "China to Churn Out Personal Cars," *International Herald Tribune*, September 23, 1994.

98   Quote on the automotive industry in Asia from "World's Car Makers Prefer the Thai Tiger," *Financial Times*, November 9, 1994.

98   Proton information from "Malaysian Car Group Seeks Fresh Inroads," *Financial Times*, January 31, 1995.

98   Ford data from "Ford to Pay $50m for 7% Stake in Indian Car Maker," *Financial Times*, October 17, 1994.

99   Lee Yuen Tseh quote from an interview by the author.

99   Quote on California Fantasy from "Rising Wealth," *Asian Wall Street Journal Weekly*, October 27, 1994.

99   Sutch and Eddington quotes from "Congee at 35,000 Feet," *Far Eastern Economic Review*, November 24, 1994.

100 IATA data, airport quotes and data all from Jay Khosla article in *Business Times* (Singapore), November 19, 1994.

102 Ebbs quote from "Middle Class Top Dollar," *Asian Business*, March 1994.

102 China's "star" rating information from "Five Stars over China," *China Daily*, April 8, 1995.

102 Pelisson quote from "Accor Sees Asian-Pacific Region as Hospitable for Expansion," *Asian Wall Street Journal*, December 20, 1994.

102– Quote on Asian attitudes toward boats, and cruise information from
103 "Slow Boat to China," *Far Eastern Economic Review*, November 24, 1994.

103 Survey information from "Lifestyles," a special report in *Far Eastern Economic Review*, August 27, 1992.

104 Quotes on food chains in Asia from "US Restaurant Chains Tackle Challenges of Asian Expansion," *Nation's Restaurant News*, February 14, 1994.

105 Roenigk quote from *Far Eastern Economic Review*, April 27, 1995.

105 Quote on Chinese consumers from "How Not to Sell 1.2 Billion Tubes of Toothpaste," *The Economist*, December 3, 1994.

105 Procter & Gamble quote from "Unilever Turning Up Heat in Shampoo War in China," *Asian Wall Street Journal*, October 3, 1994.

105 Pepsi and Coke wars described in "Cola Wars Heat Up in Asian Market," *AdWeek*, March 21, 1994.

106 List of advertising agencies and quote from "Foreign Advertising Firms Grapple with China Chaos," *Asian Wall Street Journal Weekly*, February 25, 1995.

106 Asian advertising expenditures from "The Hard Sell," *Far Eastern Economic Review*, November 24, 1994; "Winding up for the Big Pitch," *BusinessWeek*, October 23, 1995; and *Ad Age International*, April 1996, and June 1996.

107 Number of Asian homes with TVs reported in "An Asian Sky," *Asiaweek*, October 19, 1994.

Notes

107 Information on cable in Shanghai from "Asian TV Growth Sets Dizzying Pace," *International Herald Tribune*, December 7, 1994.

107 Prazwol Pradhan information from "Ready for Prime Time," *Far Eastern Economic Review*, January 26, 1995.

107 Paiboon Damrongchaitam quote from "Control Freaks," *Forbes*, April 10, 1995.

108 Faridah Stephens quote from "Pushing the Limits," *Far Eastern Economic Review*, August 4, 1994.

108 Information on Shanghai talk radio fans and Yuan Hu quote from "Shanghai," *National Geographic*, March 1994.

108 Information on Taiwan talk radio and Chen Cheng-teh quote from "Radical Radio," *Far Eastern Economic Review*, December 15, 1994.

110 T. Ananda Krishnan profile and quote from "Multimedia Mogul in the Making," *Business Times* (Singapore), December 3–4, 1994.

111 Childcare quote from "Who's My Mommy?" *Asiaweek*, March 27, 1992.

111 Toddler stress in India reported in "Flunked at 3, 1 Symbol of Middle-Class India's Angst," *Washington Post*, October 31, 1994.

111 Zhu Xiaoying quote from "China's New Rich Pay Big Money for Child Education," *Korea Times*, March 28, 1995.

112 Teen market quote from "Young and Free Spending," *Business Times* (Singapore), October 8–9, 1994.

112 Jagdeep Kapoor quote from "Changing Demographics," *Advertising Age International*, October 17, 1994.

112 Padamsee quote from *Far Eastern Economic Review*, July 13, 1995.

113 Urban Chinese money quote from "China, Struggle for Control," *Fortune*, November 1, 1993. Chinese earnings reported in "Find the Hidden Middle Class," *BusinessWeek*, June 6, 1994.

113 Kabel and insurance quotes from *Asia Inc.*, March 1995.

114 Information on auctions in Singapore from *Yauzhou Zhoukan*, a Chinese-language weekly magazine published in Hong Kong.

115 Masanori Fukuoka quote from "Indian Art Market," *Asian Art News*, May/June 1995.

116 Christie's auction in Hong Kong reported in "Jaded," *Far Eastern Economic Review*, May 18, 1995.

266

116 George Fisher quote from "Kodak's New Focus," *BusinessWeek*, January 30, 1995.

117 Vitachi quote from *Far Eastern Economic Review*, July 13, 1995.

119 McDonald quote from "Sitting Pretty," *Far Eastern Economic Review*, December 21, 1995. Ng quote and information about car sales from *Financial Times*, August 19, 1995.

Chapter Four: From Government-Controlled to Market-Driven

122 Quote on China's communists and party membership from "China's Communists Seek a New Role," *Asian Wall Street Journal*, December 20, 1994.

123 Huynh Thanh Chung quote from "Rising from the Ashes," *BusinessWeek*, May 23, 1994.

124 General information on Vietnam from "Vietnam: Determined to Be a Tiger," *International Herald Tribune*, October 21, 1994.

124 Quote on U.S. companies in Vietnam from "Destination, Vietnam," *BusinessWeek*, February 14, 1994.

124– World Bank information from "Vietnam: Determined to Be a
25   Tiger but in Need of Help," *International Herald Tribune*, October 21, 1994.

126 Ge Bulei quote from "Soldiers of Fortune: China's PLA," *Asian Wall Street Journal*, May 25, 1994. Vietnam military information from "In Peacetime, Vietnam's Army Turns to Business," *New York Times*, July 21, 1996.

126 Yuan Mu characterization from "State Business," *Far Eastern Economic Review*, February 23, 1995.

127 Quote on India's capital stock from "Spinning Out of Control," *Far Eastern Economic Review*, March 9, 1995.

127– Khoo Eng Choo, Sachs, Malaysia's program and Anwar Ibrahim
28   quotes from "Privatization Pioneer," *Far Eastern Economic Review*, January 19, 1995.

129 "Sick Man of Asia" information, including company investment, from "Shaking Manila Out of Its Slumber," *BusinessWeek*, October 31, 1994.

130   Gonzalez quotes from "Taking Off from Clark," *Asiaweek,* July 6, 1994. Subic Bay information from various sources including "The Selling of Subic," *Asiaweek,* July 19, 1996.

130   Koo quote from "Hong Kong East?" *Forbes,* August 2, 1993.

130   Leber quote from "Shaking Manila Out of Its Slumber," *BusinessWeek,* October 31, 1994.

131   Quote on India's growth from "India's 'Big Ship' Economy: Plenty of Room to Grow," *Business Times* (Singapore), October 25, 1994.

131   George statement and problem quote from "The India Boom?" *Far Eastern Economic Review,* January 19, 1995.

132   Mahathir quote from "Co-operate for Global Commonwealth," *New Straits Times,* November 14, 1994.

132   Quote on fiber-optic project from *Asia Inc.,* August 1995.

133   Freris statements from "Re-inventing the Asian Miracle," *Asiaweek,* January 13, 1995.

133   Asian investment from "The Pacific Century," *Forbes,* July 15, 1996.

133   Jennings quote from a speech in Brussels, September 16, 1994.

133   Daewoo data from "Koreans Give Vietnam a Face Lift," *Washington Post,* February 9, 1996.

133   Proton quote from "Re-inventing the Asian Miracle," *Asiaweek,* January 13, 1995.

134   Il-suk quote from "Samsung and NEC Make Virtue of Necessity," *Financial Times,* February 14, 1995.

135   Japanese data from "Into China," *The Economist,* March 16, 1996; "Exporting a Surplus," *Far Eastern Economic Review,* July 4, 1996; and "The Pacific Century," *Forbes,* July 15, 1996.

136   Courtis quote from "Japan Inc. Alters Tactics to Target Asian Consumers," *Asian Wall Street Journal,* May 17, 1994.

137   Data on foreign workers from "The Lure of Asia," "Merry Go Round," *Far Eastern Economic Review,* February 3, 1994; "Give and Take," in the May 25, 1995, issue; "Welcome Exchange," in the February 29, 1996 issue; and "Asia's Labor Pains," *The Economist,* August 26, 1995.

138   Ramos quotes from "Cross-Border 'Growth Triangles' Promote Prosperity in East Asia," *International Herald Tribune,* November 30, 1994.

Notes

139– Growth triangle information and Sopiee quote from "The Overdue
 40 Triumph of the Trade," *Asia Inc.*, April 1994. Jennings quote from a
      speech in Brussels, September 16, 1994.

141 Information on the Great Wall from "The Not So Great Wall," *Asian
      Wall Street Journal*, April 18, 1994.

141– Infrastructure projects in Asia and praise of Malaysia quote from
 42 "Building the New Asia," *BusinessWeek*, November 28, 1994.

142 Reed estimate from "The Race for the Investment Dollar," *South
      China Morning Post*, November 5, 1994.

143 Gokongwei and rejoinder quotes from "The Race Is On," *Asian Wall
      Street Journal*, April 18, 1994.

143– Quotes on Pakistan's Hub power project from "Public and Private
 44 Meet at the Hub," *Financial Times*, October 31, 1994.

145 Multinational firms competing in Asia reported in "Building the
      New Asia," *BusinessWeek*, November 28, 1994.

145 Fernstrom quote from "How to Pay for Super Projects," *Asian Busi-
      ness*, November 1994.

145 List of emerging regional players from "The Race Is On," *Asian Wall
      Street Journal*, April 18, 1994.

146 Quote on Asia's capital markets from "Here Comes the Money,"
      Asian Business, May 1994.

147 Information on Asia's stock markets from "A Survey of
      Asian Finance," a special report in *The Economist*, November 12,
      1994.

149 Quote on economic growth from "Asia's Golden Age of Growth,"
      Asiamoney, November 1994.

149 Dragon bond quote from "Here Comes the Money," *Asian Business*,
      May 1995. Additional information from "A Survey of Asian Fi-
      nance," a special report in the *The Economist*, November 12, 1994.

150 Quote about Vietnam's banking sector from "Foreign Help Wanted,"
      Far Eastern Economic Review, October 6, 1994.

152 Param Curaraswamy quote from an interview by the author.

152 Corruption in China and Western diplomat quotes from "Hands in
      Every Pocket," *Newsweek*, March 28, 1994.

152 Corruption in India information from "India's Biggest Turn-Off: Po-
      litical Corruption," *Business Times* (Singapore), March 9, 1995.

Notes

152 Goh Chok Tong statement from "Pay Raise Plan Gets a Rise Out of Public," *Los Angeles Times,* December 5, 1994.

156 Asia's wealthiest from "The Pacific Century," *Forbes,* July 15, 1996.

Chapter Five: From Farms to Supercities

157 Urban population projection from "Urbanization, Human Security and Survival," a document for the United Nations Development Program's "Asia Pacific 2000," by Anwar Fazal.

158 Many population figures are from "Asia's Choking Cities," an excellent article on the Asian population situation which appeared in *Newsweek,* May 9, 1994.

158 Rice miller quote from "Seeds of Despair," *Far Eastern Economic Review,* April 3, 1993.

159 Hong Kong information and Pryor quote from "The Lessons of Hong Kong," *Newsweek,* May 9, 1994.

159– Singapore model description and elements, and George Yeo Yong
  62 Boon and Lee quotes from "Selling Success," *Asiaweek,* July 13, 1994. Zhang Xinsheng statement from "In the City of Suzhou," *Washington Times,* July 8, 1994.

162 Government plans to move 440 million people reported in "Birth of the Instant City," *The Economist,* September 10, 1994.

163 Alice City project described in "Megacities, Mega-Solutions," *Asian Business,* February 1994.

164 List of migrants from various sources, including "China's Millions on the Move," *Newsweek,* March 7, 1994.

164– Quotes on rural migrants, including Blum, from "China Migrants:
  65 Economic Engine, Social Burden," *New York Times,* June 29, 1994. *People's Daily* quotes and Cai Haishan quote from "China's Millions on the Move," *Newsweek,* March 7, 1994. Fan Gang quotes from both articles.

165 Liu Binyan quote from "Peasants in Search of Urban Prosperity," *International Herald Tribune,* May 30, 1994.

166 Quotes on Vietnam and poverty statistics from "The Call of the City," *The Economist,* March 4, 1995. World Bank conclusions reported in "Countryside 'Is Key to Vietnam's Development,' " *Financial Times,* February 24, 1995.

167 Suchart Suksom quote from "Separate & Unequal," *Far Eastern Economic Review*, April 14, 1994.

167 Indonesian rural reforms and poverty, Asikin Mohamad and BRI quotes from "Rural Poverty Waning in SE Asia," *Washington Times*, July 15, 1994.

168 Quote on Indonesian economic development from "The Changing Face of Indonesian Agriculture," *Business Times* (Singapore), March 10, 1995.

168 Luzon rice terraces and Ifugao quote from "Progress Takes Toll on Eighth Wonder of the World," *Bangkok Post*, March 16, 1995.

169 Chinese farmland statistics reported in "Farmland Decreases Drastically," *China Daily*, February 10, 1995.

169 Xishan worker, China's agricultural upheaval, other East Asian economies and grain expert quotes from "As Industry Devours Land, China's Grain Imports Soar," *Asian Wall Street Journal*, March 13, 1995.

170 Bangkok's need for community and Dr. Ubonrat Siriyuvasak quotes from "Where Angels Fear to Tread," *Bangkok Post*, March 21, 1995.

171 Quote on urban housing from "China Discovers All Mod Cons," *The Economist*, August 20, 1994.

171 Beijing urban real estate prices from "No Place Like Home," *Far Eastern Economic Review*, July 28, 1994.

171– Quotes on Land Reclamation Act and by mother from Laem Chabang
72 from "Under Siege," *Bangkok Post*, March 5, 1995.

172 Kastorius Sinaga quotes from "Land-Love Strong Among Villagers," *Jakarta Post*, March 15, 1995.

172 Quote on Tianjin resident from "China Discovers All Mod Cons," *The Economist*, August 20, 1994.

173 Asia's emerging supercities list and Denise Yue quote from "Asia's Supercities," *BusinessWeek*, April 24, 1995.

173 World's tallest buildings reported in "The Great Asian Steeple Chase," *New York Times*, June 25, 1995.

Chapter Six: From Labor-Intensive to High Technology

176 Sri Lanka phone description from "Asian Telecommunications Guide," a supplement to *Asiamoney*, October 1994.

Notes

178– Feng quote from "New Strategies, New Industries as Taiwan Goes
 80 Global"; the ten strategic industries and subsidies given quote from
"A Leading Source of Capital"; additional information on Taiwan
from these articles and "Economic Success Set to Continue"; all from
a special advertising section in the *International Herald Tribune,* October 10, 1994.

180– Hsieh, Wu Tao-yuan, and Yau You-wen quotes from "High Tech
 82 Taiwanese Come Home," *New York Times,* July 19, 1994. Quote from
Dr. Lee from an interview by the author. Hsieh sales estimate and
little Singapore quote from "Now for Its Next Miracle," *Asia Inc.,*
November 1994, p. 50.

182 Information on engineering Ph.D.s and quotes about Asians returning home from "Have Skills, Will Travel—Homeward," *BusinessWeek* special 21st Century Capitalism edition, December 19, 1994.

183– Quotes on Singapore and Korea from "Asia Chases R&D Successes,"
 84 *Asian Business,* April 1994.

184 Pradeep Singh and G. Jagannath Raju descriptions from *BusinessWeek*
special 21st Century Capitalism edition, December 19, 1994.

184– Dewang Mehta, Vittal and Yourdon quotes from "Competitive Ad-
 85 vantages Through Indian Software Services," a special advertising
supplement to *Forbes ASAP,* December 5, 1994.

186– Facilities in Singapore, Indian engineers, education centers and in-
 87 come information, and quotes an advantages of Asian plants from
"High Tech Jobs All Over the Map," *BusinessWeek* special 21st Century Capitalism edition, December 19, 1994.

188 Made in China quote from "China High-Tech Spree Pays Dividends," *Nikkei Weekly,* November 7, 1994.

189 Quotes on Taiwan from "Very Well Made in Taiwan"; quote on
South Korea from "South Korea, the New Titan of Technology"; both
in *BusinessWeek* special advertising section, November 28, 1994.

190 Political & Economic Risk Consultancy Ltd. and World Bank quotes
from "Go-go Growth Points Up Shortage of Skilled Labor," *Los
Angeles Times,* November 29, 1994.

190– Quote on skilled worker shortage and list of graduates from "Failing
 91 Grade," *Far Eastern Economic Review,* September 29, 1994.

191 Carkeek quote from "Acute Skilled-Labor Gap Exacts a Price in Thailand," *Asian Wall Street Journal Weekly,* September 19, 1994.

192– Transmission system and Padilla quotes, AT&T sales and list of
93 high-tech purchases reported in "End of Export Curbs Spurs Tech-
    nology Sales to China," *Asian Wall Street Journal,* January 2, 1995.
    Quote on transfer of brainpower from "Telecom Firms Vie to Bring
    Latest Technology to China," *Asian Wall Street Journal* April 1,
    1994.

193 Asia gets wired section from various sources, including "Asian Tele-
    communications Guide," a supplement to *Asiamoney,* October 1994;
    "Switched On," *Far Eastern Economic Review,* November 24, 1994; and
    "Telecommunications in Asia," *Far Eastern Economic Review,* April 7,
    1994. Phone and call data from "The Technology Revolution," *Asia-
    week,* December 15, 1995; and *World Press Review,* March 1996.

194 Kan quote from "Paving the Highway," *Asiaweek,* September 14,
    1994.

194 Information on Chinese market satellite needs from "The Long
    March Back to China," *The Economist,* November 5, 1994.

196 Eight million estimate and Skeldon quote from *Asia Inc.,* August 1995.

Chapter Seven: From Male Dominance to
the Emergence of Women

201 Solo quote from "Japan Discovers Woman Power," *Fortune,* June 19,
    1989.

202 Chinese statistics on family size and decision makers reported in
    "More Young Couples in Shanghai Go for One Child," *New Straits
    Times,* May 17, 1994; and "China, No-Child Families," *World Press
    Review,* May 1994.

202 Quote on career women in Asia from "Women's Liberation, Asian-
    Style," *Business Times* (Singapore), August 3, 1994.

203 Soin quotes from "Women's Groups Here Not 'Aping the West
    Blindly,' " *New Straits Times,* March 14, 1995.

203 Charatsri quote from "Alone in a Man's World," *Far Eastern Economic
    Review,* January 12, 1995.

204 Climaco quote from "Champion of the Working Woman," *New
    Straits Times.*

204 Women in the workforce percentages from various sources, includ-
    ing "State Outlines Women's Rights and Roles," *China Daily,* June 3,

1994; Malaysia's Department of Statistics; *The World's Women Trends and Statistics,* a UN publication, 1995; "Competitive Frontiers, Asian Women in Management," *International Studies of Management & Organization,* Winter 1993–94, and *Competitive Frontiers, Women Managers in a Global Economy* (Oxford: Blackwell, 1994); both were edited by Nancy J. Adler and Dafna N. Izzraelli.

204 Studies on the need for managers in Indonesia reported in "Women in Management," *International Studies of Management & Organization,* Winter 1993–94.

205 Women in the service sector from "The Asian Economic Commentary," published by Merrill Lynch, November 1994. Korean and Japanese service sector women percentages from Joyce Geld and Marian Lief Palley, eds., *Women of Japan and Korea: Community & Change* (Philadelphia: Temple University Press, 1994). Male executive comment reported in "Leaping the Gender Gap in Asia," *Business Times* (Singapore), November 8, 1993.

205 Statistics on women managers from Adler and Izzraelli, eds., "Competitive Frontiers, Asian Women in Management," and *Competitive Frontiers, Women Managers in a Global Economy.*

206 Chin quote from "The Toothpaste and Bungalow Portfolio," *Forbes,* March 14, 1994.

207 "Where to Put Your Money" *Far Eastern Economic Review,* October 19, 1995.

207 Dr. Chow's data from an article in the *South China Morning Post,* November 16, 1993.

208 Zhang quote from "Successful Stories of Women CEOs," *China Daily,* August 23, 1994.

209 Nicholas D. Kristof and Sheryl WuDunn, *China Wakes* (New York: Times Books, 1994), p. 213.

210 Meo quote from "Network of Chinese Rim Pacific," *Los Angles Times,* July 22, 1990.

210 Statistics on women entrepreneurs from various sources, including "Japanese Working Women Strike Back," *Fortune,* May 31, 1993; *International Studies of Management & Organization,* Winter 1993–94; Adler and Izzraelli, eds., *Competitive Frontiers, Women Managers in a Global Economy;* Blackwell, "The Woman Entrepreneur's Recipe for Success," *Business Times* (Singapore), October 31, 1994; "Women's

Economic Role Grows," *China Daily,* June 11, 1994; and *Women: Looking Beyond 2000,* United Nations, New York, 1995.

211 Chanut quote from "Iron Butterflies," *Fortune,* October 7, 1991.

211– Kadir quote from "Housewife Who Built Empire from Nothing,"
12 *Financial Times,* June 9, 1994.

212 Chiang quote from "The Woman Entrepreneur's Recipe for Success," *Business Times* (Singapore), October 31, 1994.

212 Khatijah Ahmad quotes from "Into the Big Time," *Asiaweek,* December 14, 1994.

213 Ma quote from "The First Lady of Hong Kong," *Bazaar,* April 1994.

213 Mori description from "Doyenne of Fashion," *Far Eastern Economic Review,* July 21, 1994.

213 Tilaar quote from "Beauty Secrets," *Far Eastern Economic Review,* November 24, 1994.

215 D. Rounnag Jahn quote from "Asian Women Hear a Call to Politics," *China Daily,* June 25, 1994.

215– Women in office data from "Women Rising," *Asiaweek,* September 1,
216 1995.

216 Information and quote on Hong Kong women in politics from "A Woman's Place," *Far Eastern Economic Review,* January 12, 1995.

216 Doi quote from "Outspoken Doi Tackles New Goals," *Nikkei Weekly,* November 28, 1994.

216 Quote on political activism of Filipino women and information on the Philippines from "Women Power," *Asiaweek,* June 9, 1995.

217 Khunying Supatra Masdit quote from "Helping Women into Politics," *Newsweek,* May 30, 1994.

217 Chandrika quote from "Sri Lanka Swears In Woman President," *Boston Globe,* November 13, 1994.

218 Wu quotes from "Winning Ways of Madam Wu," *South China Morning Post,* March 14, July 6, 1995.

219– Quotes and materials on population demographics from "Disap-
20 pearing Girls," *Asiaweek,* March 3, 1995.

220 Charatsri quote from "Alone in a Man's World," *Far Eastern Economic Review,* January 12, 1995.

220 Viravaidya quote from "Flesh-Trade Options," *Far Eastern Economic Review,* April 14, 1994.

Notes

220 Chakrapand quote from "Thai Women Can Be Educated to Reject Prostitution," *Asian Wall Street Journal Weekly*, October 31, 1994.

221 Amihan Abueva information from "Suffer the Little Children," *Newsweek*, July 25, 1994.

222 Meng quote from an interview by the author.

222 Statistics on women and education from *International Studies of Management & Organization*, Winter 1993–94; Adler and Izzraelli, eds., *Competitive Frontiers, Women Managers in a Global Economy*.

224 Kartini quote and description of Kartini Day in *International Studies of Management & Organization*, Winter 1993–94.

225 Quote on Muslim communities from "Women's Rights," *Asiaweek*, November 17, 1993.

225 Quote on rural China and India from "Narrowing the Gender Gap," *Asiaweek*, March 17, 1995.

227 Liou Fey Ying quote translated from Global Views' Executive Women's Special, 1992.

Chapter Eight: From West to East

232 Lee and Tsang Yok Sing quotes from "China's Cloud over Hong Kong: Is '97 Here?" *New York Times*, July 5, 1995. Anson Chan's quote from "Keeping the Faith," *Sunday Morning Post*, April 23, 1995.

233 House quote from "Why Hong Kong Must Remain in Hong Kong," *Asian Wall Street Journal*, June 7, 1995.

233 Chen quote from an interview by Foong Wai Fong.

235 Keating quote and Australian data from "Australia's Place in Asia," *Asiaweek*, March 31, 1995.

236 Hunt quote from "America Is Short-Sighted on Asia," *Wall Street Journal*, July 6, 1995.

237 Rhee quote from an interview by the author.

239 U.S. Census data reported in "Southeast Asians Highly Dependent on Welfare in U.S.," *New York Times*, May 19, 1994.

239 Lai quote from a conversation with the author.

239 Ow Yang Hsuan observation made in conversation with the author.

239 World Bank data reported in "Asia's Welfare," *Far Eastern Economic Review*, June 23, 1994.

Notes

240– Fukuda and survey on Asians in business quotes and Asian film-
 41 maker information from "Hot and in Demand," *Transpacific,* November 1994. Profiles from "Masters of the Deal," *Transpacific,* November 1993. Some Asian numbers reported in "The Pacific Century," *Forbes,* July 15, 1996.

242 Asian-American and Yu quotes, and data on Asian-Americans in the suburbs from "Asians in the Suburbs," *American Demographics,* May 1994.

243 Lam quotes, list of Silicon Valley companies started by Asian-Americans and Asian organizations from "Asian Immigrants, New Leaders in Silicon Valley," *New York Times,* January 14, 1992.

244 Yaohan Plaza information and Asian mall quotes, and Kono statement from "An Asian in the Great Midwest," *American Demographics,* May 1994.

245– Issey Miyake quote, quotes and information on other designers, Feng
 46 and Tam quotes all from "Asian Designers Go West," *Asian Wall Street Journal,* July 15, 1994.

248 Mahbubani quotes from "The Pacific Way," *Foreign Affairs,* January/February 1995.

249 List of forty-something leaders and quotes about them from "Generation 2000," *Asiaweek,* October 5, 1994.

250 Anwar Ibrahim quotes from "Anwar, We Need a Truely [sic] Just Order," *The Star,* October 7, 1994.

252 Wong quote from an interview by the author.

253 Ho and Singapore's university requirement quotes from "Learn the Language That Has Economic Value," *Asiaweek,* December 15, 1993.

255 Sun quote from "Will China Play by the Rules?" *Business Ethics,* May/June 1995.

ACKNOWLEDGMENTS

Any acknowledgments for contributions to this book, and there are many, must begin with my debt to Foong Wai Fong, who has been my partner since the beginning. Not only could I not have finished *Megatrends Asia* without her; I would never have taken it on. Wai Fong is an outstanding representative of that new Asian phenomenon— young entrepreneurial women. She is the founder and managing director of the Transforma Group of Companies, based in Kuala Lumpur, Malaysia. Wai Fong has been my collaborator from conception through research, the dialogues, writing and editing. Her extensive knowledge of Asia and her extraordinary intelligence have instructed the creation of this book every step of the way. While the final judgments are mine, I could not have made them without her. My advice to almost everyone who wants to do business in Asia is to get an Overseas Chinese partner. I could not have chosen a better one.

My second large debt is to my longtime researcher, Joy Van Elderen. I doubt that there is a better researcher in the book world than Joy, who performed superbly again this time around. My heartfelt thanks and gratitude go to Patricia Aburdene, who edited the entire manuscript, and whose support of my work on this project will always be cherished. My thanks also goes to Corinne Kuypers-Denlinger, researcher and writer, who was there yet again as she has been on project after project for the last fifteen years. My old friend Steve Rhinesmith read the manuscript and, as always, had valuable advice and comments. To Linda McLean Harned my grateful thanks for managing my office, my itinerary and thousands of complicated details and arrangements, and for reading and commenting on the manuscript.

I must give special thanks to my German-language publisher, Doris Dinklage, of Signum Verlag in Vienna. Her entrepreneurial verve and attention to getting the job done resulted in *Megatrends Asia* being published first in German, and thereby helped me make the deadline for the other editions as well. Nick Brealey, founder of Nicholas Brealey Publishing in the United Kingdom, was an early supporter and, as always, very helpful on the editorial side as well. Fred Hills, my editor at Simon & Schuster, New York, is a joy to work with, a true professional, always on top of his game. My agent, Bill Leigh, orchestrated the business side with these and other publishers, and also provided invaluable editorial advice and counsel, for which I am very grateful.

My grateful thanks goes to Gordon Crovitz, the brilliant young editor and publisher of the *Far Eastern Economic Review,* who offered early support and convened a wonderful dialogue meeting in Hong Kong. Under his stewardship the *Review* is today by far the most important source of information and intelligence about Asia (as the many references in this book attest).

I send very special thanks to Dr. Noordin Sopiee, the director general of the Institute of Strategic and International Studies (ISIS) Malaysia in Kuala Lumpur, the head of the Asian institution where I serve as an International Fellow, for his steadfast and generous support throughout this project.

Lastly, my thanks to all the participants in the dialogues that were held throughout the region, and especially to the conveners of these extremely fruitful sessions: Ambassador Tommy Koh (Singapore); Jusuf Wanandi, Chairman, Supervisory Board of Center for Strategic and International Studies (Jakarta); Gloria L. Tan Climaco, chairman and managing director of Sycip Gorres Velayo (SGV) & Company (Manila); Professor Charas Suwanwela, M.D., president of Chulalongkorn University (Bangkok); George Fields, whose books in both Japanese and English have served us all so well (Tokyo); Diane Ying, editor of

Acknowledgments

Commonwealth (Taipei); Gordon Crovitz, editor and publisher, *Far Eastern Economic Review* (Hong Kong); Dr. Cha Dong-Se, president of Korea Development Institute (Seoul); and Prakash Hebalkar, president, ProfiTech (Bombay).

My deepest gratitude to the following participants for their contributions to *Megatrends Asia:* **Singapore:** Professor Tommy Koh, Alan Chan, Professor Chen Charng Ning, Chew Kah Guan, Mrs. Chin Ean Wah, Associate Professor Chin Kin Wah, Chong Huai Seng, Leslie Fong, Theresa Foo, Goh Kian Chee, Richard Hoon, Vikram Khanna, Koh Buck Song, Associate Professor Koh Tai Ann, Peter Kong, Kua Phek Long, Kwa Chong Seng, Dr. Lee Suan Yew, Lee Teong Sang, Dr. Catherine Lim, Lim Jim Koon, Lim Wen Chyi, Gretchen Liu, Low Beng Tin, Stuart Merrilees, Harpreet Singh Nehal, Ng Gek Nga, Ng Seng Leong, Sutjahjo Ngaserin, Gophinath Pillai, Gordon Seow, Dr. Kanwaljit Soin, BG Tan Yong Soon, Tan Cheng Gay, Tan Hup Thye, Tan Kwi Kin, Wilson Tan, Dr. Teh Kok Peng, Tong Chong Heong, Associate Professor Wee Chow Hou, Alfred H. K. Wong, Wong Meng Quang, Steve S. V. Wong, Y. Y. Wong, Mme. Yeong Yoon Ying, Zainul Abidin Rasheed, Arun Mahizhuan, Ooi Giok Ling, Yap Mui Teng, Gwee Wee Chen, Prof. Dr. Chan Heng Chee. **Jakarta:** Dr. Djisman S. Simandjuntak, Professor M. Sadli, Professor Haryati Soebadio, Mr. Wijarso, Dr. R. B. Suhartono, Lieutenant General Poerbo Soewondo, Major General Pandji Soesilo, Dr. Johan Syahperi Saleh, Colonel Mulya Wibisono, Colonel Sardan Marbun, Marzuki Darusman, Djoko Sudjatmiko, Ambassador A. B. Loebis, Wahid Supriyadi, Major General Soebiyakto, Jakob Oetama, Ms. Toeti Adhitama, Ms. Annie Bertha Simamora, Professor Suhadi Mangkusuwondo, Ms. Pia Alisjahbana, Ms. Myra Sidharta, Professor Magnis Suseno, Dr. Mudji Sutrisno, Sofjan Wanandi, Dr. Willem B. Wanandi, Ms. Shanti L. Poesposoetjipto, Steve Sondakh, Ms. Clara Joewono, Djohan Effendi, Soendaroe Rachmad, Neil Martin, Ms. Natalia Soebagijo. **Kuala Lumpur:** Y Bhg Tan Sri Zainal Abidin Sulong, YB Mr. Chua Jui Meng, Dr. Rozali Mohamed Ali, Tuan Haji Ramli Othman, Dr. Stephen Leong, Professor Dr. Ariffin Bey, Y Bhg Tan Sri Ramon Navaratnam, Y Bhg Tan Sri Geh Ik Cheong, Dr. Chandra Muzaffar, Abdul Rahman Adnan, Abu Bakar Hj Abdul Karim, Dr. Chong Kwong Yuan, A. Navamukundan, Dr. Peter Shephard, Professor Shamsul Amri Baharuddin, Rustam Sani,

Acknowledgments

Anwar Fazal, Dr. Tan Tat Wai. **Taipei:** Diane Ying, S. C. Ho, Huang-Hsiung Huang, Wen C. Ko, Dr. Lee Yuen-Tseh, Y. C. Lo, Casper Shih, Yen-Shiang Shih, Shen-Nan Tong, Hsung-Hsiung Tsai, Yung Wei. **Hong Kong:** L. Gordon Crovitz, Anna Wu, Ronnie Chan, Jimmy Lai, Alan Smith, John Hung, Professor Wang Gungwu, Professor Ming K. Chan, Martin Lee, QC, Daniel Ng Yat-Chiu, Barry Wain, David Li, Richard C. M. Wong, Winston W. Y. Siu, Luis P. Lorenzo Jr., Willy P. Y. Shee, Patrick Chong, Ma Vivian Yuchengco (Locsin), José Antonio U. Gonzalez, Anurut Vongvanij, Edmund Cheng, Chuck Theisen, Emily Lau, Paul Cheng, Peter Clark. **Bombay:** Prakash Hebalkar, Kishore Chaukar, Nadir Godrej, Parvez Damania, Kiron Kasbekar, Ms. Nazneen Karmali, Dr. Kirit Parikh, Shrikant Inamdar, Professor Suhas Sukhatme, Darryl D'Monte, M. R. Pai, Ms. Meena Menon, Pratap Padode, Prakash Idnani, Albert Lewis. **Seoul:** Dong-Se Cha, Dae-Whan Chang, Dong-Sung Cho, Kyung-Won Kim, Kwang-Doo Kim, Bon-Ho Koo, Suk-Chae Lee, Bong-Sung Oum, Ung-Suh Park, Sang-Woo Rhee, Byung-Nak Song, Sang-Mok Suh, Soo-Gil Young. **Manila:** Gloria L. Tan Climaco, Washington SyCip, Peter Garrucho, Felipe Alfonso, Emil Javier, José L. Chuisia Jr., Jaime Augusto Zobel de Ayala, Cynthia Rose Bautista, Dr. Ledivina Carino, Dr. Ma Luisa Doronila, Dr. Florangel Braid. **Tokyo:** George Fields, Thomas Ainlay Jr., Glen S. Fukushima, Professor Gene Gregory, Derek A. Hall, Yoji Hamawaki, Yoshisuke Iinuma, Yoshikazu Ishizuka, Thomas F. Jordan, Mikio Kato, Ms. Yuri Konno, Noritaka Moriuchi, Ms. Akiko Murai, Kiyoshi Nakamura, Toshishige Namai, Ms. Merle Aiko Okawara, Dr. A. A. Sultan. **Bangkok:** Professor Charas Suwanwela, M.D., Dr. Krasae Chanawongse, Dr. Supachai Panitchpakdi, Khunying Supatra Masdit, Dr. Chai-Anan Samudavanija, Professor Dr. Sippanondha Ketudat, Professor Dr. Vicharn Panich, Phayap Phyormyont, Khunying Thongtip Ratanarat, Professor Dr. Phaichitr Uathavikul, Professor Dr. Yongyuth Yuthavong, Staporn Jinachitra, Professor Dr. Jetana Nark Vachara, Staporn Kavitanon, Mrs. Chutaporn Lambasara, Mrs. Vasana Mututanont, Professor Nitaya Suwanwela, M.D., Associate Professor Dr. Salag Dhabanandana, Associate Professor Dr. Pranee Kullavanijaya, Associate Professor Dr. Amara Pongsapich, Associate Professor Suchata Jinachitra, Associate Professor Dr. Usanee Yodyingyuad, Associate Professor Puangkaew Poonyakanok, Achan Panadda Pongsurayamas.

Acknowledgments

Nanjing: Chen De Ming, Professor Lin-Yue Lu, Professor Chen Yi, Professor Colin Chiu, Professor Marielle C. C. Teo, Hingrong Lian, Professor Yu Shoyi, Professor Zheng Ming Yuan, Charles G. Rogalske, Hu Si, Professor Shuming Zhao, Professor Yang Xiu, Wu Rui-Lin, Huang Xiao Ping, Professor Zhang Yongtao, Professor Wu Keming, Professor Wang Zhiguo, Zhang Jian Feng. **Suzhou:** Chen Hao, Zhao Qiubo, Wang Shi Qing. **Shanghai:** Wang Dao Han, Dr. Tang Yunwei, Professor Cheng En Fu, Professor Wei Guo Zhang, Michael Sun, Jin Shun Fa, Yue Yao-Xing.

INDEX

Index

Index

Index

ABOUT THE AUTHOR

John Naisbitt is the world's leading trend forecaster. He speaks annually to thousands of business leaders and opinion makers in the Americas, Europe and Asia. The author of several major bestselling books, including *Megatrends* and *Megatrends 2000*, Naisbitt divides his time between Telluride, Colorado; Cambridge, Massachusetts; and Kuala Lumpur, Malaysia.